Praise for

*Ride the Horses, Feed the Lions*
One Man's Crusade to Humanize Selling

"Bill Hatch's book *Ride the Horses, Feed the Lions* gives us a sense that the author is on a kind of personal crusade to help salespeople be more gentle and helpful to their prospects than they are usually perceived. Hatch argues that by being helpful rather than pushy, salespeople will be more successful, customers will get more of what they want and the reputation of the sales profession will be enhanced as a whole. The role that sales leaders play is significant in this transformation. I enjoyed Bill Hatch's easy, conversational style. The many stories the author tells make his core message more tangible and accessible for the reader. It is good to find a book on Sales Leadership that comes at the subject from a stylistic perspective, when most others are forcing attention on the hard facts of sales performance."

**Peter Strohkorb**, author of the OneTeam™ sales productivity booster program:

"*Boost your sales with* Smarketing®"
PStrohkorb@Peterstrohkorbconsulting.com
www.linkedin.com/in/peterstrohkorbsalesmarketing

"What interests me about *Ride the Horses, Feed the Lions* is I recently inherited one of these personalities at a new Vice President of Sales position I had just taken, and I was looking for greater insight on how to manage and lead this challenging, unique, undisciplined but remarkable talent. This rep of mine is an enigma. I loved this guy but wanted to fire him. I was unsure how to handle him. In Bill's book, *Ride the Horses, Feed the Lions*, he takes you through a journey on how to *champion this maverick* and embrace their *stylistic* personality. *Ride the Horses, Feed the Lions*, **indeed!** Through Bill's eyes and his *stylistic*, but easy writing style, I was able to better understand what makes this personality profile tick and what I could do to harness their full sales potential without me allowing this 'maverick personality' to become a distraction or a deterrent to me and the overall health of my sales team. Bill astutely points out 'you may get frustrated if you don't understand the asset they are and can become.' *The Stylistic Salesperson* has given me a much greater understanding of this rare gem. If you don't have one in your sales team, you're missing out on the real **'rain maker.'** Bill walks you through how to identify this talent and what they bring to the equation. They're a game changer for sure! Thank you, Bill, for sharing your wealth of knowledge and helping me better understand and be able to better manage The *Stylistic Salesperson!*"
**Matt Kelly, VP of Sales,** Fairway Architectural Railing Solutions:

"Matt excels at recruiting and developing 'A-player' talent to exceed company sales and revenue objectives."
www.linkedin.com/in/matt-kelly-a7897b7

"Every *Stylistic Salesperson* should buy this book and give it to their manager. They would be doing both a favor. My company required each salesperson to have a manager ride with them annually. We were scored from 0-100 on our use of *their sales process.* I sold on every *manager* ride, never earning more than 55, a failing score. Ha-ha! I like the story-telling conversational tone. It's how we think and understand best. Your comment was the key to it all: 'Management knows the uniqueness of each individual and establishes a relationship with them' (Rare!). I liked your family history in the introduction. You made me feel like you understood me because of the psychological ping-pong you

went through yourself. This is a book I could read many times and use as a reference."
**Geoffrey D. Riddle;** Sales professional, speaker and voice-over artist
geoffriddle@cox.net

"I learned a lifetime's worth of wisdom from you in the short time we spent together. It's hard to believe with all the sales skills I picked up, they are only a small part of what you taught me."
**Christopher Atkinson, AAI, AIC,** Risk Management, Insurance Law, Marketing professional, Entrepreneur;
ctatkinson@gmail.com

"Sales management is the weak link in the revenue chain and Bill explores how to inspire the very best in salespeople by understanding and leveraging their strengths."
**Tony J. Hughes**, renowned sales industry commentator, Author of *The Joshua Principle–Leadership Secrets of Selling*; Keynote Speaker; consultant;
tony@rsvpselling.com

"I have had the pleasure to work with Bill, the author of '*Ride the Horses, Feed the Lions*,' over the past year. The impact he made on me while training me for my job was beyond profound. Bill's examples and his poise in writing style and positioning what he is selling puts his customers at ease and creates a comfort level in the purchasing process. I was lucky enough to have the opportunity to learn from him and be able to implement his teachings in my own day to day operations, which has been a large contributor to my own personal success. Bill is certainly an asset to any business, a leader, trainer and friend. I wish he was still [working] with us."
**David Wolfe**, Champion Windows national trainee. Champion Sales Achiever; now with Anderson Windows
dwolfe@getchampion.com

"Bill, I really enjoyed our conversation and appreciated the time you made for us to explore how to be better for others and to each other in the working space. There is so much fun in discovering how to help someone bring their whole self to work and allowing that specific talent to influence others on the team. Honestly, it warms my heart to meet people like you who can reach deep comfortably and know their own selves. It is truly an awesome experience to be able to 'live full on.' I look forward to your book and witnessing your passion further."
**Monica Pritchard,** VP Sales, Marketing and Product Development, Quality Edge Corp.
pritchardsuite@gmail.com

"In today's fast paced, social media driven, digital marketplace, all our sales executives must have the ability to adapt to technologies they don't understand, identify markets that never existed before and grasp buyer behavior that is always evolving. The quick and nimble will be the first to the finish line. I know your book will be a success and on my new website I can sell it as an affiliate."
**Don Straits,** CEO at Corporate Warriors
don@corporatewarriors.com

"Bill was a catalyst for so many large growing experiences for me. He puts his personal touch on adding value to relationships, ensuring that his sales force feels appreciated. When I've needed advice I've always been able to count on Bill."
**Joshua Thomas Daniel,** Mortgage Officer—formerly with Champion Windows
josh.daniel@fairwaymc.com

## Also Authored by William Dilworth Hatch

*The Conversational Close*—A Linear Closing Clinic for Sales Professionals takes basic sales skills and provides a closing system adaptable to all salespeople in our industry. Mastering this system opens all doors to conversation. With a training manual version, this treatise also offers consulting.

*The 97 Club*—A unique approach for managers to encourage writing down three lofty bucket-list items of personal goals as it unexpectedly improves professional performance. It's your opportunity to meet informally with your associates. Experience the power in writing down goals together and creating mini vision boards. Do you believe it will make a difference? It does and it will! What's the difference? Don't focus on business goals. This is personal.

*Forgive - The Third Great Commandment*—A discussion of the emotional, personal, spiritual and religious basis of forgiveness as a commandment and how it impacts the forgiver.

*The Prodigal Parent*—There is an old Biblical story about a son who gave up his entire birthright for a life of instant gratification. This well-known story of The Prodigal Son has a happy ending because his father forgives him, welcoming him back to his family home. In stories of parents who failed families, remorse is unanswered on a dusty, prodigal road, denying them mercy when we withhold forgiveness.

"We spend our youth trying to find ourselves only to lose ourselves in the pursuit of power, affluence, and worldly influence."

—William D. Hatch

"There's no question success comes to us from opportunities. What we do with our talents is what defines us."

—William D. Hatch

"Authenticity brings us all things in life that are of real value. You can't be successful being someone else. Just be yourself!"

—William D. Hatch

# RIDE THE HORSES, FEED THE LIONS

## "One Man's Crusade to Humanize Selling."

William Dilworth Hatch

Author of *The 97 Club* and
*The Conversational Close*

Ride the Horses, Feed the Lions—One Man's Crusade to Humanize Selling
Copyright © 2018 William Dilworth Hatch

**Published By:**
Genius Book Publishing
31858 Castaic Road #154
Castaic, California 91384
GeniusBookPublishing.com

ISBN-13: 978-1-947521-06-3

Edited by: Leya Booth

# Contents

William Dilworth Hatch, a graduate of Brigham Young University with a BA in Economics, worked at Sears Roebuck & Company in the field and headquarters. As VP of Strategic Client Services at Titan Global Group, LLC, his consulting firm, he offers sales training services. Founder/publisher of *Nuestra Gente, the first ABC-audited national Spanish-language magazine* published in America from 1993-2005, he's the author of two other key business management books *on personal goal setting* and *training*: *The 97 Club* and *The Conversational Close—A Linear Closing Clinic for Sales Professionals*.

One Man's Crusade to Humanize Selling is the subtitle of this book, *Ride the Horses, Feed the Lions*. As you will soon come to understand, the *Horses* and *Lions* are identified by my experience as those I refer to as *Stylistic Salespeople*. This book is a study of sales professionals who don't fit into the box but sell elegantly. The intentional building of meaningful relationships is found to be the #1 high performance characteristic cited by the sixteen executives interviewed in *Ride the Horses, Feed the Lions*. Written specifically to help sales managers and sales executives recognize, recruit, relate-to, motivate and retain the *horses and lions* of professional selling, the story-telling style makes it easy reading. As managers we often mistake *Stylistic Salespeople* as hard to manage, resistant to structure or change. As we try to keep them under our thumbs, we drive them to more flexible competitors. Learn how to recognize, recruit and retain "*the horses and the lions.*"

*The 97 Club*—"*A Revolutionary New Approach to Management through Goal Setting*" is a true story about ten average salespeople experiencing the impact of writing down and visualizing personal goals. An oft-quoted *Harvard Business Review* study indicates that the top 3% of Harvard MBA graduates write down goals, have specific plans to achieve them, and are most successful. The issue is not the accuracy of the Harvard study; it is the reality of the power of writing down goals. After reading *The Stylistic Salesperson* join Bill on his adventure with ten average sales professionals.

His other book, *Forgive - The Third Great Commandment,* asks: "*Why is it so hard to forgive our parents?*" (Matthew 16:14-15 KJV).

WDHatch1.titanglobalgroup@gmail.com; (925) 337-0853; *lives in the Denver area.*

https: //www.linkedin.com/in/william-dilworth-hatch-45538637

For me, one burned out match inside a row of un-struck matches symbolizes the importance of sales managers lighting a flame under those working with them. It becomes the validation which transmits the energy, through personal relationships, between employer and employee, even an average performer. It gives emotional license, actually enabling all *Stylistic Salespeople* to unleash flames in their interpersonal skills and talents.

This symbolism is taken from my impressions of the front cover of *Talent Unleashed* published by the Franklin Covey Company.

# Dedication

Seldom does a man in his fields of labor have the chance to honor those who he worked with, learned from, who guided his path. Seldom do any of us have a venue like a book to express a humble "thank you."

This book gives me a way to acknowledge the positive influence of many individuals from family to business. What is interesting about life is how little we plan or prepare for its challenges. Each talent I've developed played a role in my growth as a professional, marketer, public speaker, writer, author, entertainer, composer, and national sales trainer.

My father, **Burton D. Hatch**, had a great influence on me by setting examples of integrity, responsibility, and the importance of hard work and education. A humble man, he thought little about himself. He won the battle over how to parent and then how to be a grandparent.

My father, Burton Dilworth Hatch

March 1, 1915—September 10, 2005

"Key man in the guidance systems Quality Control—the Atlas Missile."

Electrical, Mechanical & Aeronautical Engineer—General Electric

Perhaps it was when I was twelve years old and stayed up late on Christmas evening to play with an American Flyer electric train. It was the gift I'd hoped for. That year my parents had forgotten my birthday. Even with seven children it'd never happened before. Parenting is an amazing journey in humanity; the most meaningful, demanding job in the world. For me, family is my life! It is the foundation of every compassionate society.

That Christmas night, a large deep blue wool rug lay in our living room where the Christmas tree stood, glimmering, glistening, lighting up imaginations and dreams of the season. I had left the train transformer on and acid had leaked out overnight. It ruined the rich, navy blue living room rug.

He never said a word.

At 90 years of age, he asked that we file one more patent. His brain was sharp. He just kept inventing. His message: "Never retire your mind."

***Carl Stiber***, though he may not have realized it, became the business mentor who gave me not only courage and confidence in my abilities but also the opportunity to escape my disappointment at law school and rise to great heights in the corporate world. When the world punished me for standing up for principles, integrity and honesty, this mentor stepped up.

***Bruce Abrams***, Automotive Merchandise Manager of forty stores in the Northeast Zone, he soon became #1 in Automotive in sales increase in Sears nationwide with me as his regional buyer. Bruce was promoted to headquarters. He offered me a corporate job the following year. Were it not for Bruce, my career in The Sears Tower would never have happened.

# Acknowledgments

Thomas E. Morris was Sears VP of Marketing in 1984 when I came to headquarters. He became my champion and mentored me as I rose in the Marketing Department under Ralph Hoch in 1985. They both would open doors, provide my budgets, and pave the way for departments to accept my ideas, my programs, and my initiatives. Tom invited me into many high-level management meetings. Ralph accompanied me to meet Michael Bozic, Sears President, as I delivered marketing ideas to have a "Grand Reopening" of all 800 Sears stores with Everyday Low Pricing. Each assignment helped me grow. Be open to opportunities for growth!

Hoch was Sears National Manager of Retail Advertising and Visual Merchandising in 1992. As I went in for my annual review, paranoid, expecting the worst, Ralph praised my efforts. I had expected to be critiqued, yet he lifted me up. His example of management style is one that I would emulate. He saw the whole picture and appreciated the scope of my contributions.

Glenn L. Moore, a loyal friend and businessman, has earned my respect. He stands as an example of human integrity. I dedicate this book to him and the men and women who influence and develop others almost selflessly. During his career, he promoted more than forty Sears managers into key positions. He was the man who sat across his desk from me and said these immortal words: "I think you can do this." That gave me the courage to begin my journey into the world of commission sales. Glenn was promoted and recommended me to national leaders at Champion after he left Sears. He often reaches out to me with business opportunities. I'm so grateful for Glenn.

I am indebted to my first wife, Jolyne Vest Hatch, who had faith in me. Her love for theatre and music opened me up to develop my talents. Without her love, I would have no children. Without family, what is life? She is the mother of our six children, my first love and a pillar of physical and emotional strength. The physical challenges she went through and her persistent faith in God has been an inspiration to thousands. We sang together, often along with our children, from college through the days we began sending our children to college.

I then met my second wife, Linda Kay Sutherland Hatch, in 1999. Since our marriage, Linda's support, forgiveness, and encouragement have opened my heart to writing. Because of her I've expanded my abilities even further. To this day, on my journey to publish my life's work and share it with as many sales executives who open their doors to the message of *Ride the Horses, Feed the Lions*, she is by my side. "Saddle up!" The race is just beginning for me and for those who read this book and discover the wisdom in its message. Thank you, Linda!

# Foreword
# By Ben Gay III

Since I was a boy, I've been fascinated by amazing salespeople I've had the great fortune to meet with, train with, and sell with. Those men and women could move mountains based solely on their ability to talk. I've spent more than forty years selling and teaching what I've learned to others. Based on my experience, I am proud to be able to recommend another sales professional and teacher, William D. Hatch. In his book, *Ride the Horses, Feed the Lions*, he shares experiences and insights that I recognize from my own background in sales.

A good sales manager can take most low-achieving salespeople from acceptable to good, and they can help the good to achieve success in sales, but Bill Hatch has a different kind of salesperson in mind. The *Horses and Lions*, as he calls them, are the truly exceptional salespeople who can transform a sales department and achieve a kind of success that most others don't. The *Horses* are the salespeople who win the races time after time, and who serve as an inspiration to the rest of the sales team. The *Lions* are the salespeople whose ability to sell is simply transformative. Some of them can be difficult to work with and challenging to manage, but boy, can they sell!

The sad truth is, many sales managers don't know what to do with *Horses and Lions*, or how to provide them with the support that they need to really excel. Human Resources screening processes routinely weed out these superstars because their talents—their ability to listen on purpose, to intentionally seek to understand their client's needs, to overcome objections and get to the sale time after time—don't show up as keywords on resumés.

In writing this book, Bill draws on his own experiences as a salesperson and the manager of three Sears Home Improvement #1 ranked districts, but *Ride the Horses, Feed the Lions* goes beyond one man's point of view and professional opinions. He also extensively interviewed sixteen LinkedIn "Influencers," including Dr. Marshall Goldsmith; Australian sales great Peter Strohkorb of Smarketing® fame; Shawn Moon, Executive VP of Franklin Covey; Matt Kelly; Chad Rawlins; and other fascinating voices of sales wisdom. You won't find another book that brings you this level of sales experience and insight.

What I think is most significant about this book, in a world awash in sales books that push techniques that require you to reengineer your entire sales process, Bill Hatch's approach focuses on bringing out something that your sales team already possesses but probably never utilizes: Authenticity. By seeking authenticity, team members from the front-line sales people, sales managers, and human resources personnel can promote the kind of sales results that most organizations can only dream of. An authentic salesperson is one who connects with everyone—not just the client—at a personal level. They invest in personal relationships with others and encourage those around them to invest in getting to know them as well. Bill describes ways to recognize this kind of authentic, stylistic salesperson, and gives practical advice on how to recruit, retain, and work with them to everyone's benefit.

It's not often that I come across a powerful, easily accessible, transformative book like *Ride the Horses, Feed the Lions*. If you're a high performing sales professional who finds themselves micromanaged by a supervisor who just doesn't "get you," give them a copy of this book. If you're a sales manager with a superstar that you can't find a way to work with and, like Matt Kelly, have a sales maverick you want to fire, you're holding the answer to your dilemma in your hands. And if you're a Human Resources executive whose elaborate "artificial intelligence" algorithms still bring you mediocre sales staff, I encourage you to learn the characteristics of Stylistic Salespeople and get to know them personally before you decide their resumé doesn't stack up. You may just find that you've been turning away the superstars your software is supposed to find.

Sales is about relationships. Bill Hatch's excellent book teaches what so many have forgotten: you can achieve sales success if you focus on the people on both sides of the sales equation, rather than debating endlessly over whether sales is an art or a science. You might find what you've been looking for all this time. I highly recommend you read *Ride the Horses, Feed the Lions*.

Ben Gay III, Salesman, Speaker, Sales Trainer at "The Closers" / Coach / Consultant.

https://www.linkedin.com/in/bengayiii/

Ben Gay III started his first business at age 14, and by age 25 was the president/CEO of what was then the world's largest Direct Sales/ MLM/Network Marketing company. He was personally trained and closed sales with fellow sales giants such as J. Douglas Edwards, Fred Herman, Earl Nightingale, Zig Ziglar, Napoleon Hill, Merle Fraser, Mel Lanius, Bill Dempsey, Gladys Terrell, Hal Krause, Cavett Robert, Gladys Smith, Ray Considine, Larry Wilson, Bill Gove, Walter Wells, Barbara Dempsey, and James H. Rucker, Jr.

# Characteristics of a *Stylistic Salesperson*

1. They are **creative!** They only need your guidance on policy. They are problem solvers.
2. You can't **make** them; you **find** them. This is the best part of your journey. Training new people to become like robots is simply *not* fun, for you or them.
3. They are **people-people**. They are naturally sincere, authentic, warm and **charismatic.** For them each appointment is like a first date.
4. They sell with **integrity**, honesty, are concerned about the customer's needs more than their own, and they feel they cannot be dishonest and succeed.
5. They need to be **motivated,** not managed. How would you manage Michael Jordan? Take an interest in them so they will "get you."
6. The need for **recognition** is different for each person. The challenge is how to reach them. In this sense each manager must be stylistic too.
7. Want to **adopt them** or invite them for dinner? These are my tests. I hire on this basis when looking for a superstar. Eyes wide open? Yes!
8. You can't find these characteristics on their **resumé.** I admit that I never read resumés when hiring a salesperson. I look and listen for who they really are.
9. They're **happy** by nature. **50%** of how we handle rejection is how we are raised. **10%** of events are out of our control, but **40%** is our choice!
10. They want to **help** people. This is an intangible. Look for it. You don't have to push someone who **pulls others up**. They'll help you if you establish a relationship with them.

Know these *thoroughbred*s personally; don't rein them in right out of the gate. Let them set their own pace. Be on their team so they're on yours. Like most things, learning how to manage *Stylistic Salespeople* is on-the-job training. Each person is like a book with something unique on each page. Don't rush. Listen to stories they tell. Watch, learn, have fun!

**Note to Sales Managers**: They want you to get to know them! What about the *lions*? They're the one-in-a-thousand who sell millions! They're salespeople operating outside of the box procedurally, yet they drive tremendous sales revenue. You don't train them. FEED them and learn from them!

# Chapter One

## My Journey

My journey into professional selling began as I stood in the women's shoe department in the Sears Roebuck & Co. store in Albany, New York. I had just finished my first year at Albany Law School, established around the same time as Yale and Harvard in the 1800s. It became clear to me by the middle of my first year that I wouldn't be happy as a lawyer. Some of my close friends had counseled me never to pursue law as a career. "You are too much of a people-person," they said. At the time, I didn't really know what that meant. What was a people-person? Were they right?

The many lawyers in my family include Abram Vermont Hatch (1893-1959), Uncle Mont. After graduation from Harvard University and Columbia Law School, he worked for White & Case in New York, a firm ranked today as first among top law practices by the *Law360* list firms. White & Case is known for its global reach and expertise. He rose to become a banking specialist and was general counsel at Columbia University.

As a young man, like so many of us, I always thought I was right. During my struggle to know what I wanted to do with my life, my sister gave me a birthday card. It was timely. The graphic on the front showed a young man whose head was exploding like a volcano. Her message was that I always argued to prove I was right. Should I become a lawyer? Uncle Mont was part of my struggle to define my future. I was born with many talents and interests, making it hard for me to choose just one career path. What I discovered later was we are all given talents for a reason. What were mine?

My father, Burton Dilworth Hatch, was an aeronautical, mechanical, and electrical engineer for General Electric for forty years. He had 100 patents in his name. I didn't know he had a position waiting for me in the patent office at GE upon graduation from Albany Law School. I wasn't interested in being an engineer. I didn't know yet what I wanted to do. I started a commission sales position at Sears just to make ends meet. Was this to be my new career?

While I was learning to sell shoes at Sears I auditioned for lead roles in musical theater. It was my love of singing and performing that propelled me. My wife was the professional actress in the family and we loved doing this together. Whenever I performed, my parents would be in the front rows in some old Vaudeville theaters like Proctors Theater in Schenectady and The Palace Theater in Albany—165 miles north of New York City—to cheer me on. Dad complemented me once. "I have never heard a better male voice than yours." Their encouragement strengthened my commitment to marriage, family, education, and my desire to contribute to society. My father's philosophical parenting was most clearly felt through his example. At the end of the work day, my father was always home for dinner and attending faithfully to his church duties. My father was a humble man and not one to push his children in one direction or another. He was a religious man committed and dedicated to his family.

My grandfather, Edwin Dilworth Hatch, was the District Attorney of Wasatch County in Utah and had a thriving farm in Heber, Utah. While my grandfather was taking his sheep to be sheared in Chicago, the support price of wool under President Wilson dropped from thirty-three cents to three cents a pound despite a promise never to remove the price supports for wool. Edwin was now bankrupt. He had to sell his sheep just to earn passage home. He had to start life all over again. His wife, Vernico Burton, was frail. Her health continued to suffer with the great stress as she helped him study law. Within two years, he passed the bar exam despite never attending law school. He accomplished this by studying at home, known as "reading law," after completing his daily work.

My uncle, Sheridan Lamar McGarry, served honorably in the Air Force during WWII, surviving thirty-five bombing runs over Europe. As a lawyer, he became Attorney General of the State of Utah.

I was surrounded by the law on all sides. Had I graduated from Albany Law School, would I have been different? It wasn't meant to be. As an undergrad during my third year at Brigham Young University I studied Economics. I quickly realized that this should be my major. That decision later opened doors.

At BYU's Opera Workshop I pursued my love of singing. An interesting aside, my Uncle Mont Hatch's wife, Nita Cowlishaw, was rumored to have sung in the Metropolitan Opera. We often find validation in talents residing in family members. When my sister Seila took singing lessons at BYU–Provo, she gave me the courage to do the same. That opened another door to developing my talents.

I remember a kid in my eighth grade class at Tredyffrin-Easttown Junior High School in Berwyn, Pennsylvania. He annoyed me. By then, he already knew he wanted to be a doctor. I had no clue what I wanted to become. I wasn't certain I wanted to be a lawyer like others in my family. In my struggle how to best to use my talents I would even consider singing in Broadway musicals. Growing up, I didn't like history or creative writing. Today I love them both. Life is our greatest journey.

My father's brother, Calvin Shipley Hatch, worked for Proctor and Gamble for twenty years. Prior to retirement from Proctor and Gamble, the Chairman asked if he was willing to accept a promotion to become CEO of the Clorox Corporation, owned by Proctor & Gamble. At that time, sales were tanking dramatically. Cal took the job for five years with the understanding that someone was waiting in the wings when he retired at age 65. My uncle soon turned Clorox around, increasing sales and profits by forty percent. Maybe if I had played my cards right, my uncle would have offered me a position at Proctor and Gamble in Cincinnati and I would even have a golf club membership. The problem would be that I hated golf. However, I would soon discover that I loved retail, not law.

My parents' friend Don Spence was running Sears' shoe department in Albany, N.Y. After my first year of law school, married with two kids, living in a two-bedroom apartment in my parents' basement, and saddled with law school loans, Don hired me for a summer job. I began selling shoes on commission at Sears. Then a funny thing happened. My very first day, I asked Don Spence, the shoe department manager, for books on how to sell shoes or even how to size a kid's shoe.

It was "Back to School" time and I didn't even know the first thing about shoes. My feet were narrow. My mother had to order my 12B shoes from a catalog. I understood how important it was to find shoes that fit, so I wanted to know how. Don stood in the stock room, extended his arm and pointed to the sales floor. He smiled and said, "Go out and help the kids. You'll learn soon enough." In just three days I had handled over 100 kids' feet. I loved it! Soon I was promoted to women's shoes. The first thing one stately woman said to me was, "My, you have great teeth." I must have been a real charmer. Are teeth the real secret?

I want to debunk the myth that success is just handed to anyone. Success is hard work. What if nobody teaches you anything? How do you become successful then? Would learning how to sell be some secret kept from me until I stumbled over it? Where was the *University of Selling* I could go to? With two kids, a wife, and a B.A. in Economics, I still needed help!

When you start your first job you're given problems to solve. And in sales organizations it can be even more challenging. You need to grow your business but where do great salespeople come from? Any company that sells a product needs "boots on the ground." In residential sales, which was my profession, it is only as you add salespeople or improve the quality of those you recruit by *"riding the horses and feeding the lions"* (I'll explain that soon enough) that you grow the bottom line. Could I become one, a *Horse* or a *Lion*? It almost seems like outstanding salespeople have to be born that way. From my experience, over 15 years of professional selling and sales management, the great ones smile, help you, and listen, as if they're really interested, hanging on your every word. Great salespeople do all these things with ease. For managers, executives and HR professionals who want to hire *thoroughbreds* who love selling and are responsible, the previous list of characteristics of *Stylistic Salespeople* is where to start.

Life is like Don Spence's school of shoe sales, and I learned early on that selling is about people, not just product or price. Business is often on-the-job training. My excitement? Every day I had a new challenge to solve I had never encountered in any classes in college.

I remember attending the forward-looking Meacham Elementary School in Syracuse, N.Y. There were sections in each grade in all subjects. On the first day of second grade, a student may be placed, for example, in Section 2-1 reading group but could move ahead to Section 2-2 reading group if they were willing to read more books. Students could move to the Section 3-1 mathematics group too. Each group sat together at their own table, like a club. It was a real incentive to make an effort! I remember asking Mrs. Baron, "How do I move to the next group?" It excited me to think if I read more books to catch up I could be part of a higher reading group. It was the same in music. In 4$^{th}$ grade I was playing violin with 7$^{th}$ graders.

Elementary school classrooms were actually separated into two categories with academic students on one side of the hall and those we called, at the time, "blue collar" kids classified today as vocational in the classrooms on the other side of the hallway. I remember in first grade I was told to go to the other side of the hall to the vocational group. My father was a professional electrical, mechanical, and aeronautical engineer. I was not going to be some vocational blue-collar worker or a businessman!

I refused to go. The school principal called my mother and had her come to school. I knew I belonged with the academic students just like my two brothers and my older sister. I would not allow my teacher to classify me differently. I wrongly viewed those who would go into business as different than an academic or professional like my father. My mind was made up. The Hatch family had always been leaders. In that situation, I suppose I was too. My mother came, visited with the principal of Meacham Elementary School, and my filibuster worked. This "Bill" passed from kindergarten to 1$^{st}$ grade on the professional side of the hall.

After law school, while working at Sears Roebuck, I discovered a love for retail. My economics degree prepared me to respond more accurately to customers' needs by recognizing sales trends and adjusting my local inventory. Soon I was made Division Manager of work clothes and menswear. My men's work clothing department was soon ranked 15th in all of Sears. Annual sales grew from $80,000 to $250,000. I later became the youngest $1,000,000 Division Manager in the Albany store's history. I still have that sales plaque today.

What I didn't realize was that the store manager, Carl Stiber, was watching me. I made a mistake one day and he came by, acknowledged it, and said, "Bill, everyone makes mistakes. What I expect is that you learn from them and not make the same mistake again." I took Carl's advice seriously and he began to support me to be Division Manager and eventually be promoted to Northeast Zone Staff. It finally happened two years later. That changed my retail career forever.

At that time I hadn't realized I had entered an exclusive club. I never went to Harvard, wasn't a member of the Elks, and never went golfing with the boss. I was never part of the gossiping inner circle of managers. I hadn't read any books on sales. But my natural abilities with people would lead to many future successes. This was important because when we enter homes or offices of customers in residential or business-to-business (B2B) sales, our relationships outweigh politics in the office. Success in building relationships will ultimately win over the managers we report to. Customer focus is an interesting characteristic that relates directly to what I will be discussing about the unique skills of *Stylistic Salespeople*. While they may seem to be undisciplined, what you'll find is that their interpersonal skills are unique, and lead them to success in ways most people can't fathom.

I believe now that I was developing into a *thoroughbred*. What was to happen to me next? Well, even *thoroughbreds* can stumble, and I did. After two years at Sears, Carl Stiber, my first mentor, was promoted to Group Manager of five stores in Rochester and Buffalo. My new store manager, Walter Murray, hated Carl. He had always been one step behind Carl through his entire career. Before Carl left, he told Walter, "Bill should be the first one you promote." Guess where I ranked on Walter's list? Dead last. Walter held me back two years, promoting anyone and everyone else. An entry level executive position opened up in Sears' Zone Office, located in the Albany store. In my personal life we were struggling. I made $14,000 a year. Median income for college graduates to support a family of four children was almost $26,000. A couple with only two children qualified for $17,700 in goods and services from government assistance. If I had been unemployed our standard of living would have gone up. I felt stuck. Ironically, even though there was an opening, Walter Murray wanted to give it to an 18-year-old high school graduate who was Department Manager of Boys Clothing. In the past, promotions went to college graduates. When our Security Manager found out, he went to Walter and told him if he promoted her, he'd "have his job." Walter had no one else distinguished in sales to promote but me. My departments ranked nationally. He begrudgingly recommended me.

**Note to Walter:** *"Knowing how to value and manage people is a bigger key to success."*

## I had been Patient and my Career Exploded.

After Walter was forced to recommend me, I became a trainer on the Northeast Zone retail staff, and my career exploded. My first assignment was to implement computer registers in all of the small Sears "C" stores from Rome, N.Y. to Presque Isle, Maine as well as every small Sears retail store in New Hampshire and Vermont and Maine. Things quickly changed in my life. Soon I was required to be away from my wife and, by then, five children five days a week. My assignment put me four or five hours away. We had recently acquired a golden retriever puppy. Including the dog, my wife now had responsibility for six she had to care for all by herself.

I soon discovered the excitement of a dinner out on the road and a nice hotel faded fast. It worked something like this. First you drive five hours. Then you train eight hours a day. You eat more than you should and fall asleep with the television blaring. A call home that's too short ends with "Sorry honey, I have to put the kids to bed." When I came home at the end of the week, my wife would explain, "Bill, your picture is still on the mantle for the kids to see." My wife was trying to tell me

I wasn't to engage in parenting on weekends. It was hard for them, but even harder for her. Mom was the voice they heard all day, five days a week. Dad was now "just a visitor." I was now a road warrior. It felt like a demotion.

"Necessity is the mother of invention" is a famous proverb. I became the "Father of Invention." I got creative and highly organized. I'd never been accused of being organized, just ask my wife, but if I was going to be away from home, I'd better make this career successful so I could be promoted and get off the road. I was going to make things happen! In my new drive for efficiency, I found a way to convert each C-store, the smallest retail Sears stores, to computer register systems in five weeks vs. the planned two or three months. I got a two-year assignment done in nine months. I was soon promoted to the position of inventory control merchandise manager with many more responsibilities and no travel. I was thrilled.

© Schenectady Light Opera Company, used with permission

A year later I was a regional buyer for twenty-seven Sears Men's Sportswear departments and then the buyer for forty Sears Automotive Centers. Now that I was back home, I could make my wife's dream of acting and singing in musical theater a reality. Because I no longer worked nights, we joined *The Schenectady Light Opera Company* as part of the cast. Seven years later in my ninth leading role I played Harold

Hill in *The Music Man* and sent an invitation to see the production to my new boss Bruce Abrams. He invited Cliff Hooks, who was then the Northeast Zone Manager in Albany, N.Y. My performing talents were seen by my manager as unique abilities, which led to promotions as a regional buyer and softlines manager in Pittsfield, MA. Carolee Carmello, pictured above playing Marian the Librarian, has starred on Broadway for 25 years. I was 165 miles from Broadway but I decided to take a very different path and was promoted to Sears Chicago offices to work on the 25th floor of the Sears Tower. The CEO of Sears was Edward A. Brennan during my corporate career from 1984 to 1992, and Arthur C. Martinez from 1992 to 1996.

Edward A. Brennan

January 16, 1934 – December 27, 2007

The business world now excited me even more with new challenges and opportunities. At Sears Tower in Chicago, I had unique assignments that required all my abilities and some talents I didn't know I had. The key was not to fear new talents, but to use a sort of "Discovery Channel" in my brain. Try things! Make mistakes! Learn from them. Each day was unique. When I first started in the Albany, N.Y. retail store, complaints weren't handled quickly. Complaints often went to Carl Stiber, the store manager. His message: "Handle them at the lowest level of management possible." What he was saying was "take care of it yourself." That philosophy fueled my success. My key mentor in the Sears Tower, Thomas E. Morris, VP of Marketing, was no longer at Sears in 1996 when my job description changed and I was not allowed to interview for my own position. Tom had taken me from my position in the Sears Marketing Department and raised my visibility to the point that when Tom Morris left, many Sears associates thought I would be the next V.P. of Marketing. John H. Costello, President/COO, Nielsen Marketing Research, USA., got the job instead. At first things were okay. I was the Acting Director of what was called ethnic marketing at the time. I had been promoted to that position in May 1992 and my creative Hispanic Marketing and Advertising programs resulted in Sears being recognized in an L.A. Times Business Section article in January 1996 as *"The Best Ethnic Marketing Retailer in the United States."*

That would soon change. The new VP was looking to cut Hispanic marketing funds. I chose to defend the crown jewel of my ethnic marketing, *Nuestra Gente*, Sears' proprietary Spanish-language magazine that I had created from the ground up. It was the first national ABC-audited (or rated, as some would say) Spanish magazine in the United States. But Costello wanted to eliminate it or have a friend head up the project. After 12 years in field organization and 12 years at Sears corporate, a sudden re-organization occurred. Ironically, just when I was at the top of my game with Hispanic store sales climbing, John eliminated my position. They had to hire three people to replace me. I was offered a lateral move or a severance package. I could see the writing on the wall with this new VP. so I left Sears and became a consultant. Because of the loss of a consistent salary and some personal choices I made in our marriage, my wife was devastated. We divorced a year later.

Robert Armband, co-owner of *La Raza,* Chicago's Spanish-language newspaper, offered me a job. I was grateful for the offer since it took eleven months and multiple interviews before I was offered a marketing position with Kraft Foods as Corporate Ethnic Brand Manager in Northbrook, Illinois. Just four months after that my boss at Kraft was promoted, and the executive who replaced him let me go.

I finally accepted an Account Director position with a Spanish advertising agency, *La Agencia de Orci*, in Los Angeles, CA. After four months, the accounts were reorganized and my boss was fired, and I was quickly out of a job. This was hard to handle. My father was a GE "company man" for forty-four years. I had been a company man for twenty-four years at Sears. Now where could I use my talents?

Surprisingly, unemployment drove me to Denver, Colorado. I had started dating the woman who would become my second wife, and she lived in the Denver area. Things began looking their darkest, though I didn't know that an exciting *"world of sales"* awaited me just around the corner. Little did I know that a second Sears career was where I would become a *Stylistic Salesperson*, making more money than ever before. I moved from L.A. to Denver with no job and no idea what I'd do with my life. I remembered that eighth-grade kid who knew he would be a doctor. What would I be when I grew up? This question always seemed to haunt me, but I have learned that there are many opportunities and doors that can open for you, if you believe in yourself and you persist. No matter what our age, race, ethnicity, gender, financial, or social status, we can succeed and flourish—if we seek out our talents and magnify them.

At one point in my corporate career with Sears I was known to 800 store managers and flew around with corporate officers. Each assignment opened doors for me. There is no question that success comes to us from opportunities. But what we do with our talents is what defines us.

Looking back, I had been divorced, fired three times, and offered severance while my marketing was recognized nationally, but I never gave up! Quoting Alexander Graham Bell, "When one door closes, another door opens, but we so often look so long and regretfully upon the closed door that we do not see the ones which opened for us."

## *Persistence and Patience are Partners!*

*Ride the Horses, Feed the Lions* is my one-man crusade to refocus the sales profession on relationships or, in other words, to "humanize" selling. I found by choosing to be a professional commission salesperson that it was critical for me to be my authentic self. When I left my home each morning and would meet complete strangers, it wasn't long before a relationship was created. I worked for a company people trusted, but it was critical that each customer, client, or potential business partner trust me. How did that happen? Why do some salespeople hate their jobs? Why do some succeed and others fail? In the rich talent pool of potential sales candidates, you'll find the next *Stylistic Salesperson*. Each is an individual. Will you wade in the waters and become one yourself? Managers face the challenge of understanding *Stylistic Salespeople*. Get to know them. As sales executives at a district, regional, or national level, you must need and want to listen, to like, and to love people to be successful. I did. You can.

# Chapter Two

## "I Think You Can Do This."

Now in Denver with my girlfriend, it was time to prove my worth by finding good employment. I landed two interviews from job postings in the newspaper—one with Sears and one for assistant manager for the Cherry Creek Mall with a salary of $65,000, quite a bit less than the $115,000 I had been making at *La Agencia de Orci,* which matched my salary at Kraft Foods, and less than $96,000, my highest salary at Sears. Tough to swallow? Yes. Starting over was emotionally hard for me. My ego had been beat up pretty good. Four jobs in four years was just not like me. At the time I didn't know my next interview with the Denver District Sales Manager for Sears Home Improvements, Glenn L. Moore, would change my life's path and open a second career of fourteen more years with Sears.

There I was, sitting in Glenn L. Moore's office as he described a commission sales job with no base salary, no gas money, and a week of unpaid training. Then he said, "I think you can do this." What I would do next surprised even me. I took the commission job. After a week of training, I was partnered with another new hire for my first appointment. He knew product, and I knew the paperwork. That's all! What was I doing there?

After showing a newly married couple in a single-story starter home with eight windows what Sears could provide them, I said to the husband, "This is normally when we would call in to get you approved on credit."

Referring to discussing the matter with his wife, he asked, "Can we talk about it?" In a knee jerk moment, I said "Yes." As they went back to the bedroom, I turned to the guy with me and said, "Should I have said no?" Every salesperson dreads hearing "I have to think about it."

It wasn't long before he and his wife came back and sat down. Then all of a sudden he said to both of us, "Okay, let's do it." The rest is history. One easy sale, as unlikely as it was, had just happened to two rookie salesmen. It was amazing. We had sold eight windows for about $8000 and the customers were thrilled we could get them financed. I had my first happy Sears window customer. My self-confidence grew as I sold $132,000 worth of windows my first month. I exclaimed, "No one could stop me now. If I loved sales before, now I really I love sales!" When we left that house, I thought to myself, "I'm God's gift to selling!" I started at Sears Home Improvements February 21, 2000, and that year I earned $65,000, what I would've made as assistant manager of the Cherry Creek Mall.

In all seriousness, I am convinced that commission selling is the best career in the world. For anyone who is stymied in their career path, even if you have never sold anything in your life, sales will open the doors, smash the glass ceiling, and provide a future you can only imagine. *Sales is indeed the lifeblood of every business. Saddle up for the ride!*

## "You don't Sell...they Buy!"

I remember at some point talking with my oldest son when he said to me, "I can't do what you do, Dad."

I was puzzled and asked him, "What do I do?"

He said, "You sell!"

As much as I love my son, I have to say he was wrong. I discovered one simple truth veteran salespeople have come to understand: **"You don't sell, they buy!"** What I would later discover is that *Stylistic Salespeople*, the *horses* and the *lions*, know this too. If you know it without being taught, if you love people, have innate interpersonal skills, and naturally enjoy meeting people and listening to find out their needs, you are a **Stylistic Salesperson**! These are all things that most new salespeople have to be taught, but they come naturally to us.

For sales executives, managers, and HR professionals, allow me to define the characteristics of *Stylistic Salespeople* from a gender perspective. While the salesperson usually looks for "who controls the pocket book" when closing a sale, today that is no longer usually a man. Things continue to change. Likewise, there are no longer stereotypes of what kind of salesperson will succeed. This places more responsibility on whoever is interviewing a new sales team candidate. There are many different types of people who have successful careers in selling. The issue is often one of perception, both for applicants and managers. Anyone can screen a resumé, look for experience in sales and a pattern of success with other companies, but how do we find *thoroughbreds* in embryo? Where do we find the *lions* who can explode our sales? How do we recruit *Stylistic Salespeople*?

Often, an average candidate, interviewed for a commission selling position, believes there is a cookie-cutter approach or some magic system that, if learned, will turn them into a sales guru. This is never the case. Usually this results in the new salesperson stumbling and losing interest in selling. You can't just plug in a system and expect success. Selling requires more of you emotionally, intellectually, and culturally than perhaps any profession.

Too often executives approach sales as if it were a science. It's easy to be convinced by any one of the many successful sales evangelists to believe in the next newest system: *"If we have this new selling system our success can come from presenting more product information so our brand or company reputation makes the sale. We don't need talented salespeople. Just use this method!"* Creating a successful sales team requires much more than that.

For years the success of Sears Home Improvements had come from training salespeople with the famous *Sears Ten Step* selling system. The majority of those who failed went to their competitors, who were grateful to have someone Sears had trained. It was like a calling card on a resumé. "You worked for Sears?" Immediately they were hired. When I started selling in February 2000 it was for American Home

Improvements, a Sears wholly-owned subsidiary. I was excited to return to Sears. In a formal Press Release, January 6, 2001, Sears announced: "All salespeople in our forty-eight offices are now Sears employees." Since I'd worked for Sears and left with a severance package, normally it would be against HR policy to hire me to work again for Sears. But the announcement made it possible for me to return. Miracles do happen! Believe! In this second Sears career in the home improvement industry where salespeople often go from company to company as if on a merry-go-round, I didn't think it would be easy and I didn't know if I could do it. At least I knew Sears as a company. That would be a foundation to build on.

Indeed, I would go on to have great success running three #1 ranked profit districts for Sears. Take it from me, if you are disciplined, take accountability for your success, care about people, and if you are authentic and if you sell with integrity, you will never have to worry about food, housing and the good things in life.

Quoting Richard Brenkley, *B2B Marketing Magazine*, July 25, 2011, "If sales is the lifeblood of every industry [and it is] don't fear social media, embrace it. It is just relationship marketing after all."

This timely quote emphasizes the focal point of *Ride the Horses, Feed the Lions: Stylistic Salespeople* have mastered relationship marketing of themselves to the customer. They do it naturally. Go find *Stylistic Salespeople*! Recognize them, recruit them, relate-to them and retain them.

In an interview with Jim Schleckser, CEO—Inc., CEO Project, I asked him how he finds great salespeople. Jim said, "When I was Group VP and President of Spirent Communications, it was hard in job interviews for me to tell the good ones from the great ones, because they're [all] good at selling themselves. Things I looked for first? Prior success, particularly selling in different fields. Also, salespeople can be successful at one firm, but if they can sell across multiple fields, go to another business and do the same thing, a pattern of success in multiple products really interested me."

He continued, "With someone who's been successful at only one firm over an extended period of time, sometimes it's hard to understand all the support systems and factors that were going on, and who was around helping them. [Their success] could be a bit of a coincidence. Because of that it is hard to tell how much they were a part of it. But it's certainly one pattern of success. Another is I'll actually have them describe what the most significant sale was that they made. I would say, 'Let's dig into how you made that sale happen.' What I'm looking for is the nature of how they sold. I want that to match up with how the firm that I'm running sells. There are times a sale is an individual process, and I want sort of a hunter-killer to get out there [and] ink the sale without a huge amount of support."

I asked Jim to summarize. "Tell me, after almost all sign-offs, one last person has to close the sale, what characteristics make them great?" I added, "We throw trust around a lot, don't we?"

Jim hesitated. "Yeah, I was going to go there for a minute, but I chose not to."

I continued, "Jim, on the way into work I was listening to a guy on the radio. He said consequences. I heard, **Trustiquences™**."

Jim said, "Wow, that's a good term. Is it yours?"

I stated, "It is now. We say we buy from people we trust but until a sale is closed and all the paperwork is signed, do we still make our decisions to buy from those we like?"

Jim stated, "Yeah, I like you, I trust you, I buy from you."

Then I went in for what I call the kill shot, the real question we all want to have answered. "Let me ask you, Jim, how do you see talent in a job interview? How do you first distinguish or recognize their greatness in that first visit? Obviously, it's not that hard to come across poised. They look like you, dress like you, and represent someone who is going to sell like your company sells. They've done their homework. You're sitting there across the desk. What intangible says to you, *this person is a superstar?*"

"Yeah, now this is going to sound stupid, but [I wonder if] I'd buy from them. As an executive, as a guy who ran a bunch of companies, now I look at him and sometimes I'd say...I wouldn't buy a paper clip from this guy. I believe my customers wouldn't buy a paperclip from him. But if he or she's poised, smart, has good answers, transfers enough confidence to me that I would buy from the person across the desk, I'd give it go. It's a real 'gut-check' moment. If he's my kind of guy, he gets me and I'd buy from him, what makes me think my customers wouldn't buy from him?"

I also spoke with Tony J. Hughes, a best-selling author, blogger, and well-known keynote speaker who has over 200,000 LinkedIn followers. His worldwide consulting business is based in Sydney, Australia. After some introductory questions, he explained three key things he looks for in hiring. "I want to see how they prepared for the interview. First, have they researched my company? Second, did they check my LinkedIn profile? Third, did they ask time-relevant questions?"

I went for the close. "Tony, if you got more than one who passed your criteria, how do you choose?"

He paused and said, **"Gut feel."** The greatest will always recognize the value of personality!

# Chapter Three

## The Power of Perception

Anyone who has been in business understands the importance of structure in their sales training. That's why *Stylistic Salespeople*, by virtue of being the most productive members of the team, become a challenge to most sales managers. Many *Stylistic Salespeople* are let go from sales organizations because of perceived "lack of discipline" when that's the furthest thing from the truth. They're the *thoroughbreds* and *lions* of the sales world, and a breed of their own. They're greatly admired and command respect. They also evoke jealousy and may be harder to manage. That is part of the characteristic signature of *Stylistic Salespeople* who can single-handedly make your career a great success. They did mine. They don't come along very often.

"*Ride the Horses, Feed the Lions*" is a phrase I borrowed from Peter Bulger. He hired me at Champion Windows headquarters in 2015 as one of three national sales trainers. I fondly call him *The Professor*, as he is the most amazing sales guru I have ever met. Throughout his sales career he's exhibited amazing interpersonal skills. He's a *Stylistic Salesperson* with his own unique sales process.

If you have been a sales trainer or in sales management long enough, you know as I do that we have a gender-based issue in many of our sales teams. The salespeople we hire are predominantly male. This can cause problems on many levels, not the least of which is that women sell as well on average as men—there are many female *Stylistic Salespeople*, and many who are not. In addition to that, it has been shown statistically that men don't listen to women as closely as they do men. Sexism aside, this is a problem for your sales team because the majority of purchases are made by women. We typically listen to our female customers just long enough to get a word in edgewise. Conversation at times may be perceived as sort of an inconvenience until "it's our turn to talk." It's very human, but in my experience training sales professionals for two decades, listening "on purpose" is something that I had to focus on.

In contrast, it has been shown that women are often more consultative in their approach as managers and in relationships. Women often seek out opinions of others and weigh those perspectives against their own. What I had to learn at the time was the female brain is not only wired differently, it is not that way by accident. In a graduate class at BYU we actually saw a preserved male brain next to a female brain. We learned that the *wiring difference* we discovered gives women an advantage in relationships, which can reveal itself in conversation. Statistically, women *reason together* and listen to each other. This becomes more important when training men to focus on listening. If we want to attract and retain great salespeople, the one trait that we should be looking for is their ability to listen and collaborate.

"*The listener*" who has the power of perception becomes a *pot of gold* for you as a sales manager. However, regardless of gender, all *Stylistic Salespeople* have greater intuition and listening skills than average new hires. This makes them extremely valuable. Can *listening on purpose* be trained? If you can reach the sales candidate on an emotional level, yes! Also, in the case of male members of your sales team, if men understand that it is in their interest to understand differences in how women approach issues, they can learn active listening behavior. "*Active listening*" isn't a new concept. Customers perceive they're being heard when we listen, but validation comes by understanding their needs. I know that I had to learn to *listen on purpose* as I rose up the ranks to be rated #12 out of 1500 salespeople at Sears Home Improvements.

Managing salespeople also requires the *manager to become a people-person*. *Stylistic salespeople* are conversational and value people more than "just being in it for the money." They enjoy getting to know people. That's why they stay in sales. They intentionally foster and encourage this interaction. Meeting new people and earning their trust in a short time is a sign of their people-person skill set. They exhibit outward listening skills by being present in conversations. This interpersonal skill helps anyone seeking to gain a better understanding of their customers reach an increased level of communication. When someone "gets" that the relationships we have with people during a career in sales is the real enjoyment that keeps professional salespeople getting up each morning to meet a stranger, they're a *Stylistic Salesperson*. They enjoy people and the entire process, with or without a sale.

**Note to Sales Managers:** Accurate paperwork is usually *not* among the common strengths of these unique *Stylistic Salespeople*, so more support is often needed for them. It is crucial to understand how much of an asset they are—and can become—to your team. When I was running the Sears District office in Livermore, California, covering the San Francisco Bay Area, one salesman had been a "*walk-on*" with the Oakland Raiders and the San Francisco 49ers. If you are unfamiliar with the National Football League, this meant that he was never drafted. He didn't go to college but he went to an open tryout and made both teams. Because of his community volunteer work, local Oakland kids knew him. He held the Sears company record for the most sales in a day, seven. *Mr. Football* turned in contracts in stacks of paper, rolled up in rubber bands, covered with coffee stains, missing some initials or with signatures in the wrong place. When discussing this with him, I suggested, "Why don't you hire someone to help fill out paperwork for you? You'll make more money." While this former walk-on Oakland Raider and San Francisco 49er ignored my suggestion on how to improve his performance, nevertheless our management team saw value in this unique *Stylistic Salesperson* who other sales managers may have let go. He loved to sell.

As managers, we may lose sight of what our real goals should be. We became managers based on our sales achievements. We may think we can manage best by using what made us successful. Some procedures we require our sales team to implement may complicate a sales proposition:

"Go see the customer. Listen to the customer and be perceptive to determine their needs. Master new technology. Have a disciplined sales process. Make a friend. Help the customer make a decision. Give clients a reason to trust you. Invest time building relationships. Have fun. Then write up the agreement you made."

Often this rewarding process is interrupted in a sales meeting by "Do it my way and follow through. If not, you're fired. Now go out and sell."

Once again, as sales managers and executives, "are we losing sight of what our real goal should be?" Sales!

Where does it say to jettison any salesperson that doesn't fit into the mold that we, as new managers, have just constructed? Nowhere! How do you manage these *Stylistic Salespeople*? To develop these skill sets of intentionally listening, caring about people, having fun, and investing time in relationships, we need to apply these principles to how we manage our sales team. The only effective way to be perceptive and meet their needs comes from ***"listening on purpose to our professional salespeople."***

Why listen to our employees? Why work on our own interpersonal skills? Because of the profound impact, and importance, of validating the *self-image* of our salespeople. Validation is not commonly understood as a key to the connection to our sales teams. Managers rarely tell us what a great job we are doing. A negative environment is an *open door* for **us** as sales managers to change.

The importance of positive reinforcement became popular in Ken Blanchard and Spencer Johnson's book, *The One-Minute Manager*. Their basic idea is almost counter-cultural now. I will put it in my own words: Negativity is human nature, but a process outlined in *The One Minute Manager* is an empowering approach to managing people.

Referring to *The One-Minute Manager*, Eric Spamer from the Bruin Leaders Project, UCLA (January 1, 2011), said, "This brief volume tells a story, recounting three techniques of an effective manager: one-minute goals, one-minute praisings, and one-minute reprimands. Each of these efforts may take only a minute but is purportedly of lasting benefit." While we may all have read *The One-Minute Manager*, and somewhat understand the premise, by *going back to the roots of the concept of servant leadership* we can only manage our sales teams effectively if we recognize and value them as people. *Ride the Horses, Feed the Lions!*

## Managers: *"Spend more time with those who produce!"*

Let's focus on discussing *The Power of Perception* for just a moment. What's required of managers to motivate *Stylistic Salespeople* who operate their business careers and lives "outside the box"? Remember, these sales professionals value relationships. That should be your clue. The answer is that you, too, must be a "people-person." And if you understand that, the time and attention you give to *thoroughbreds* and *lions* will pay off handsomely.

I remember my then twenty-year-old son asking me for some advice on something important to him. He was serving on a church mission, having responsibility for fourteen young male missionaries. Management issues focused on encouraging and supporting them. These young men were leaving their friends and families, some for the first time, to serve the church. They were often sent far away from home, worldwide. In my son's case, it was New Mexico. Morale becomes critical in such an environment. Many missionaries may not have gone to college, worked, or lived alone before. Even though the young men worked in pairs, it didn't mean they'd get along with each other or deal well with feelings of isolation and rejection that often occur when discussing religion with complete strangers. With a deep conviction that what they were doing would benefit those they taught, they were believers. Have you ever had anyone wonder if you believed in what you stand for? They have, I'm sure. Perhaps it's because your conviction didn't seem sincere.

Rejection is hard to handle for anyone but it is a part of professional selling, missionary work, performing on stage and in all relationships. My son wanted to know where to spend his time and how to motivate men that may not be dedicated or reliable. Where would his efforts make the biggest impact? I suggested he spend his time with those who took responsibility, who were already productive. Those who worked the hardest believed openly in what they were doing. Soon my son was appointed an assistant to his church mission president.

My advice turned out to be correct. When it comes to belief in what you are doing, perception is reality. Belief generates commitment and integrity. Integrity attracts like to like, which improves the quality of your recruits.

## Belief is important for Managers too!

It may seem strange to bring belief or personal conviction into this discussion of the perceptions you have of your salespeople, but in truth it is the most critical part of the process. Remember, managing people is built on a foundation of how they perceive you, too. New sales managers are often selected from a pool of highly successful sales professionals. Perhaps you were chosen for that reason. Where do you start? Or what do you turn to if you're failing as a manager?

Commissioned salespeople experience challenges each day. First, they don't know how to identify who will listen and be receptive, and—truth be told—neither do the sales managers who assign them their leads! Residential salespeople and even new B2B account executives meet complete strangers, not knowing if the outcome will be a sale. They may not believe strongly in what they're doing. Is it just a job for them? Do they sell just to make money? Are they the kind of person who will do or say *anything* to make a sale? Quite often they will model what they see you do as their manager. What are your convictions? Do you believe in the people you work for? Can they believe in you? Do you really believe in yourself? Do you believe in what you're offering? Your product? Your company? Are you authentic in all you do, all you say, and who you are? Belief becomes transparent. When you were a salesperson, did customers ever say to you, "You really believe in your company, don't you?" Then you know you have one key quality that will connect not just with a *Stylistic Salesperson* but everyone.

## Three Ways to "Ride the Horses and Feed the Lions"

1) Establish a relationship with Superstars. Get to know them on a personal or close business basis. Understand who they are and what makes them tick and then validate their abilities.

2) Utilize them. This frightens most sales managers. *"You can't train others to do or be what he or she does or is..."* is a common claim of middle managers.

3) Ride with them on sales calls. Learn from them. Use any *golden nugget ideas* you see they have. Challenge others to emulate their interpersonal skills. When you see them contribute, validate them so they support you.

## *One Caution:*

Some will say, "Don't let salespeople ride with him. He's got his own style. He doesn't follow procedures. He'll just confuse them." This is a common thing you hear from sales managers and even other salespeople. Only follow this advice if a *Stylistic Salesperson* doesn't want you to ride with them. Otherwise ignore it. Deserve their trust. Learn from them and connect! Wait it out. In time, even the most skittish, prideful *thoroughbred* racehorses trust their trainers.

We often fear super-achievers because they do things in ways that aren't in our basic training manuals. They may seem to be in conflict with what managers teach them in their disciplined, mechanized, step-by-step, stopwatch type of way. Managers who don't insist we follow procedures are also labeled by executives as mavericks or being "off the rails."

If you're a sales manager who still sells in the field, runs leads, calls customers and addresses emerging needs then you can reach these superstars more easily. If you lead from the past and insist on using old approaches that may not be relevant today, then the creativity and interpersonal skills of *Stylistic Salespeople* may challenge you as a manager more than others. Also, it is important that you don't let them perceive you are intending to check on them. The goal is to earn their trust, be able to utilize them and strengthen your team. *Stylistic Salespeople* are usually the most productive in a sales office. When a sales manager challenges them in a meeting, others watch to see how they react. Often in what we call parking lot meetings after lunch, sales managers either gain or lose salespeople's respect and disciplines put in place can fail. You sink or swim based on relationships you have with your superstars. I need to say that again. *You sink or swim based on relationships you have with your superstars.* Implementing the secrets mentioned above can lead to success for both parties. If a sales manager is riding along with the *Stylistic Salesperson* on a lead, what he or she learns will elevate any team.

Successful sales managers have the courage to grow their business by recognizing, recruiting, relating-to, and retaining *Stylistic Salespeople* who seem to have the ability to "close at will." Supporting and validating them can earn the respect of members of your team who aspire to be like *"the horses and the lions."*

## *"Sometimes it's Not a Matter of Degrees"*

A Master's Degree is far superior and commands more respect than a Bachelor's, but we shouldn't be recruiting a sales team of those who feel they have *Master's Degrees in Sales*. Actually, I know of no school you can attend to get that degree. The toughest type of sale is the "one-call close." It has to be awarded by the school of hard knocks, by learning on the job and observing other sales superstars. The good news is, in selling, even a high school education can become the launching pad for a successful sales career. Those over fifty can reinvent themselves and become of great value to a new company. It's possible in sales, by working hard, to master *"The One-Call Close."* In addition, using or developing people-skills, having an authentic, honest personality, and sincerely believing in your company opens doors to customers and a great standard of living.

As sales managers our goal should be to advance our new hires, regardless of degrees, from recruitment to the highest level of excellence they're capable of achieving. By doing this, we have the best chance of retaining a talented team. The alternative is high turnover. There are costs to continuously recruiting, training, motivating, and losing salespeople. How do we escape the costly recruitment cycle? Even though one of the realities of sales management is to weed out those who consistently underperform, in order to retain salespeople on your team and reduce turnover, use your most talented performers as examples for them to follow.

What can your team learn from *Stylistic Salespeople*? What turns a good salesperson into a superstar? Unfortunately, the skills of a *Stylistic Salesperson* are not so obvious that they can be taught. These skills are shown by example. Only if your *horses* and *lions* are loyal to you as a manager will they typically let others ride with them. Can your team benefit from emulating a *Stylistic Salesperson*'s investment in building relationships? Yes, but this may require a change in approach to your personal relationships before you can apply it at work. To get a bit symbolic, an *"On-the-Job Master's Degree in Sales Management"* requires every former sales pro to be *authentic* in People-skills, Personality, Persistence, and Patience. Authenticity is key. The rewards are great!

## *How to Recognize Unusual Talent*

Look for reliable people with a track record of being responsible. Then recognize personality types a client can feel comfortable inviting into their home. Would you invite them for dinner? Can you trust them? Why? Do you trust them? Is it a "Gut Feeling" like Tony J. Hughes mentioned? Is it the "Barbeque Factor" you will read about later from Shawn Moon, one of the most productive sales team builders at Franklin-Covey? Is it that your dog or cat seems to like this stranger? Customers notice. In a LinkedIn article by influencer Peter Strohkorb, as he noted, "The new trend seems to be a dependence on technology, when we should really be investing time and resources in our people." Peter is someone to emulate and to consider having present his message to every corporation that faces the challenge of marketing and sales working together.

One day, while I was managing the Denver Sears Home Improvements District that included all of Colorado, Wyoming and half of Nebraska, I was training a class of seven new people that included a man named Greg. As I got to know him, we became friends. Today, I'd trust him with my personal safety. Now, that is trust! Who can you say that about? Which one of your employees? *Great salespeople aren't just trained, they are found.* In Greg's case, he was clearly disciplined and followed the selling plan. He honestly hated the interpersonal part of sales. Obviously knowledgeable of every aspect of construction, he became #6 in the company. We rode that *horse*. Another true *Stylistic Salesperson*, James, in the Washington D.C. office, was almost entirely self-taught. He was disciplined and could sell anything. He was a true *lion* and was ranked #3 nationally in his second year. He was trainable, but because of his unique talents, I decided to *feed this lion*.

Any manager—whether a sales mentor or a CEO—is often evaluated, promoted, and respected based on the people they hire and promote. Why be afraid to hire the individual who is smooth or has the charisma we wish we had? Why question the high-level performer who has been released from another sales organization? Well...because we don't know this person so we depend on the input from others. Today's HR practices limit our ability to get unbiased input, positive, negative or even objective. Is it a gamble? Yes, of course. The key? Build successful relationships with *Stylistic Salespeople* rather than only recruiting people who adapt to your structured training model. When you gain the trust of *Stylistic Salespeople* they will become invaluable to your success and your entire sales team. The upside? Life changing. Relationships are the answer.

This requires a lot from a manager if that manager is stuck in their ways. Sometimes these types of managers will play it safe, train the basics, and never deviate from the outline or plan. In John Maxwell's *Success Magazine* article, March 4, 2015, *6 Tips to Develop and Model an Abundance Mindset,* he said, "*The Scarcity Mentality* is the zero-sum paradigm of life. People with a Scarcity Mentality have a very difficult time sharing recognition and credit, power or profit—even with those who help in the production. They also have a hard time being genuinely happy for the success of other people." In managing salespeople, having a scarcity mentality rather than abundance might be demonstrated by expecting salespeople to just spit out words of a sales script. In other words, "*Don't be creative. Close, close, close.*" Some management styles make the sales team think they are in the Army. "Salute the boss!" Selling simply doesn't always work that way. In one case at Sears, I discovered there are some superstars who are disciplined to the point of being regimented.

Robert worked for Sears Home Improvements in the San Diego office. He was so disciplined you could set your watch by when he started each selling step. He did the same things, said the same words, and told the same jokes to each customer. He had a great personality. He went on all company incentive trips. He lived to sell! Robert's nephew, Zach, was still a surfer at the age of twenty-eight. Robert went to speak to him about what he wanted to do when he was "done playing around." He was concerned about Zach's future and wanted to help him. Everyone in Zach's family knew of Robert's success—of his trophies, the baubles, and his wife's glitter.

Robert invited Zach to San Diego to run sales appointments with him for three weeks. What happened next was unexpected. He respected his uncle's success, and tried to copy exactly what Robert taught him, step by step. Discipline and structure is what Sears taught Robert.

Sears' "Ten Step Selling Plan" is well respected and universally known in the Home Improvement industry. While you may not be familiar with it, famous corporations engaged in residential repair and upgrade both on the exterior of homes and the interior, such as kitchens and baths, have copied Sears' training programs. While running the Sears San Francisco Bay Area District, based in Livermore, California, 2004-2007, we hired a man who a big box store had sent to take our training. He was to copy everything, the way we approached the customer, closed the sale and even our contract paperwork. After mastering Sears' sales plan he was hired as their Regional Manager.

Robert, Zach's uncle, had mastered Sears' "Ten Step Plan." He was disciplined, not creative, not flexible and not stylistic. But dependable? Yes. As Zach ran appointments with his uncle Robert, he thought, "That must be the way everyone succeeds in the world of sales." Not surprisingly, it didn't work for this handsome, suntanned surfer. Zach seemed gifted with personality and charm. He had lived near the ocean all his life, making his home in Santa Cruz, California. He wasn't undisciplined in his personal life, but he valued relationships more than *"selling like Uncle Robert."* That regimented process worked well for Robert, but not for Zach. At first, Zach tried to be like Robert but in doing so he became, statistically, only an average salesperson for Sears. If he had continued this way, he may never have become categorized as one of the *horses* you could simply ride to the finish as a manager.

Take a note here as managers: The challenge of managing a sales team may not be new to those who have experienced it, but the

key is to approach each salesperson as an individual. Each one of us has unique abilities that, when leveraged, will enhance our ability to connect with someone and justifiably earn their trust. Authenticity is built upon our uniqueness. Zach would turn out to be an extreme example of who we call *Stylistic Salespeople*. In his case, he would become a *lion* in sunglasses, khaki pants and a sport shirt. Was he just an average salesperson? We might have seen him that way as he tried to sell like Robert, memorized scripted approaches and doubted if he could just "be his authentic self."

Zach ultimately decided to do it his own way. He used his unique abilities. He tweaked and customized his approach to each of the people he met. He was a great listener and was very successful with single women. His relaxed, sun-bronzed appearance didn't hurt him at all. While we all can't depend on appearance, that, along with his personality, active listening, and understanding of his customer's needs, made him a success at selling and extremely wealthy. He became the #1 salesperson nationally at Sears Home Improvements four years in a row, averaging over $4 million in annual sales. Is there anything wrong with stable, disciplined salespeople who average $800,000 in sales per year? Of course not. But who wouldn't want someone like Zach on their sales team? Management prior to my arrival in Livermore as his District Sales Manager let him be much more independent than the rest of the sales team, and I did the same. Did he become a *Stylistic Salesperson*, the *thoroughbred racehorse* or the *lion* by the training he received? Actually, if his managers had attempted to micromanage him, demand the same discipline and regimented structural approach that his uncle Robert exhibited, Zach would have left Sears, perhaps never entering the "Hall of Fame" sales world. He told me as much.

Some of his sales steps might have been somewhat out of order. He was much more conversational. He earned trust, solved problems, sometimes arranging for services we didn't offer yet. Zach operated in a way that was clearly *off the rails* at times. How do you manage someone like that? I gave him the space to be Zach, and he loved selling. He did whatever was required to take care of his customers. Unique? Yes. Authentic? Yes? A listener? Yes. While we all can't depend on appearance, clearly he was someone a manager discovered who became the prime example of the *Stylistic Salesperson.* If you go back and read the list of characteristics of those I am calling *Stylistic Salespeople*, you will find Zach there. Look for these characteristics and hire them. Why do we need *Stylistic Salespeople?* The next chapter will share even more about Zach and others like him.

# Chapter Four

## "Why Do We Need Stylistic Salespeople?"

I was assigned as Sales Manager in the San Francisco District Office at the beginning of 2004. Sears Home Improvements sold to customers from Santa Cruz, where Zach lived, to Modesto, near Tracy, California, where we lived. When I began working with him, Zach had already been the #1 Sales Rep of the Year, of 1500 nationwide, for four consecutive years. He was making between $300,000 and $400,000 a year.

Everyone wanted to watch him sell, and they wanted to ride with him, but Zach wouldn't allow anyone to be with him in the car, not even managers. What do you do, as a manager, with a superstar who won't come to meetings, sells his own way, and refuses to be managed in the traditional sense? *"Feed the Lions!"* Once more, developing a relationship is the key. As a sales manager, you must become a people-person. What we had in Zach wasn't a *horse* as in *Ride the Horses*. Soon we saw Zach was a *lion* as in *Feed the Lions*. You may be able to train *horses* to race, but you will never be able to ride, fully train, or reign in the *lions*. Just *Ride the Horses and Feed the Lions.*

Why are *Stylistic Salespeople* so valuable? Why are they so unique? Why does a *Stylistic Salesperson* need to work for a manager who values them and lets them run at their own pace? Why is it important for a sales manager to recognize the powerful personalities and character traits of *Stylistic Salespeople*? It is easy to declare that such a person is unmanageable and that his or her abilities and methods are of no value to your team. Should all *Stylistic Salespeople* be written off as unreachable and untrainable?

For managers who think you can't teach style, and in response to questions about talented salespeople who have a reputation for closing sales no one else can, **there's a lot you can teach about style.** We can teach more active listening skills and encourage service to others. We can promote authenticity and value each salesperson's personal talents, their accomplishments in life, their skills, interests and personality traits that we enjoy in getting to know them. These are the very things that help customers to connect with us. Ultimately, they are the foundation upon which trust is built. When we play a game of averages, do we sacrifice the future loyalty of superstars just to endear ourselves to the middle of our sales team, the ones who never aspire to greatness? Why resist the challenge that might stretch the outer limits of our own management and interpersonal style?

At meetings, some sales managers repeat a typical complaint like, "You're not listening to the customer. How do you expect to close a deal?" As managers this may give cover for ineptitude, but it stops discussion before it can yield fruit. Can't we stop insisting on doing things how they've always been done? We can't grow unless we do.

Perceptive managers want their sales teams to be perceptive. And organized managers want their teams to be disciplined, have great follow-up, and in essence, *be like them*. In fact, every sales manager has their own style. Beyond a structured sales presentation we require salespeople to learn, aren't we really also requiring them to do it "our way"? The core of a *Stylistic Salesperson*'s personality mirrors a rare but *natural salesperson*. We need *natural salespeople* because they will sell two or three times more than average new hires. Zach sold over $4 million a year, four years in a row, and was the top salesperson at Sears Home Improvements. No one else was close. Yet, remember that no one closes every sale, not Greg, me, and not even Zach. What do *Stylistic Salespeople* have in common? They're people-people!

## *Can Anyone Become a "People-Person"?*

"It's hard not to fire someone perceived as loose cannon, a maverick, someone outside of the box," Matt Kelly, VP of Sales, Fairway Architectural Railway Solutions, commented about one of his salespeople recently. "I inherited a salesperson with a unique personality upon my third VP of Sales position. I was looking for greater insight on how to manage a challenging, unique, creative, somewhat undisciplined, remarkably talented salesman. This rep of mine was my enigma."

Matt said, "I needed this guy, but I wanted to fire him. I was unsure how to handle him. He wouldn't return my calls, and when he did call back he didn't want to meet with me. I just wanted to ride with him to see how this superstar was so successful."

This was a new VP assignment for Matt. "I wanted to get to know my sales team. After a few attempts and a number of refusals, then having him avoid my requests to meet me, I called the CEO to tell him that I'd decided that I wanted to fire this guy. This was my new sales team, and he would either follow me or he had to go. I told my wife what I told my CEO, 'I'm going to fire this guy!'"

"Soon, I scheduled my first national sales meeting. He would have to come and I could address this issue, face-to-face. At the national meeting his comments were very confrontational. He was distant. Cold! After the meeting I asked him to go to dinner with me in a way that he couldn't refuse. Dinner seemed to be fine. My attitude didn't change initially, and it was certainly not my intention. Soon he began to open up and we 'just talked.' First it was about sports, then I shared things about my family. As I look back, I'm not sure when my attitude toward him began to change. I listened to him and really got to know what made him tick. I started to get to know him better as the night wore on. Did he change who he was to ingratiate himself with his new boss? Not at all. He was unique and wasn't changing who he was or how he sold for anyone. Not even me. It was me who changed as a manager. If I wanted my salespeople to *listen* then it had to begin with me, and I did.

"I started to get to know him better as the night wore on. Astonishingly, in the bar six hours later, as we stood up to leave, we actually hugged each other. You know...a *man-hug*. The same guy who I wanted to fire became a friend. I can truly say 'I loved who this guy was inside.' Best of all, I was able to understand what I could do to harness his full potential without allowing his *maverick personality* to become a distraction or deterrent to me and the overall health of my sales team. You may get frustrated if you don't understand the asset this type of salesperson is and what they can mean. If you don't already have one of these rare gems in your sales team you are missing out on the real rainmakers."

**Production soars when we as Sales Managers apply the three steps mentioned earlier:**

1. Establish a relationship with Superstars. Get to know them on a personal and a close business basis. Understand who they are and what makes them tick and then validate their abilities.

2. Utilize them. This frightens most managers. *"You can't train others to do what these superstars do...."* is the common claim of middle managers.

3. Ride with them. Learn from them. Use *golden nugget ideas, approaches or concepts* you see they use. I call them golden nugget ideas because they are priceless. Challenge others to emulate their interpersonal skills. When you see them contribute, validate them so they support you.

When *Stylistic Salespeople* are permitted to contribute in their own way, it validates them, and their exceptional achievements can motivate your middle performing team members to aspire to be like them. The question becomes *"What can the rest of the team learn from unique Stylistic Salespeople?"*

January 4, 2004 was the day I conducted my first San Francisco District Sales Meeting. This was my first day as manager of the most profitable district in Sears Home Improvements. We think we know it all. We have been successful at sales. That is why we are promoted to such key positions. But I had never come close to half the sales volume Zach produced consistently each year. After meeting him at the District Sales Meeting and visiting him at his home in Santa Cruz, my approach was to *"Feed the Lions."* When I met Zach I struggled with the same thing Matt Kelly did. Zach wouldn't let anyone ride with him except Dan Morse, who he had great respect for. I promoted Dan to Field Sales Manager as a way to manage Zach. It was the right move. Later Zach told me that if I had tried to *manage him* like *just any salesperson,* he would have left Sears. Zach was a *people-person* and I thought, "That's how I'll manage him." Was Zach arrogant or confident? Was he unique or born with certain talents? Think about the director on the movie set who has to work with headstrong but famous actors. If you have never stood on a stage in front of thousands of people before, perhaps it's hard to see what this challenge is like. To become a people-person is perhaps the ultimate interpersonal challenge.

Let me share with you what I mean when I say that to become a real, authentic people-person we all may have to change our lives. I had to change my own life so this is "front-and-center" and personal to me. The first thing I changed was how to approach my personal relationships. I don't mean I went to some kind of sensitivity training, but I realized that if I was going to teach by example I needed to learn how to listen. The great news is that people can change. Their motivation? We're paying people to *"listen on purpose"* to customers. If they do, they'll earn a bigger paycheck since customers will trust them more. Best of all, they will change as a person.

Next, we need to know that it's acceptable to discuss the differences between people. Some of those differences may be strengths waiting to be validated and leveraged in seeking and reaching excellence in any field of endeavor. Even at home. Let me use a gender example. My perception is that women use more words in a discussion than men. I believe that women have a verbally-based cognitive skill in communication with others that is different and more perceptive and inclusive than the approach that men take in professional sales. If, indeed, that is the case, how will that effect how we train men to interact with women? How can we help them gain the trust and meet the needs of their female customers? Good questions.

In 2014, Northwestern University, where I once lectured the MBA Club at the famous Kellogg School of Management about Multicultural Marketing while working at Sears corporate offices, research published in the Journal *Scientific Reports* was a study of 133 adults in both relaxed and professional settings. Each person had a device about the size of a smart phone that captured and measured social interactions. Their findings? "Women talked more when it came to casual conversations while men talked more in long conversations. Men were more likely to dominate professional conversations...." This study addressed an issue that will relate to our managing, training and hiring practices. Who should we hire? What should we train men to do more effectively?

In my experiences designing and selling kitchen remodels, I observed that women often enjoy discussing their choices, the colors and styles, the way these design features would combine with their existing flooring, paint on the adjacent walls, and how "changing the kitchen" would contrast or conflict with the next room. To me, and perhaps it cannot be statistically proven, I believe that in general women listen to others while men often prefer to decide unilaterally. Does that mean women talk more than men? And is that relevant to sales? The conclusions that I have come to are as follows:

We need to train men to *listen on purpose*, intentionally, and NOT try to dominate conversations.

We need to hire more women on our sales staffs. Casual conversations tend to generate trust and create relationships. Authentic relationships in business-to-business and in-home residential sales are critical to success as well as something even more important, "the enjoyment of a sales career."

What does it mean to *listen on purpose?* The definition of *"listening on purpose"* may be obvious even though we may not realize we are doing it or avoiding listening for the very same reason. For example, if we want to understand someone's point of view, we certainly would *listen on purpose.* If, on the other hand, we are in a business discussion and only want to convince those in the meeting that *our solution is the only solution*, then we will be courteous only long enough to *get a word in edgewise* when the person speaking takes a breath. Sound familiar? How this relates to managing will become clearer as we discuss a very important key to selling.

## *Assessing the Customer's Needs*

How can we assess the customer's needs if we don't listen with that purpose in mind? Do we just wait until the customer gets done talking so we can begin? Some people are better at listening on purpose. For example, it is my observation that women tend to enjoy engaging in meaningful conversation by active listening. In my opinion, this gives women an advantage in sales to other women. Is this stylistic? Does it matter? I believe it's a trait that is more common in women than men and therefore a reason to recruit women in professional sales career opportunities. While it may not be only found among females, this innate ability is similar to a *Stylistic Salesperson* who is naturally interested in people. A people-person, regardless of gender, is who I look to hire.

I approached this training challenge with new trainees with a laptop presentation. I used the example of an attractive woman and a handsome man to catch the new trainees' attention. The photos were used to represent customers. In each case the slide included these words in LARGE font: "Would you listen to him or her?" It was a serious question and usually received the enthusiastic response "Yes!"

I then made my point by asking, "Then, why don't we listen more?" Seem obvious? This discussion is part of the world of selling. It allows me also to emphasize that as managers we need to look for and recognize unique skill sets and abilities. I found that what was common in the *Stylistic Salesperson* was more common in women so I sought them out to add to my sales team. You may have discovered the same thing on your team. In my previous example of "getting a man's attention" in an attempt to explain that we need to *actively and intentionally listen on purpose* to everyone, it was not how attractive a person was that mattered. My trainees got that, but it generated a deeper discussion about the importance of listening. Then I zeroed in for the kill.

"When we listen *to actually find out what a person needs*, whether in sales or in our personal lives, only then can we help solve their problem and meet their needs more effectively." If we as sales managers and HR professionals look for the characteristics listed in the beginning of this book describing a *Stylistic Salesperson*, then gender is irrelevant. Physical appearance is irrelevant. Who the person is, what they are made of, and if they are who we now identify as an *authentic people-person* can change our approach to interviewing, recognizing, recruiting, hiring and retaining the *horses and lions* we might miss on a resumé. While we don't have to teach the *Stylistic Salesperson* that they need to listen, I found many new hires were not good at it.

With a few exercises in which we all paired up, the new hires would start to just talk with each other. After that, however, it was interesting and revealing how little they remembered. If we did it again, they "got the message." Do you always want to listen? What I always explain to our new hires, trainees, and middle-level sales performers is "Learn to listen, but **listen on purpose**. You will get to know your customers and find out what their interests are and what they need. ***It will change your life*** and I mean that! The impact of listening at home, and in marital and family relationships, will amaze you. Listen when your spouse, your child, sibling or parent is speaking and validate what they are saying by sharing that you understand. Repeat it back. You will be shocked at the reaction. Do you care or don't you? Then prove it."

Validation is an interesting term. My first wife, whom I still love, tried to help me understand what Oprah Winfrey would later clarify.

My wife said, "You never validated me." My look of amazement was obvious. As a child, a copy of *Readers Digest* containing a monthly list of ten obscure words and definitions was always on my father's nightstand. But it never featured "validate" at any time in its 100+ year history. If not for Oprah Winfrey and Dr. Phil, men would not know what it means. "But I have you up on a pedestal," I replied. "You had six children. You directed shows in local community theatre, you worked in church. You could have easily used your skills to run any company." What did I miss? "How have I not validated you?" I had failed her. I was confused.

What I found out was I didn't really *listen on purpose* with the intent to understand her reasoning. I only listened long enough to get enough information to ride in on my white stallion and save the day. While this is personal, in business we trip over these same obstacles.

What she taught me in that short conversation has stayed with me ever since. I am not saying that I am perfect at it. What I am saying is that I now LISTEN to understand and seek to validate what one of my children, a co-worker, or a family member has decided to do. By doing this, I am validating them, or as Oprah would say, "No one wants you to fix it for them. Listening is validation. I've talked to nearly 30,000 people on this show, and all 30,000 had one thing in common. They all wanted validation.... I would tell you that every single person you will ever meet shares that common desire." —The Oprah Winfrey Show, final episode. Learn to validate!

When it comes to the business of sales, listening on purpose isn't waiting for customers to stop talking so you can move on to the next line in your presentation. A popular sales doctrine is when you're talking, *you're taking control.* Who wants to lose control? We forget that when we ask questions or listen, we *are* in control.

Role-playing, where one person is the customer and the other plays the role of a salesperson, is one of the tools we use when training. It helps to see if those we are LEADING are following. Practice *"listening intentionally"* and validating the other person. It can be painful role playing this. Most haven't done it, so as I train new hires I challenge them to try it when they first get home. "Listen to your spouse, children, a college roommate, or elderly parents." Listen on purpose? Yes.

Relationships will dramatically change for anyone who listens out of respect, sincerely showing interest in what other people say. For women, this is the highest form of validation. Oprah Winfrey has confirmed this.

The next critical part in active listening is evidenced by sharing with the person what he or she said. Make sure you understand them correctly. A business-driven listening skill helps personal relationships too. This is not role-playing, it's respect, validation, and reality as in the statement below:

"Nobody cares how much you know, until they know how much you care" (most commonly attributed to Theodore Roosevelt but actually an anonymous quote).

The greater part of learning to listen intentionally is watching a sales career turn you into a people-person. If you're in sales to make money, you'll stay a while, until you're bored or burned out. If you love people, you will be able to go to work each day knowing it's okay that your goal is to have fun and make someone's day. Get it? Not everyone does.

If sales managers and salespeople get the message I intend, they will save themselves a lot of recruiting, hiring, and training, while not firing the best salespeople they may ever have had just because they couldn't put a square peg in a round hole. People-skills needed at work can be mastered when applied first in personal relationships. If you use this approach and teach them the *how and why* of listening, your team's performance will improve dramatically. For salespeople, increased perceptions of what makes customers tick helps create an environment in which decisions come more easily for customers. That's what we are there for; not to sell but to listen and *help them make a decision*. After thousands of in-home visits, it has been my experience that, when it comes to home improvements, clients know at least six projects that need to get done. What they don't know is which one to do first. Once they decide to accomplish one, the other five priorities will fall in place.

## Why talk about Stylistic Salespeople?

Even though I was often labeled stylistic and was told not to teach my style, I excelled in personal sales, ranking 12th of 1,500 Sears Reps my second year working at Sears Home Improvements. When looking for a future Field Sales Manager or District Sales Manager, we typically selected someone more regimented in the way they taught their sales process. While I was good at that, I always added my own approaches, some of which I have shared, such as having real love for people and listening-on-purpose.

As I mentioned, I went on to be a District Sales Manager in San Francisco, Washington DC, and Denver. The office in San Francisco was ranked in the Top Five for sales and #1 in profit at least one year during my three-year tenure. When I trained, I shared the importance of people-skills with new trainees. Those who applied them excelled. Out of 1,500 reps in the company, those I trained with the perspective of a *Stylistic Salesperson* ranked high nationally. My challenge was to train them in a way that they valued, understood, enhanced and improved their authentic interpersonal people-skills.

I witnessed million-dollar salespeople leave Sears if management launched a new project or changed sales presentations. It disturbed me. Once, we got a massive, rote-memorization of over twenty-seven pages of dialogue for a laptop presentation, and it chased away some long-time sales reps and seasoned veteran professionals who weren't technical, or weren't interested in changing the way they succeeded. Why lose any *Stylistic Salespeople*? People-skills aren't a program. Presentation books, laptops, memorized scripts and *Power Words*? What about "I like you, I trust you, I buy from you?"

## "But He Just Sells on his Personality."

You may get pushback from members of your sales team or upper management as you add stylistic, flexible, charismatic sales professionals. The average salesperson may resist examples set by superstars. They may view holding up the exceptional sales performances of others as being critical of their performance. But in commissioned sales positions, pay that is related to attaining sales goals attracts people who take initiative. At some point you'll likely hear excuses when you compare the productivity of your *Stylistic Salespeople* with lower-performing staff.

"Yeah, but they just sell on personality."

"He isn't really following the selling plan you taught us."

"She does things with clients that you don't allow us to do."

"He gets the good leads. I could sell if I got those customers."

"I saw them out with the boss at some restaurant."

"If I had his money, I wouldn't have to drive as many miles!"

When you start to hear these comments you know you are on the right track. Why are you on the right track? Are you intentionally encouraging jealousy or resentment? Not at all. You're trying to get their attention. You want motivated individuals on your team. When you have a strong game plan, one where you value everyone for their unique abilities, stick to it. Validating one person through recognition is not denigrating the performance of others. What it does is require more of you as a manager. It actually opens the door to the powerful concepts as related in *The One Minute Manager*, mentioned earlier. "One minute praisings" means you are managing each member of your team as an individual. The goal? Have them aspire to "Be like Mike"—referring to a phrase commonly associated with Michael Jordan, perhaps the greatest basketball player in history. Did he fail? That is the greater part of his life story. Failure draws the clearest and most direct *map* to succeed in the future. Fix what's wrong.

Those who complain the most find themselves at the bottom of your sales board every month. They just can't figure it out. It must be the leads or the city you keep sending them to. No, it's the last names on lead sheets. "I never sell anyone in that town and certainly not with that last name." Really?

I had this exact situation while I was managing the San Francisco District Office that was consistently ranked in the Top Five nationally. This is a reality check and how I dealt with it. The Bay Area is one of the most ethnically diverse in the country. At one of our meetings, this "last name" discussion came up. "No one sells to people with that last name!" We're all human and as we fail we often look for scapegoats—anyone but ourselves. After the meeting, I began to work on my plan to debunk this theory. I went to the files of sales we had made over the past few years. I made a list of last names that were hard to pronounce and that were of different cultures from all over the world.

We say we aren't prejudiced today, but prejudice really means to "pre-judge" others we don't know, haven't met, or with whom we may have little experience. It is the other guy's fault, not ours. I felt the same way as a salesman when I had an appointment in Boulder, Colorado. I never seemed to sell in Boulder and hated to get a sales lead there. Surprise! One day I had a sale. Then I told my boss, "You can give me the leads in Boulder now." That's all it took. One sale changed my attitude!

I decided to have a contest at the next meeting with my sales team in San Francisco. If they could pick at least twenty last names out of my list of fifty that actually were sales made in our office over the past few years, they could win $20. Instant cash was a motivator for any salesperson. I had their attention. I decided to choose the longest last names in every one of a dozen cultural groups in the Bay Area, perhaps the most diverse metropolitan area in America outside of Washington DC. This would be a challenge. What was the obstacle to them winning? Let's admit it. We all judge. History is history, experiences are experiences, and attitude is attitude.

What happened? Jack, who went on to manage two different offices for Sears Home Improvements and Champion Windows in the Northwest, raised his hand. "Hey, you called out more than just twenty last names that you said we think we can't sell. I think I won the $20 but it looks like so did some others who are raising their hands." I paused and said, "Exactly the point I am trying to make. All of these were sales. All of them! Remember the phrase 'Your attitude will determine your altitude'?" They got the message and never once complained again about who they were going to see.

We are about helping others, not prejudging them. Right? In my high school we chose languages we wanted to study. Latin was my first choice as most colleges expected it. Why did I choose to take Latin? I did it because it was hard! It was a challenge. I took two years of Latin. Later, it took three years to complete two years of Russian and I barely passed. When it came to sales, I thought I'd do well with Russian immigrants in America. But, like my experience selling in Boulder, Colorado, when I tried to sell to Russians, I quickly went "o for 14" on fourteen appointments. Finally I sold one young Russian couple some windows, but then they cancelled. I guess was guilty of prejudging too.

# Chapter Five

## "It Wasn't You, Bill."

By virtue of my divorce, I was single—which wasn't something I'd anticipated would ever happen to me. But life went on, and I discovered the interesting attitudes of the singles community. In the shadows of the greatest failure of my life, divorce after twenty-eight years of marriage, I felt a vulnerability that I had never experienced before. As I look back at this failure, the greatest lesson I learned was to accept total responsibility for the choices I made and own my part in them. We all can chose differently at any point in life. Even in failure, seeds of success can be planted and take root. Secondly, I realized that I can choose differently.

I recommend a phenomenal, insightful book, *Daring Greatly* by Brené Brown, that shows how *having the courage to be vulnerable* can transform the way in which you live, love, parent, and lead. Vulnerability is not exactly at the top of the list for crusty, hardened sales generals standing in front of their troops each week when giving them the next *Glengarry Glen Ross* speech about how they're lucky to get a lead. But in today's environment, vulnerability can play a role in your rise to excellence. To your team, you want to project strength externally but need to use your interpersonal skills internally.

If you aspire to be an exceptional manager of salespeople, this is an important tool in your work chest. You teach others to listen on purpose, be perceptive, and take an interest in what customers are interested in to connect with them and earn their trust. Not in a mercenary way just to get the sale, of course. Rather, you use this tool to reach them on a personal level with emotional integrity. What they see in you, they may be willing to emulate.

Ego has its place in sales. But it is only one of the fuels that drive salespeople. Numbers mean something. The sales board and rank each month motivates us to persist and learn something new in this lifetime vocation. We learn and we forget. We rediscover a piece of magic that we learned earlier as if it were brand new. Being able to learn from our coach and co-workers is a quality critical to our continual growth and development.

A quote about Casey Stengel, the long-time coach of the New York Yankees, is relevant to our basic discussion. I'll paraphrase it for effect: In his later years, Casey Stengel forgot more about baseball in a year than anyone else in baseball knew.

When sales superstars get bathed in their achievements, humility is not commonly found in their war chest. But for me, it would soon come in handy. I don't know about you, but I have a healthy respect for anyone who has the innate ability to remember people's names. What I am good at is recognizing and remembering faces. They always tell you to use people's first names in sales, but I wasn't good at it. One time, I called a woman Barbara when her name was Betty. That ended the trust I was hoping to build. No sale!

One day, I actually got a callback from a prospective client. We *never* get callbacks in residential home improvement sales. If they don't buy during the first visit, they are shopping for price. We used to laugh about sitting in a corner and turning blue waiting on a call from someone who claimed, "We'll be in touch."

But in this one case a woman did call me back. She asked me if I remembered her and asked if I'd be able to come back to see her. She was ready to make a decision. I sat there stunned. I didn't know who it was. How could I save this opportunity? The sound of her voice brought her face to my mind, but no name. She had been divorced twice and now had another new boyfriend. It had been about four weeks since I had met with her and her former boyfriend who was living in her home to offset the cost of rent.

It was a Thursday night, and I was in Denver, heading to my next kitchen appointment. "You want to meet at 6 PM? Sure, that will work." I'm in my car. I don't have my appointment book with me. "What's your address again?" One thing I did religiously was keep a spiral notebook with copies of my lead sheets in date order. Armed with her address, I was able to find her name. Now I was all set, but how embarrassing. Perhaps that's why at the time I was a salesperson and not managing the business.

Here is where this story takes an interesting turn. The young woman was just thirty-one years old and had been divorced twice. She lived with her former boyfriend to offset the rent and had a new boyfriend. The appointment went fine. It turned out it wasn't the price that held her back initially from signing a contract with me for a new Sears Kitchen Cabinet Refacing job. During our first meeting she actually told me, "Bill, I'm not buying tonight." Then she said, "I'm going to get ten estimates." We all have heard the normal "I'm getting three estimates," since the insurance industry has made it a standard.

But ten? That had me really confused. Ten estimates? Really?

We all have customers who seem to have little sense of urgency or who want a lower price, but what was her real reason to get ten estimates and to sit there for two to three hours with each salesman?

When I finally wrote up the sale during our second meeting she and the former boyfriend even added $1,200 more to the original estimate and signed the paperwork. He even helped us pick out the countertop colors. I left with a signed work order. What more could I ask for? Something seemed to be missing. It was like playing an old game of "Clue" and me thinking that Colonel Mustard did it with the knife in the ballroom. What was it? If it wasn't me, what was it? Why did she call me back? Was it product? Was the Sears kitchen just better than the other nine companies? Perhaps it was our warranty. We do stand behind our work.

My mind was all abuzz. Okay, I got the sale. But why did she call *me* back? It wasn't the price. We had added over $1,200 beyond what she first wanted. During the original contact I had asked her if she was really going to sit through ten three-hour appointments. She had said yes. And amazingly she did get ten estimates. But what bothered me was I did not know why she needed to do that. Why get ten estimates? No one gets ten estimates. Wow! Then she actually called *me* back. We almost never go back. This was a "one-call-close!"

As I sat across from her, she said something that retracted my ego into a humble, emotional box it where it belonged. When I asked her why she was going with us, she said, "It wasn't you, Bill."

Oh, Great! What she said next was the answer. "I didn't trust any of the ten men that came to my home, but I trust your company. When you leave, it will be Sears that will stand behind the work, not you."

Trust! She didn't trust me but she trusted Sears. The company you choose to work for is a significant key to your success. Choose carefully. Your integrity is one key, but the company's integrity is the other.

Teaching the importance of earning the customer's trust becomes a key component of a sale. This intangible need for a customer to trust the representative of a company must be authentically earned by salespeople. I worked for a company with integrity. But why did she feel the need to get ten estimates? Now I *was* Colonel Mustard in the Ballroom.

Let's review: She was thirty-one years old, divorced twice with a former boyfriend helping with rent, and with a new boyfriend in the wings. She may have wanted ten estimates because she didn't trust men! The salespeople who visited her were all men. It is also possible that she didn't trust her ability to make a good decision, but men were clearly a part of it. She had made at least three choices that didn't work out. I'm no psychologist, but her message was about TRUST. Why was trust so important? If we think that she was the exception to the rule, we would be wrong.

How do we EARN the trust of a stranger after only three hours in their home? The *Stylistic Salesperson* knows innately. Bring in the *horses and the lions*. They are both stylistic in their approach to selling, they focus on the customer, they listen on purpose, they earn and deserve trust. Perhaps when she said to me "it wasn't you Bill" what she was saying was "You didn't earn my trust on the first visit. I had to compare you with nine other salespeople." In the end, she trusted a company and not its salesperson. Trust is the key!

# Chapter Six

## What Do We Look For?—Covey Insights

Usually after an author completes a book, it gets edited to correct any spelling or grammar errors, the cover design is approved, and marketing begins so the creativity of the author reaches its intended audience. I was well along that path with this book when I interviewed Shawn Moon, Executive VP, Strategic Markets; Former VP, General Manager of all Franklin-Covey sales professionals; and co-author of *Talent Unleashed*. In his capacity as General Manger, his personal approach to managing a national sales team was evident. Sales exploded! The retention rate of their salespeople went from 54% to 80% over a three-year period, based on tracking salespeople remaining with Franklin-Covey after at least three years.

I spoke with Shawn regarding his management approach and learned that his style is compatible with the premise of this book. The legacy of Stephen R. Covey is alive in Shawn Moon.

Shawn shared some meaningful and insightful thoughts about those he might identify as *Stylistic Salespeople*, who seem to have something unique about the way they conduct business. Then he clarified it even further.

"They come in all sizes and shapes. Some are extremely organized. They're successful because of their relentless follow-up."

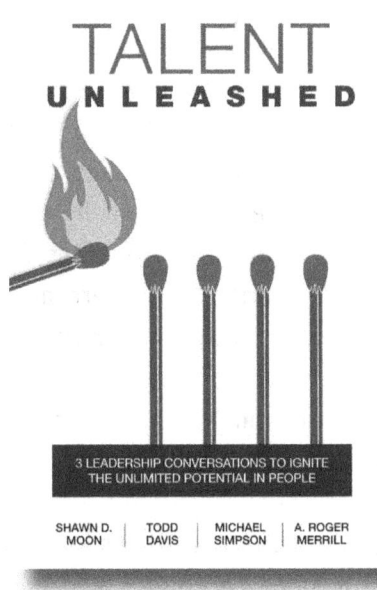

© Shawn Moon. Used with permission.

There were great performers under Shawn's leadership at Franklin-Covey. He paused for a moment. Then a specific example came to mind.

"I can think of one particular salesperson who consistently generates three times the average sales of a good Franklin-Covey professional. She hasn't paid the price to learn our products and service at great depth, but when she visits a client, she's not the one doing the product presentation. She will always bring an expert to help with that."

According to Shawn, she does two things superbly well. "First of all, she is absolutely relentless in following up on details. She doesn't let a single detail drop. Secondly, she's exceptional at using the resources she has, and leveraging other people's expertise to help provide clients the needed information. Another type of highly successful sales professional is the one who may not have the same organizational skills but has a way with people." Shawn expounded, "What we try to create as we develop our salespeople is both the Art and the Science of salesmanship. At Franklin-Covey, it's not just 'everyone follows the same formula and checks off all the boxes on the sheet.'"

As we continued to discuss how to identify exceptional examples and the importance of interpersonal relationships, even at a company as large and diverse in its worldwide influence as Franklin-Covey, it became apparent there were a number of pieces to his personnel puzzle. I asked him how a company's sales process played a role in their success. "Yes, they have to engage in the process. They have to understand each step in any sales process. They also have to be effective in front of their clients. And there are certainly some core behaviors of people you must model that, in my experience, have made the difference:

"Give people effective training about what to do.

"Then you build a relationship with them."

The more I spoke with Shawn, the more each basic premise of our overall discussion regarding characteristics and "bottom-line qualities" of the most successful sales *thoroughbreds* were validated. Shawn continued:

"In client relationships, the critical step is really understanding [the customer's] needs and being able to ask effective questions in order to become a True Advisor. The next critical aspect is **'go in with the right motive.'** If your motive is just to make a sale you will be far less effective than if your motivation is to provide services necessary to help the person, team, or organization achieve something they're not currently achieving.

"We believe that motive counts more than technique."

As a sales executive, sales manager, or human resource professional, there's a conflicting paradigm in the selection process. Do these qualities show on a resumé? Are there different personality profiles for superstars? As we continued our discussion, Shawn seemed to read my mind when he said:

"They have different personalities. We don't try to make everyone into an automaton. We can't do that. We have to run with our people's strengths. We are a lot more flexible with those who have the character component [and are] willing to *pay the price to grow.* If they don't produce, or are not making progress, they don't last. At Franklin-Covey, even if they are super salespeople, if they don't model our values and our behaviors, they don't last long. Our focus combines *Character and Confidence.* One without the other isn't sustainable." Shawn then shared how Franklin-Covey views, manages, and values people. If you take a page right out of their belief and management culture, it reads:

"People are inherently capable, aspire to greatness, and have the power to choose."

At this point, our discussion may be the best advertisement for *Stylistic Salespeople* to apply to work for Franklin-Covey, with their eyes wide open. Franklin-Covey knows that **building personal relationships is key** with their customers, but more importantly with their employees.

Process is important! In fact, it is essential. If salespeople have no interpersonal skills and do not focus on building relationships, they will not earn trust that will develop in the client's heart or mind. Today, if you ask customers about their experience with a salesperson, very few will report having an authentic experience. Trust? That's a term that we throw around a lot in sales. The reality is that trust is the key factor in all the decisions we make. It was even highlighted in a 2002 study by Watson Wyatt which showed:

"Total return to shareholders in high-trust organizations is almost three times higher than the return in low-trust organizations." In my Sears experience, if sales professionals were all about achieving significant wealth, they ultimately burned out. Money eventually has little meaning. For sales to become more than a source of financial security, to become a lifelong career, there must be an enjoyment of meeting and connecting with people. It was in reading the book that Shawn Moon co-authored, *Talent Unleashed*, that I appreciated this almost as much as the highly impactful *7 Habits of Highly Effective People*. *Talent Unleashed* reflects the spirit of *7 Habits of Highly Effective People*, written by Stephen R. Covey. On the cover of *Talent Unleashed* is a single match aflame and four other matches as if waiting to be touched and go ablaze. Why is this visual image important in our discussion? Symbolism sometimes is more powerful in delivering a message than what we might write to describe it. The reason for the match and its symbolism? The match is you as a sales executive or sales manager. The other four matches could light themselves, I suppose, but your influence, your support and encouragement, and how you treat each one individually and "give them space" to be creative and sell with their own sense of style is powerful, empowering, validating and critical to their success and yours.

It's quickly apparent that both Stephen Covey and Shawn Moon share beliefs in principles and practices of their company. These people continue to lead. With almost a *"flow of consciousness,"* Shawn shared what he believes about people: *"Some may doubt that you can marry character into a corporate culture. After all, doesn't everyone ultimately believe 'business is just business'?"*

What's unique at Franklin-Covey is the focus on people. That spirit and management style of its founder lives on even after the death of Covey on July 18, 2012.

I don't think that I am overemphasizing the impact of this symbolism but, for me, placing the burning match on the cover of *Talent Unleashed* symbolizes the importance of each manager lighting the match of those working with them. It becomes a validation which transmits the energy, through personal relationships between employer and employee, even with an average performer. It gives them emotional license; no, it actually enables all *Stylistic Salespeople* to unleash the flames of their interpersonal talents.

In my personal experience, a sales career can be interpreted by a new recruit as either being about people and serving their needs or just about making a sale. After all the long hours and the emotional demands that come with being on this career's almost theatrical stage each day—with its disappointments, losses, violations of trust and, in some cases, broken relationships—if it's just about sales, it's not a career at all. It's just a job. Drawing on memories and experiences enables me to confidently and sincerely say that selling is the greatest career of all.

Shawn put the proverbial nail on the head of our discussion:

*"Finding a sales superstar is important but developing a person into one is also a value we subscribe to."*

Remember that those we ultimately call *thoroughbred horses* were once colts or fillies with raw potential. We are not just looking for fully developed *lions* that may require little of us as managers except to support them. We are also invested in "recognizing, recruiting, hiring, training, motivating and retaining" *Stylistic Salespeople.* Can you hear yourself almost screaming, "How do we find them, recognize them and retain them?" After my interview with Shawn Moon, I want to challenge current HR practices and follow his lead, but express my own observations in my own words. Let's be clear, while Shawn seems to have mastered finding and developing top sales talent, and retaining 80% of them three years later, the next part of this discussion is my thoughts alone.

Today, HR algorithms filter resumés by looking for key words. Is that the answer? Is it just to save time for Human Resource professionals to generate potential new hire interviews that will be productive? Well here is a *News Flash* of sorts for HR. The person looking for a specific job will hire an expert in the field or a professional recruiter. Guess what that person does? They revise the prospect's resumé to contain all the KEY words that Human Resource professional are looking for. HR algorithms pick up those key words in the resumé and set up an interview. This process does not filter or capture the unique qualities we look for in *thoroughbred horses and lions*. Algorithms, key words and HR resumé filters can miss out on superstars. If you charge HR with finding you great candidates with the potential to be superstars, they can fail. Where does it say on the resumé, "This person is someone you would invite into your home"? What resumé template format inserts these words: "She easily earns the trust of everyone she meets" or "We wanted him to come back when the project started. Frankly, we wanted to introduce him to our niece. Even the dog liked him." We must empower our HR professionals to interview three times as many candidates so they can sense this. If you are sitting across your desk, slide your chair around, adjacent to the person you are interviewing. Then ask yourself, "Would I invite this person into my home?" This is a process that finds *the horses and the lions.*

There was one final relevant issue for me, so I added a follow-up question in my interview with Shawn. I asked him, "When you're sitting across the desk from a potential new recruit or new hire in your organization, what are you looking for?"

Shawn paused for a moment, then said, "What I finally want to know in an interview is **'can they do it?'** Then I want to know if they have **'done it before.'** In other words, did they have the qualifications and any achievements in the past? That is important to me. Any candidate needed to show me what I would describe as sustainability."

## *Are there really any Coincidences?*

It is seldom that two contemporaries in the same industry will share the same approach in the selection process of a new sales team member. We each have our ways of identifying key capabilities or warning signs. In our conversation, one criterion that Shawn and I had in common is **The Barbeque Factor.** This was no coincidence. I sat there quietly stunned, but sort of chuckling. I couldn't hold my smile back. "You do that too?" I'd identified this very quality as a characteristic of potential or budding *Stylistic Salespeople*, and that Shawn looked for while interviewing a potential new hire. As you read about *The Barbeque Factor* in the next few pages, I will share how a barbeque question, and what I will call "The Adoption Papers," play a key role.

## *Shawn's "Barbeque Factor"*

"You're sitting there in the interview, and you don't have a whole lot of time left to get to know them. There's this thing at Franklin-Covey we call *The Barbeque Factor.* You ask yourself, 'Do I want to hang out with this person after work on Friday night?' Do they seem like the kind of person who would be fun to be with, even if they're not like you? Maybe they have other interests, but would you invite them over on Saturday for a barbeque? If they fail '*The Barbeque Test*,' I usually wouldn't hire them." It told Shawn whether the person could connect with people. Shawn continued with:

"So much of selling's about relationships. Now, as a caveat, that is my area of strength, so I don't want to superimpose that on everybody and suggest that everyone has to be just like me. That's not what I'm saying. For me, one intangible, conclusive characteristic that I look for in a potential new hire is what I call the '*Scrappiness Factor.*'"

That may not be a real term, but for Shawn it described an essential work ethic quality. Selling, by its nature, is ambiguous. It's not formula. It usually requires us to "figure out" how to "make this happen."

As Shawn continued, it became clear how invested he is in people. He went on to explain, "I ask them, 'What have you done that shows me your ability to create something where nothing existed before?' From my perspective this is called creativity. It's like being on stage. No, really. A sales professional is always 'on stage.' Every action, gesture, expression, and word you use, and even the personal references, are scrutinized by this stranger you're meeting. Selling isn't exactly Saturday Night Live, but it's close. This *scrappiness* skill is critical to both engage your client and earn their confidence in you, your abilities, your knowledge of product, and your ability to meet their needs."

Shawn then engages the prospective new hire again:

"After setting the stage for their response, I would ask, 'Give me examples showing me you are *scrappy*. Or are you someone that needs a lot of hand-holding?' I want to know if they would be willing to take a risk, willing to do the hard things. I want to know if they have done that and if so, what had they done? 'What was it like?'"

At this point in our interview, I was left to imagine what it would be like to be a *fly on the wall* as Shawn intentionally "grilled" each prospect he might hire to see if they valued both **people and process.** He continued, "In my experience, all companies, including Franklin-Covey, have Human Resource competencies that, if they exist in a new hire, allows them to 'map people' into certain HR quadrants. You have probably seen these graphs or these analytical models before. But I found them not to be helpful. Another set of questions which I don't find to be effective are, 'What are some of your strengths?' And especially when HR asks, 'Now, tell me some of your weaknesses.'" These questions are not effective? He said that? I was thrilled. In a few sentences, an executive vice president of one of the most prominent, well respected companies in the world hit a HR home run. Why do I say that? For my money, Shawn unlocked some doors that needed to be opened, concluding with a comprehensive description of the intent of the process he uses, "That's what I have done to try to find that 'right person.'" Notice that Shawn interviewed people to measure people-skills. And it worked.

"You know what? I've had pretty good success, and not just by finding those who passed *The Barbeque Test*."

Shawn had one critical story to share that may complete the picture he painted on how important it is for sales executives and managers to have the interpersonal skills they are seeking to find in new hires. And also why it's important to listen and observe those around us in our pursuit of the different sizes, shapes, and cultures they exemplify.

"There was a young man who worked as an administrative support in our office. He was a hard worker. One day he came to me expressing his desire. 'I would like to try sales,' he said. If someone is willing to take a 'sales quota' upon which their compensation will be based, I will give them an opportunity to prove themselves. This young man turned out to be one of our best producers."

Shawn described him with a story that reminded me of dialog from the musical *How to Succeed in Business Without Really Trying.* "Each morning at 7 a.m. he goes in his office and closes the door. He never starts the day with a game of ping pong, though Franklin-Covey has game tables for their employees. He doesn't go around slapping people on the back. He doesn't go to lunch with people. He just eats a sandwich at his desk." Shawn said, "It's been 15 years. He's excelled at sales. He remains one of the company's top producing Client Partners." Of course, Shawn likes to have him over for barbeques! "He's not a rah-rah guy. He's SCRAPPY. But you know what? He would've failed all the HR matrixes and algorithms, but I hired him."

I'm suggesting the approach we use institutionally to screen potential sales candidates is upside down. Shawn basically described a factor in his process I'd call "like-ability." I may be a disrupter in decrying the HR algorithms we as managers allow to be used, and I am suggesting a radical change. Invert the process. Have HR screen for "like-ability" first, process second.

**Shawn Moon**, Exec. VP, Strategic Markets at Franklin-Covey
     www.linkedin.com/in/shawn-moon-3473983

### *An Author's Open Letter to Shawn Moon*

Shawn, I want to thank you for having the picture of one single, burning match placed on the cover of *Talent Unleashed.* The subtlety of this simple graphic sends the message to all managers who are seeking to unleash the talent in their sales organization. Sales *potential* is represented by a ring of matches. In our own imagination, by striking one match and placing it next to a discarded pack of matches, once one catches fire, the ring explodes. The reality in big business is like in the Army. Generals give commands, Captains pass on orders, Sergeants bark instructions, and the Privates take the hill.

The key to all future sales growth is always people. The title of your book *Talent Unleashed* barks out an instruction to all sales managers: Encourage potential *thoroughbreds* to leave the starting gate and get into the race. The compatibility of your hiring practices, Shawn, right down to *The Barbeque Factor*, made me smile. I would identify *Stylistic Salespeople* by asking them, "Did the customer invite you over for a barbeque?"

Franklin-Covey's—or rather Shawn Moon's—criteria opens the door to believe that managers soon will be able to *Ride the Horses and Feed the Lions.* The key questions is

### *"Who are they and how do we find them?"*

# Chapter Seven

## The Power of Personality

What should sales managers look for when recruiting? Who should we add to the team? Today our industry's biggest problem is **salesperson turnover.** The cost of acquiring a new hire was around $6,000 per new salesperson at Sears Home Improvements in 2014. This added cost must be factored into a long-term R.O.I. (Return on Investment) revenue model. When done right, recruitment can result in very little turnover. That makes it much more important to focus on your team, move the poor to average, the average to good, and the famous business category of "good to great."

When I began selling for Sears, the Dallas office was what we called a "closed shop." It had the largest sales volumes in the nation. It wasn't closed to new hires but literally no **turnover** had occurred for a number of years. The management was strong. The Field Sales Managers ran leads with the current sales representatives to make them stronger. The District Manager focused on just a few exterior products and excelled with quality installation and real customer service. What was the difference between operations at other Home Improvement offices? Dallas had disciplined, regimented sales professionals and a few *Stylistic Salespeople.* But the real difference was the Dallas office management knew how to recognize the uniqueness of each individual and establish effective relationships with them.

I interviewed Chad Rawlins, creator of a process for salespeople called *The Success, Sales Engagement Acceleration Envoy.* He said, "I am an envoy, or a messenger. *I know what I want in salespeople."* He explained *how he sells* and *how he trains others to sell.* "These methods were developed over years. I've borrowed from people. I didn't invent any of this. I sell using what I call a *pivot method.* I need to know if my customer is what I call a *Commander,* a *Performer, an Analyzer, or an Empathizer."* Then I asked him, "What kind are you?" *I pivot as if I'm a big psychology guy.* Then I pivot my presentation and just talk to make sure I communicate so we connect. I talk based on how I've profiled them.

Similarly, the *Hartman Personality Profile* explains that people possess one of four driving "core motives." They are classified in four colors: Red, motivated by power; Blue, motivated by intimacy; White, motivated by peace; Yellows, motivated by fun.

https://brandongaille.com/explanation-the-hartman-color-code-personality-test

**Red:** The power wielders in the world, Reds will use logic, vision and determination. From a *Red perspective,* emotion has nothing to do with completing tasks. Reds are Action-oriented, Assertive, Confident, Decisive, Determined, Disciplined, Independent, Logical and Pragmatic, Obsessive, Proactive, Productive, Responsible, and Task-Dominant. Reds often have to be right. They may come across as harsh and critical, even when they don't mean to. Reds can also be cheap. They may tend to give priority to work over personal relationships. Reds may be poor listeners. They also exhibit controlling and/or domineering traits.

If your background is in sales you're probably nodding your head right now. Smile, pause, dig a little deeper, read on.

**Blue:** Life is a sequence of commitments for those who thrive on relationships, and Blues willingly sacrifice personal gain. Blues are highly demanding perfectionists. They can be distrusting and worry prone. They are complex and intuitive and can be opinionated as well as emotional and moody. They can be self-righteous yet be self-disciplined and sincere. Blues are steady, ordered, and enduring. They love with great passion and bring culture and dependency to society and home.

Highly committed and loyal, comfortable in creative environments, they strive to be the best they can. Blues are the most controlling of all four Hartman personality profile colors. They can be insecure and judgmental. Lacking trust, they also find themselves resentful or unforgiving. They often fail to see the positive side of life. They want to be loved and accepted, and constantly seek understanding while often refusing to understand and accept themselves.

**White:** *Motivated by Peace in Relationships*, Whites will do almost anything to avoid confrontation. Their only demands from life are things that make them feel comfortable. That feeling fosters a need to feel good inside. Kind, considerate, patient and accepting, they are devoid of ego. They are also good at constructing thoughts that did not exist before. Whites are careful to listen and will take time to think things through. They don't commonly share what they are feeling, understanding or seeing. They won't express conflict and may be unwilling to set goals and dislike working at someone else's pace. They can be self-deprecating. (*See any "stylistic characteristics" here?*)

**Yellow:** Motivated by fun and here to have a great time, known as being spontaneous, optimistic, and sometimes self-centered, Yellows are enthusiastic. They're persuasive. They're always looking for some new challenge. They develop friendships easily but can be self-centered, often interfering with having meaningful relationships. With superficial friends they'll have difficulty getting down to business.

It's obviously important to Chad to understand people on a deeper level.

Chad questions new trainees, "Are you an auditory, visual, or kinesthetic learner? How do you make decisions? I have to find that out. I love interacting with people. It's one of my passions."

I got specific. "What types do you usually to hire?"

"We often hire people who are like us. That may be a mistake or may marginalize sales potential. What I've mostly done recently is include report-direct managers in my interview process. It gives me someone else's perspective." Note: Here's something that Chad and I also have in common.

At the end of my interview with Chad, I asked for his bottom line: "Who was the greatest salesperson you've ever known? What is it inside that made them great?" Chad responded, "The person who comes to my mind is a great man by the name of Rick. Interestingly enough, Rick worked for Franklin-Covey back in the 1990s and he has been the most successful sales guy I've ever met. I believe he was successful because of two things. First, his absolutely clear vision of what he wanted to get done. Not just every day—every week, but every month. Just like as I categorize customers to understand how to communicate with them, I do the same with salespeople I train or manage. I classify him as a 'commander,' but he understood people. He was definitely a *people-person* and understood the value of relationships. He poured his soul into those relationships. By doing so he yielded the results he was seeking. What he taught me has been an amazing thing that I have lived by ever since. It was originally a concept from the great Zig Ziglar (1926 - 2012), a WWII veteran, an American Baptist, a salesman and who integrated his Christian beliefs into keynote speaking motivational tours.

"'You can have everything in life you want, if you will just help other people get what they want.'"

Chad added, "That's what Rick instilled in me in my sales career about 25 years ago. He could talk with people. He knew how to listen to people, to find out what their pains were and how to solve them. Rick was great!"

After I heard Chad explain what made Rick tick, I asked him how he managed the *mavericks* that I'm calling *"lions."* These are the salespeople operating outside the box procedurally, yet they drive tremendous sales revenue. Chad easily recalled hiring a guy who sold millions. Because he wouldn't let you ride with him, he was difficult to manage.

That question seemed to spark fond memories for Chad as he reminisced:

"In my sales management career, I've held two different positions. One was Director of Sales. I started in sales and was a sales manager in two different organizations. I've managed over one hundred salespeople and hired a couple hundred. I had a salesperson I hired like you describe. His name was Jay. He was crazy.

"Was he hard to manage? And how! I had to manage that guy since he was such a maverick in every aspect of his life, not just as an employee. I mean the guy just was 'out there.' You know what? I learned to let him do his thing. I didn't make him conform to my way of doing it. What we cared about more was the result. He was never harmful to people around him. That's not what he was about. He was a funny guy." Looking back on our interview, Chad is what I would call a Middle Manager or, even better, a Manager in the Trenches.

Chad then described his basic management style and philosophy of how to manage people. At first it sounded like something in a Western movie, but it is effective: *"Give them enough rope and give them the skills that they need to be successful but leverage their strengths."* He expanded on this theme. "I just leveraged Jay's strengths and let him do his thing. You know, people buy into that which they help create. When you let them create their own vision and they go get the results, they go get it done. You check your ego at the door and just worry about the results. Sometimes managers don't do that. Sometimes managers will be like... 'You know what? You're going to do it my way or the highway!' I think that's such a short-sighted mindset because there are other ways of getting results in order to win. I hired Jay because of a good reputation, and he did a great job. It was definitely not my style, but he got it done.

"There's a *must-see* movie, *White Squall*. It's got a line I'll paraphrase. Their advice goes something like this: *'Where one of us goes, we all go.'* I chose to buy into that philosophy and that's how I manage."

Chad B. Rawlins; www.linkedin.com/in/chadrawlings

I loved my 14 years at Sears Home Improvements as a salesperson, a field sales manager and district sales manager in three cities, San Francisco, Denver, and Washington DC. Ironically, I heard about too many cases of managers firing million-dollar, obviously *Stylistic Salespeople* because they didn't conform to their manager's selling system. **I never understood it.**

## *What is Unique about Stylistic Salespeople?*

As you study characteristics of *Stylistic Salespeople* as described on the list at the beginning and repeated later in the middle and at the end of this book, experiment incorporating these qualities, talents, and, abilities in what you look for when hiring.

Observe members of your team who have the qualities described there. Ride with your sales team one by one to see if their personalities represent the system you now work with. Your purpose should not be to critique or change them. See if you can learn from them. What creativity do they employ during an appointment and what flexibility do you notice?

Do they exhibit any of the key characteristics of *Stylistics Salespeople*? Perhaps you have one or two who you would say are the *horses and lions* you could build your future sales success on. How do they handle objections? Do they approach difficult and objectionable customers in a unique way? How do they earn a customer's trust? Are they persistent after receiving a negative response? Observe who's the best and adopt as many of their skills, approaches, and abilities they exhibit as you can. Adapt your team's selling techniques to improve interpersonal skills. If you're observant, you'll recognize these qualities when interviewing a new hire.

When a sales professional came back from an appointment, I would ask them three questions: "Did the customer fill out the paperwork?" If they had a contract in hand they'd say, "Sure," and they would hand me the contract. I would ask, "No, I mean, did they fill out the adoption papers?" My point was, "Did they like you so much that they almost wanted to adopt you?" If the customer had a pet dog, I asked, "Did their dog like you?" If they missed the point entirely I'd ask them, "Did they invite you over for a barbeque on Saturday?" In other words, did they like you, trust you, want to hang out with you?

In a March 5th, 2015 *Entrepreneur* magazine article, Mark Zuckerberg, notable, controversial *Facebook* founder and CEO, explained his hiring criteria this way: "I would only hire someone to work for me if I would work for them." If a new hire is hard to work with, do you have a relationship with them? If not, establish one. If nothing else works, ask them to help you. That's a start!

Remember, you assign *"company leads"*! Don't give up your power. Ask one of your sales superstars to help you. They want to be important. If you can get their help, you have managed and channeled their power.

Ultimately customers trust and buy from people they like or they have something in common with. But some clients don't even want a conversation. That is a challenge *Stylistic Salespeople* know how to handle but, for most of us, the following scenario tests our mettle. How would you suggest handling a customer like this? After your salesperson enters the home or their home office in a B2B appointment the following dialogue ensues:

"Hey buddy, how long have you been doing this?"

"For a long time...why?"

"You probably know about what this is gonna cost, right?"

"Well, I have a pretty good...."

"You have a business card? My office is at home, and I've got a lot of work to do. Just write your estimate on your business card and leave it with my wife. Thanks!"

"Sure...but...."

In sales meetings, have superstars help others practice overcoming objections. This accomplishes two things: First it builds relationship between you and the influencers on your sales team. Second, it allows them to help those who aspire to be superstars. Your perception of being approachable, authentic, inclusive and confident in managing your team increases. If you learn how to recognize, recruit, relate-to, and retain *Stylistic Salespeople*, your success will be because you "*Ride the Horses and Feed the Lions.*"

In 2001, starting over at the bottom as a sales representative in what I hoped would be my new career in sales, I sold cabinet refacing at a net close rate of 27% and was recognized as a Masters Winner and was awarded a week-long Sears Home Improvement Trip offered to only the top 3% of 1500 salespeople. Not long after that, Tim, the "Mid-South Region General Manager," invited me to train at some of his offices how to sell this unique product. It wasn't a paid position, but my volunteering opened doors to future promotions. I started with the Sears basics.

In Sears' Ten Step selling plan, Step One is "The Warm-up." If we get to know our customers and they like us, if we address their concerns and overcome their objections to moving ahead, then they will buy.

Step Two is to "Determine their Needs." While this obvious part of solving problems is in every sales plan and sales book ever written, it's the "*one-two punch.*" Determining needs is what *Stylistic Salespeople* do best. Why do *Stylistic Salespeople* do this best? They *listen*. They get to know people. They sincerely ask what customers need and solve their problems. They care. Creativity is a key characteristic that all *Stylistic Salespeople* have.

A one-call close is the doctorate of selling. Sears' *"Circle Close process"* dealt with objections. We are trained to ask customers open-ended questions to isolate any objections and reasons customers wouldn't move forward. We identify all concerns, write down a complete list, analyze, and then resolve each one. Then we ask, "If we can resolve your concerns are you comfortable moving forward today with me?" Some classic objections were these:

"I have to get three bids." "It's too much money." "My father owns the home." "I never make rushed decisions." "I need to think about it." "I need to check my finances."

The reason most consumers raise objections is to get you to leave their home, to relieve pressure they feel from the salesperson, and to give them more time to *think about it.* Resolving objections, one at a time, we move to the next and the next until we isolate the last objection. The best time to buy is when you have information you need, and when the company and sales professional you trust can resolve the affordability issue. My question, "Is it process, personality, honesty, integrity or authenticity that closes the deal?" **Yes, all of the above!**

More on the Circle Close and the Circle Sale in the next chapter.

## *"He never writes. He never calls."*

Remember the 31-year-old woman who didn't trust men and didn't trust herself? Most of all, she just didn't trust "sales-**men**!" I am intentionally referring to male salespeople because men, historically, have pursued sales, earning a reputation of dishonesty, taking deposits and leaving customers with nothing or promising anything to get a sale.

One woman I know agrees with this social media claim: "90% of all salespeople are crooks." Many misrepresent what will be done and say anything to get a sale. That is why most customers don't trust salespeople. This type of slick, faux salesperson never lasts and costs every company lost profits long after they are found out. They earn home improvement salespeople a reputation far below that of lawyers and used car salesmen. I could never be that kind of salesperson. A short segment in this book, *Selling with Integrity*, describes a strong foundation for a successful career in sales. Integrity is one key characteristic of the *Stylistic Salespeople* you want to hire.

## *Selling with Integrity*

Selling with integrity means *never compromising your ethics.* Don't promise a customer you'll come back for a visit if you don't plan to. The *Stylistic Salesperson* goes back during installations and after a sale. If you ask average customers, even those who trust their salesperson, about the ongoing relationship they have with their salesperson, they'll likely say, "He never writes.... He never calls." If you hire salespeople who will make sure the customer is satisfied, they are worth holding on to as an example to others. It's a mark of discipline you won't find in every superstar but is common among high performers in sales and other business relationships.

In my first year at Sears my goal was to "find out if I could make a living." One successful salesperson suggested I make a photo album of before and after pictures of all my projects. I ignored his suggestion. After my first year he suggested the photo album again. This time I listened. By accepting his counsel my income went from $65,000 to $92,000 that year, changing nothing else. That *Stylistic Salesperson* shared an idea unselfishly.

In home improvement and residential in-home selling, you're alone with customers. No one is there to hold you back. No politics. No micromanager. Why not call customers back or visit them after the sale when you can solve customer issues and get referrals from happy customers? Does your team do it? *Stylistic Salespeople* do. Managers, take note: Your *horses and lions* set examples. Recognize them in private—and public if they allow it.

In 2015, as National Sales Trainer at Champion Home Exteriors in Cincinnati, I met a man named John they called an *Achiever.* He sold over $1.5 million annually. He would send postcards with his photo on it to targeted neighborhoods. He called them, set appointments, and called back anyone he didn't sell on the first visit. He ended that year, 2015, as a *Super Achiever,* with $2 million in sales. This $6,000 investment for a year of mailing postcards got him $50,000 more sales and an added $6,000 bonus plus a company trip.

Let me share another story. Dan was a classic *Stylistic Salesman* who worked for me in Sears Home Improvements' San Francisco District. Dan consistently sold $1.5 to $2.5 million a year. He was with a couple in Mountain View, CA. The Sears kitchen they wanted was $35,000. As the sales call continued, dinner time approached. Dan could tell they were hungry. He asked, "Do you know La Fontaine, that French restaurant on Castro Street?" Both customers knew it well. This *Stylistic Salesperson* politely added, "Let me take you to dinner. This is an important decision. After dinner if you want your new kitchen, great. Either way we'll have a wonderful French meal together." Did he get the sale? Of course! It's about building relationships. Dan's a *lion.*

How many salespeople invest in their success?

### *Stylistic Salespeople do!*

# Chapter Eight

## "The Circle Close" and "The Circle Sale"

*The Circle Close* is a *process* that allows customers to describe, one at a time, their concerns. Seldom do we ask, listen, or take enough notes when spending time with the customer. You must realize the importance of the relationship with your customer. We can design a solution to their needs and hear "hot buttons," but what really concerns them? If we can resolve and satisfy their needs, the customer will trust us and the company we work for. After discussing each concern, we must be able to provide a resolution for it and, one by one, solve the problems. When each objection is resolved to their satisfaction, when you employ the basics of The Circle Close, you should ask this clarifying question again: "Is there any reason you wouldn't be comfortable moving forward *today?*" Structured and organized, the Circle Close system allows you to ask the customer for their business **today.** There is no way the customer will remember how they feel now or the answers to their concerns by tomorrow. Earning business today is like having a Ph.D.—a *"Doctorate of Selling."* Even if you only graduated from high school, if you enjoy relationships with customers, justifying their trust in you and your company, the best news is you will always have a job!

When I began to describe to people how I sold, every manager told me I was *too stylistic.* In other words, my sales approach was more personality than process and my unique approach was my *connecting with the customer.* That was just who I was. Was that wrong, somehow? I operated within a structured system, based on what I'd learned at Sears. Haunting me, in the back of my mind, was the same management echo after each conversation, "You can't teach that, Bill." I didn't know whether to take that as a compliment or drop my stylistic, interpersonal approach that had been successful for me. The message from almost every *Stylistic Salesperson* to their manager is, "Can't I just be myself and sell?"

There were a lot of super salespeople in Sears. Some were very structured while others were like me, *Stylistic Salespeople.* Very few sales managers knew what to do with us. Some managers would isolate these key contributors. They would give them leads but restrict them from attending meetings. Managers create the office environment. We either enhance performance of *Stylistic Salespeople* or we micromanage them, which will ultimately result in them leaving. Is that smart? Then how do we replace their sales volume?

Remember Matt Kelly, a new VP of Sales who had a guy who just would not respond to him? He was going to fire his top salesman after the national meeting. At dinner that night, after a few drinks at the bar, before they said goodnight, an unusual thing happened.

They...hugged? Believe it or not, Matt said, they hugged.

Matt had taken the time to get to know this *Stylistic Salesperson.* He was not a *thoroughbred* racehorse you could train, who would then win, place, or show. This *maverick* was clearly a *lion.* It's challenging to you as a manager or executive, but instead of giving up and letting them go, each person needs to be handled differently. You may think you're sending a signal, "Everyone fall in line behind their Boss," but what happens if the best-of-the-best decide to leave? What then?

Caution: The most destructive thing for some *Stylistic Salespeople's* morale is not allowing them to associate with the entire team, especially when you initially *"Ride the Horses, Feed the Lions."* You either leverage the influence they have by earning their respect and loyalty, by connecting with them, or you'll suffer consequences when they unavoidably interact negatively with the sales team offsite. Make sure this doesn't happen. If you discover a salesperson undermining you, further disciplinary action must be taken including, but not initially, separation from your company. When they test your ability to manage, what they usually want, just like we did as second graders, is your attention but also your respect. You deserve to give them both. In return, respect for management is a sales discipline.

## *"The Circle Sale"*

When I was asked to describe how I sold, which upper level management called *stylistic,* I called my process *The Circle Sale.* Sears' Ten Step selling plan was very structured. We memorized each of the Ten Steps and delivered them in sequence to the customer. Although it may seem logical, delivering a memorized script, even if you know it well, seldom comes off as conversational. *The Circle Sale* is instinctive and creative. My approach as a *Stylistic Salesperson* was to listen to customers and then occasionally deviate from the Ten Step selling plan structure to address a customer's concern. By being creative, flexible, open to ideas, and interested in what customers really need and want, you will sell more often. You can't be like some professor who indignantly says, "Hold your questions until the end." If you do this, by the end of the sales presentation, customers often forget their questions in the context of what you are later discussing. The result is that they say, "Well, we'll have to think about it." They are right. And what you have done is left some concerns unaddressed. They still do have a question! Because of the approach of not listening or responding to the customer's needs as they arise, they'll always default to a delaying tactic. They will sleep on it and the next salesperson will answer their question and, by the way, will always get the sale. In stark contrast, for your customers, *The Circle Sale* does not feel scripted or memorized because you are having an open conversation and addressing needs when they are raised.

The reason why I describe *The Circle Close* and its approach to resolving customer's needs one at a time is to show how structured the sales process was at Sears. Structured sales processes are common and basically effective. But when a manager encounters a sales professional that operates "out of the box" like me, a *Stylistic Salesperson*, a choice has to be made on how to manage this type of over-performer. Each professional salesperson needs some structure and a scripted presentation with which to begin covering the information the customer needs to know in order to make an intelligent decision. By "circling back," you have every right to see if your customers have any unanswered questions. By doing this they will appreciate you "asking for the order."

Another reason why I describe *The Circle Sale* is to demonstrate how, in my case and in the case of other *Stylistic Salespeople*, you'll hopefully *recognize, recruit, hire, train, motivate and retain* them. Potential sales growth outweighs the challenge of managing these people. In my case, it was not that I was bucking the system or intentionally being one of those we call *mavericks* that *operate out of the box*. My intent was to connect with each customer, to get to know them first, to earn their trust and establish relationships that make selling the best career I ever had.

## Unanswered Questions are Landmines

The customer needs to know the company they're dealing with.
You must earn a customer's trust so you meet their **real** needs.
You determine exactly what the customer wants to accomplish.
They need to see your products and choose what **they** want.

Your solution must solve their problems, including financing, product quality, contractual details, and warrantees. How the work will be done and how problems are addressed is decided by you and your company.

I learned Sears' Ten Step selling plan in 2000. It's so effective it has been copied, redeveloped, changed or imitated by Home Improvement companies for years. The names or functions of the steps in any borrowed selling plan may be easily copied by a competitor at another company. I saw Sears' sales plan divided into smaller steps at one company. Some of the basic Ten Steps may be eliminated completely to make room for the bright ideas of a sales manager. But in the end, as managers we have to ask ourselves, "Is it the process that is the key to increasing sales or is it the interpersonal skills of the members of our sales team that is the key?"

## *"What's the Secret? Should I Hire Horses and Lions?"*

*Stylistic salespeople* are not all about artificial rapport, fake charisma or how they look in some expensive suit. Selling is about trust. Earn trust! If you just want a job, fake it until you make it, then continue faking it. Want a career? Be authentic. You can enjoy sales for a lifetime. Be yourself, embrace honesty, have integrity, love people, listen on purpose. Desire to help others more than yourself.

Those key qualities are an accurate description of *horses and lions. Stylistic salespeople* are likeable and deserve your trust. If your close friends, employers or people you've met the first time use terms mentioned above when describing you, then I encourage you to consider a sales career. You'll never be bored as a *Stylistic Salesperson* if you really "connect" with people.

## *It takes all you've got, so give it all you've got!*

Remember, any "one-call-close" is like a Ph.D. in selling. In order to master this "degree" of expertise, you must of course become an expert salesperson. Even a *Stylistic Salesperson* can't be successful selling with no product knowledge. Remember Shawn Moon's Franklin-Covey story of the woman who outsold everyone else? Did she have great product knowledge? Not really. Did she meet the customers' need for information? Yes. She always had with her experts who could answer all of their questions. If you're not an expert, this is not an area in which you want to *fake-it-until-you-make-it.* Customers use the internet to research products and services today more than ever. Once the basic foundation of the sales plan and knowledge of product is mastered, the possibility exists for new hires and potential *thoroughbreds* to be successful in at least one of these approaches with their customers:

**Structure**: Consistent sales Delivery without Deviation.
**Personality**, *over function*: Earning Customer's Emotional Trust.
*Stylistic* **Skill Sets**: Merge these two approaches into one.

Creativity for me was like becoming a juggler. I delivered Sears' Ten Steps as well as anyone, but as I presented, instead of being strictly structured, I'd use those procedural steps like tools. I followed them in sequence but was flexible enough to hear customer's conversations and made adjustments to the sequence if needed. As soon as it was possible, I would bring the customer back into the Ten Steps by asking questions that returned the customer back to where we left off. I call that adventure like "*taking a left turn*" or leaving the highway, only to return to the main highway again and proceed on my way. Let me give you an example:

Often you'll have a customer that intentionally does not want to spend any time with you. "Hey Bill, that's your name, right? You've done this before, so you probably know just about what my project will cost?" I knew what was coming next. "I've heard this all before and I have a lot to get done. You just go ahead. Call me when you have a price. Okay?"

**Question:** What are you going to do now?

**Answer:** You are going to agree with him. Really? Yes. Then you are going to ask him to help you. Most people will agree to help you. Ask for help.

**Example**: "Bob, in order for me to get you accurate numbers, I'll need to get some measurements, so I know much square footage of siding you'll need. I don't want you to pay for more than you need. Would you please help me outside for five minutes?" Reluctantly, he'll come outside to help you. After all, you didn't ask much of him. I am using the example of a man here because women are typically more respectful of your time. Okay, so he comes outside. What next? Ask him to help hold the other end of the tape. As you walk from one side of the house to the next, he watches you write down measurements. **Just say nothing**. Wait for it...! Finally, when you've measured the third side of the house, invariably he'll say something like, "How long have you been doing this, Bill?"

At times, you never got a chance to speak with him before, to "warm up" or even shake hands. This is what I refer to as the REAL "cold call." It's not about how you got the appointment, as in cold calling, it's more important what reception you get when you come to the door. After all, sometimes one person who lives in the house purposely does not tell the other about your appointment. That's who wants to buy. You may not be familiar with a residential sales call, but whether it is Sears or another company you work for, "warming up" should never be over!

## *"How long have you been doing this, Bill?"*

Continuing our example, he opened the door for you to talk, so go for it. Find out about what he does for a living, how long he has owned the home or what his favorite sports team is. Don't make it obvious. **Just talk.** Now, since he has actually started a conversation, you're way ahead of where you were, but you deliberately haven't told him about your company or products. Keep going.

Don't be too anxious to "get down to business." People buy from those they like and trust. Have you earned his trust yet? Not really. Be comfortable just having a conversation with the customer about anything they want to talk about. That's what I meant by "taking a left turn." You've left the highway, the shortest distance between a knock on the door, a contract, and a check, but you two need to get to know each other first. That is how "The Circle Sale" works. This is *"intentional flexibility."* You may feel out of control at first but your ramp back onto the one-call-close highway is "asking questions." *You are in control when you ask questions.*

A true story: After three hours a customer thanked, complimented, and enthusiastically expressed their admiration. "Bill, you're sure a great salesman." *Watch out for that phrase.* I knew exactly what was coming next. It was like waiting for the Death Star to explode at the end of Star Wars. It's coming!

No contract? No sale? Why? What just happened? I connected with these people, or so I thought at the time. But the husband had quickly retreated to the family room before I could give them the numbers. He was 80 years old and wanted to watch a baseball game while I spoke with his wife. I could hear the excitement of the crowd on TV. The look on his wife's face said it all. She had heard it all before. What do I do now? I walked downstairs and spoke to her husband. "You know, my job is mostly working nights, so I seldom get to see a game. Would you mind if I watched with you for a few minutes before I leave?"

What could he say? We both laughed, yelled at the umpire, and even argued over bad calls as we watched the game. If any approach to closing a sale ever was *"stylistic,"* this was. I was tired and almost left. Then something strange happened. You can't make this up. Write this down. During a long TV break, this man said, "Mary, do you want to sit through two more of these things? Should we go just with Sears?" They signed a contract. They got financed. Why did they decide to move forward? What would happen next taught me an important *"stylistic"* lesson. More important than making the sale, this experience gave me a principle, a characteristic or perhaps better stated a disciplined behavior that now would be part of my style. It may not appear to you to be revolutionary, but it was for me. Even *Stylistic Salespeople* never stop learning. I found a way to stay. *Stylistic Salespeople* always do. Don't be offended when I call that act of persistence *The Lead Butt Close.*

After that success, whenever I trained residential sales professionals, I added a simple commandment, if we can use that procedural sales term:

"When things aren't going your way, find a way to stay 30 minutes more."

The *Lead Butt Close* **wasn't** the classic instruction sales managers teach: "Ask for a drink of water." Nothing really happened differently than at any other appointment, except I stayed with the guy and watched baseball with him. He felt comfortable. Trust had been earned. As I look back on it, I didn't know if the wife really wanted to go with Sears, or whether the husband was defending the fort by sticking with the plan to not buy that night, but she had agreed with him. I didn't see that coming!

Discipline is part of the Science of selling. Flexibility, your native interpersonal skills, becomes the Art. Let me share another true story:

I arrived at this beautiful home where this woman was dressed up like she was headed for a corporate meeting to give a presentation. She wore a wool skirt, a jacket and scarf, somewhat like a suit coat, slacks, white shirt and tie. Oh, and don't forget the shoes. She dressed to impress, but not to impress me. No. The minute I saw how she was dressed I was sure she was going to tell me that she'd forgotten about an important meeting at work and had to go. But she invited me in. Surprisingly, she told me that she works from home. Okay, she is obviously serious about her work since she is definitely not dressing casually, even on casual Friday. But she did have one odd accessory. She had a clipboard, a note pad, and a pen.

We spent some time getting to know each other and she asked a lot of questions as I told her about my company, the process of her kitchen project, how it would proceed. More questions came forth as I showed her the choices of cabinet door styles and wood grains, the countertops and everything right down to the antique brass door handles and knobs.

Throughout the appointment she had her clipboard out and took detailed notes. That really bothered me. I hadn't seen anyone do that before. Keep in mind that all these stories come from when I was a Sears Sales Representative. I was successful, but when you think you've "seen everything" you haven't. Gnawing away was the thought:

"Great, I already established that all she wants are the details so she can compare what we have to offer with two or three other companies. Maybe she'll say, 'I'm getting TEN BIDS,' like that other woman had before." My mind kept delivering imagined *Tommy Boy* movie dialogue to my brain. This is not a quote from the movie but me quoting an imagined dialogue with myself in a similar situation to the movie. If you haven't seen this sales classic, Chris Farley plays the part of a rookie salesman. When he first gets into a stressful encounter with a customer who is not interested in buying the product he and David Spade are selling, he is the first to get up to leave. In this dialogue, imagine I'm both David and Chris. In this case, it is from a real appointment of mine. Here I am arguing with myself:

"Bill, you must have had this happen to you once or twice."

"No! Not really."

"You feel like shortening up the presentation, giving her a business card and saying 'give me a call when you're ready' before she does."

"Yes! Okay, yes, I have, haven't you?"

"Dinner's hot on the table. It's been two hours already. 'Well, why don't you just thank her for her time and politely pack up your samples and leave?'"

"Because I'm a professional. I punch my emotional time card, do a complete two-and-a-half-hour presentation, and answer all of her questions. I may become a sales manager someday."

"Come on, give me a reality check. What are you really thinking?"

Actually, I'd pretty much decided to pack up my samples and thank her for inviting me into her home when something unusual happened. She spoke clearly a declarative phrase I thought I would never hear: **"Okay, let's do it."**

Inside my mind, for a moment I was shouting, "Let's do it? Are you kidding me? You're not supposed to say that. Stick to 'I've got to think about it.'" What next? She bought her kitchen. Now she was a *stylistic customer*! Why do I say that? Because she didn't "go by the book." Most customers have a great disdain for any salesperson. They have "heard it all, seen it all" and only want two things, to see the product and the price. Just like when we said that *Stylistic Salespeople* aren't *cut out of the same cloth*, sitting there in her wool suit and her clipboard in hand, she obviously was not a customer cut out of the same cloth either. She had her own style. Professional, respectful and decisive. Therefore I call her a stylistic customer. Remember this story, because it's an important lesson to learn.

We work with consumers who have had salespeople come to their home before us. We have no idea what each customer has taken away from those experiences. When we enter a home, we inherit all that past history. Our challenge is to be the one salesperson they can trust. "It wasn't you Bill. I didn't trust any of them," that one woman said. Statistics on customers calling salespeople back are minimal. The Ph.D. of Selling is the **"one call close,"** because if we don't sell on the first appointment, we don't get called back. If there's no incentive or urgency for customers to make a same-day-decision, our closing percentages (% of sales made vs. appointments) don't increase. In other words, historically, if we don't sell on the first visit, they don't call back and we don't get an additional sale after we leave the home. Customers have the same needs and motivations to buy before you arrive as when you leave. Your job is to help them make decisions. In my experience regarding home improvements, what all consumers struggle with is the "value equation" of the project. Price plays a role. Once I have been able to help customers focus on getting a project "done," and they sign a work order, they feel a great relief from just "deciding." A *Stylistic Salesperson* helps relieve pressures of price (affordability) with clear communication.

I never thought I was a good closer like those in some of the scenes in *Glengarry Glen Ross*. "You're *stylistic*, Bill," was the echo in the back of my head from my managers when I began to sell at Sears and when I became a Field Sales Manager riding with sales representatives. At Champion Windows, Peter Bulger taught me a truly LINEAR process of closing a sale. Customers will say, "I have to think about it," but what they're really saying is, "It's too much money." So do we say, "No it's not?" No. What they are really saying is, "We need more information. Answer our questions." This linear closing system keeps open conversations so that customers CAN think about it while you're there. We often spend hours with them but may not know questions they still have. We think to ourselves, "So what do I do now? I did a great presentation. Do I leave?" Be careful. You've invested this much time, why give up? Stay! Help your customers make decisions regarding affordability, the value of the products and the services they want to purchase. This experience inspired a manual titled *The Conversational Close*. I use it for sales training. In a later chapter, I'll outline the basic principles.

# Chapter Nine

## The Power of Vulnerability

I used to tell people that *"sales is the best job for a divorced man."* Since I was going through a time when it was hard for me to get a job, this statement about sales seemed to be perfect for me. The only one who could lose this job was me. Even though this statement may be too gender specific, men are often not the greatest listeners. And I include myself in that conclusion. I teach men on my sales team and we re-learn the importance of *listening on purpose.* In order to develop better interpersonal skills, swallowing a large dose of humility doesn't hurt men either. My large dose of humility came in a unique way I'd never expected. Very few writers will share personal feeling or failures, unless writing a "self-help" book or if they are psychologists themselves. Nevertheless, I will get personal here in the story I'll relate next.

My first priority has always been my family, even in the wake of a separation and ultimately a divorce. My first wife, whom I still love, had a life-threatening medical condition that only seventy people in the world had at the time. Without going into details, her digestive system had been paralyzed by parasites, lodging in the entire digestive tract, and had gone undiagnosed for over ten months. My priority: To provide for her needs. This gave me a wake-up call. Leaving Sears corporate after a distinguished career, it took me fourteen months to land a lucrative executive position at Kraft Foods headquarters in Northbrook,

Illinois as the Corporate Equity Brand Manager of Multicultural (Ethnic) Marketing. I was calm but excited that I had finally made it. I was hired! The wake-up call?

I was making a positive impact at Kraft when the man who hired me got promoted. The woman who took his place then let me go after only four months. Okay, life happens. I left Chicago and helped my son in Utah refinish his basement. The CEO of *La Agencia de Orci* and his son had become my acquaintances while I worked in the Sears Tower and they invited me to be the Keynote Speaker at The Association of Hispanic Advertising Agencies Convention. Soon we came to terms and I was hired as Account Director for Allstate Insurance's Spanish campaigns. Allstate's advertising agency, *La Agencia de Orci*, specialized exclusively in Hispanic marketing, which was my area of expertise.

*La Agencia de Orci*, like Kraft Foods, required multiple interviews in considering anyone outside their company who's applying for a high-level executive position. At both Kraft and at *La Agencia de Orci*, I had fourteen interviews before I was hired. I had experience directing, approving, and putting together advertising strategies at Sears but had never worked in an agency. In fact, in retrospect, I remember some college friends telling me:

"Don't become a lawyer and don't get a job at an advertising agency. You're a people-person!"

I didn't know what they meant, but after just a year of law school I knew it wasn't for me. What would happen at an advertising agency? *La Agencia de Orci* seemed perfect but soon something went very wrong.

After my divorce, and after Kraft Foods, a big wake-up call came to me at *La Agencia de Orci.* I didn't know that before I started at the agency the Sr. Account Director had already promised my position to a Jr. Account Executive for Allstate Insurance's Spanish account, who was now working under me. They conspired to withhold information from me. "He'll be gone in ninety days," they said as they planned my exit. After three months I got called into the CEO's office. He told me he'd discovered their conspiracy and fired my Sr. Account Director. Regarding the Jr. Account executive, he said, "You can either let her go or you can work with her. I should have fired her. In business someone disloyal seldom changes." I made the wrong choice to rescue a relationship that wasn't there. What happened next? The account executive convinced the client to complain. Thirty days later she called the CEO, saying, "We have the wrong Account Director," and I was fired. Was there a message? Relationships are the key to success in life and in business. Bill, wake up!

That was a very personal story. Why did I share it? Years after this happened, someone close to me sent me a book and I was ready to LISTEN. Remember the critical nature of listening-on-purpose? She said, "You need to read it! You need to read it to make *your journey* to vulnerability." I didn't know at the time that I would share what I learned in *Daring Greatly,* a book by Brené Brown, but here goes. It brings home a need, as people, to allow ourselves to be vulnerable. If you read it, you too will discover that what we used to call humility, compassion, empathy, or today, validation, are actually strengths we need in order to become great leaders. It even applies to C-Suite executives. How

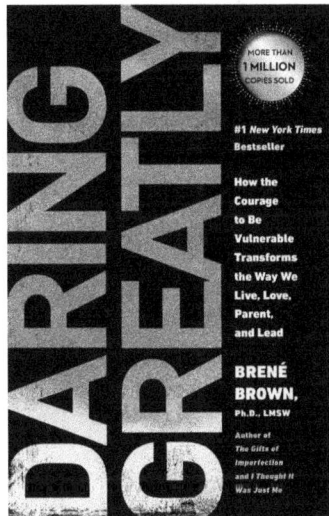

© Brené Brown. Used with permission.

can we develop meaningful personal relationships without becoming vulnerable? An *aha moment* question? Now, stay tuned for a true-life story from Weldon Long. He learned the lesson that Brené Brown was trying to teach us. Why am I talking about vulnerability? Because it is a powerful tool in our interpersonal skill set, as salespeople, sales managers, sales executives, and people.

Who is Weldon Long and why is his story relevant?

## *Weldon Long's Profound Story of Vulnerability*

It was my privilege to interview Weldon Long, who has an amazing life story, leading him not only to the inspiring world of vulnerability, but to unexpected success in sales, creating his own company, selling it and starting another, and the list goes on.... In his first book, *The Upside of Fear*, Weldon tells an unlikely story of dropping out of high school in 9th grade. He lived on the streets and was sent to prison for thirteen years for three different crimes. A chapter in Brené Brown's book would have clarified the impact of humility on Weldon and on all of us, but it is better told in Weldon's own words.

"I got out of prison, ended up in a homeless shelter at forty years of age, and started a successful career in sales, right from a halfway house. In the story of my life, *The Upside of Fear*, recognized by Writer's Digest as a #1 Best Selling self-published book, I talk about the lessons I've learned.

© Weldon Long. Used with permission.

"I was still in prison in June 1996 when my father died. It was kind of my moment of clarity. Stephen Covey's *7 Habits of Highly Effective People* was the first book I read after he died. That book became my roadmap back to a truly responsible life. Franklin-Covey now has a program called *7 Habits on the Inside*, for incarcerated individuals. After I had written my book, *The Upside of Fear*, by a chance encounter with

Stephen R. Covey, a man who had been friends with him for forty years got a manuscript of my book in his hands. On June 10th of 2009 I got his endorsement agreeing to write the forward to *The Upside of Fear*, thirteen years to the day that my father had passed away."

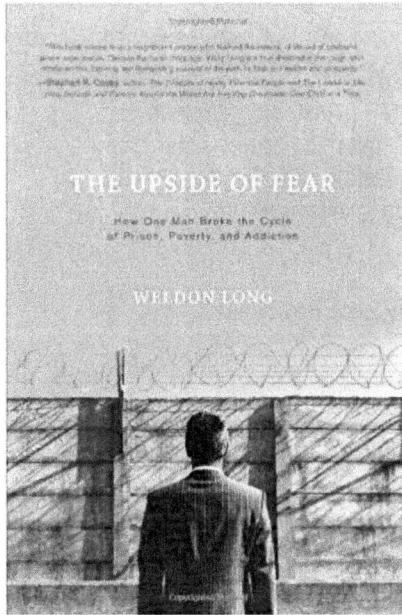

© Weldon Long. Used with permission.

When Weldon finally got out of prison, he thought, "What I need to do is get my mind straight. After I get my mind right I need to have a simple process then execute every single time on that simple process. It's just doing some simple things.

"I [now] live on the south side of Colorado Springs, Colorado, fourteen miles away from the homeless shelter where I lived in 2003. At that time, I developed a great relationship with a guy who had just retired. He was the Deputy Director of the Department of Corrections for the State of Colorado. He's got me access to some of the prisons where I served time in my twenties. In the late 1980s, I was able to get to my room in an old cell house. It was in that cell when I decided to live.

"My second book, *The Power of Consistency*, a Wall Street Journal and New York Times Best Seller, focuses on the mindset that transformed my life, personally and professionally, through simple processes I developed."

THE POWER OF CONSISTENCY

A *NEW YORK TIMES* BESTSELLER

★ ★ ★ ★ ★   amazon.com

"This book is awesome, **dare I say life changing.**"

ROBERT, *Amazon.com Customer Review*

© Weldon Long. Used with permission.

As you continue reading this chapter you might wonder why I am sharing so much of the life of this amazing man, Weldon Long, his books, and the accolades that come to any best-selling author. How does Weldon's life story compare with that of Brené Brown's deep wisdom in *Daring Greatly*? Some things Weldon shares with us will answer that question. Weldon's stories leverage his experiences selling air conditioners, starting his own company, growing it to $20 million in revenue, and being asked by distributors and manufacturers to do two-day training programs and keynote speeches.

His overall message isn't *"sales is the best career for someone who got lost as a youth and went to prison."* His real message is one of turning his life around which started with having faith and hiring his first employee.

To stay relevant to subject matter in *Ride the Horses, Feed the Lions*, I asked Weldon questions about how his hiring practices might parallel other LinkedIn Influencers. I hadn't grown my business to $20 million and then sold it. I grew up in a middle-class family and never had to pull myself out of poverty or prison. In business we make a "turn-around" as glamorous as a Hollywood movie. Whimsical characters emerge from the imaginations of the screenplay writers when we talk of Bill Gates as some sort of *garage-to-greatness god.*

Yet Weldon Long's life turn-around perhaps makes his experiences in business as poignant and relevant as any Harvard graduate born with a silver spoon. Weldon's life story is a journey. Not *good to great* as in a book by the same name but more like *unlikely to unbelievable.* Let me start with a few questions that I asked him to get a bearing on how his experiences might include some wisdom in managing people:

"Weldon, what were the best salespeople you hired like? What was their personality type? Did you run your own heating and air conditioning company with salespeople like *plow horses* or *thoroughbreds*? Who did the job following your simple processes exactly as you taught them?"

His answer was unique, unexpected, and worth noting: "I tried, for the most part, to hire salespeople *outside our industry.*"

That relevant piece of advice seemed to come out of nowhere. He continued, "In my own personal experience, when we hired salespeople inside the home improvement industry they often brought with them bad habits, poor training, and a focus on price instead of service or our value equation of product, warranty, and trust in our company reputation. My best HVAC salesman had been a life insurance salesman. Another really good guy I hired had been the finance manager at a car dealership. One man came from the window business. They tended to be better about sales than former HVAC salesmen. One was actually a boiler technician. That guy was from back East and he understood my sales process. He was also an excellent problem solver. What distinguished him from others was his ability to build trust and establish relationships.

"All my other salespeople just assumed the guy from back East was 'high pressure,' but instead he was always about 'high service.' When we would have Home Shows here in town, although his customers were by far the ones who spent the most money on very sophisticated solutions, he was the one whose customers were coming up to him at the shows giving him hugs. He was fantastic at building relationships. The others sold cheap HVAC systems based on price and didn't have customers coming back to them. In fact, they didn't even remember their names.

"One additional characteristic that made him most successful, and I used to kid with him about this, is this gene that we have. You know the strand of DNA that makes us feel uncomfortable or sometimes awkward? Well he didn't have that piece of DNA. He didn't have that. You couldn't make the guy uncomfortable. He never got nervous about big numbers, a price that might seem high to other salespeople, and he never was nervous about asking for the order, where a homeowner would say, 'Well we can't do it right now, we're going on vacation' or 'We have to think about it.' He didn't ever let it get in his way. He was about sixty years old when he came to work for me. He had this very distinguished silver hair and he wasn't too flashy. He took the company truck to his sales calls."

Weldon went on describing that salesman. "When he asked a homeowner for the order, he had an expectation the answer would be a 'yes.' Then if they didn't start signing the paperwork, he would slump down in his chair and pull his eyeglasses down onto the tip of his nose. He would just stare at his customer until they got so nervous, they couldn't sit still. He would just wait. You know *Whoever talks first loses*? While customers considered what to do, he stared at them down gnarled nostrils. Normally the *Tommy Boy* in most salespeople, responding to this pressure would say, 'I've got to go now. Give me a call when you're ready to go,' and leave."

That reminded me that, in training new salespeople, I would describe a guy that worked for me at Sears who we called *The Admiral*. He just did his job. Was he stylistic? No. Was he a *plow horse*, just doing his job, pulling the late-night load! Yes! Was he reliable? Always! Where does he fit in? Was he a *lion*? No, he was a *plow horse*.

Weldon picks up the narrative here as if he was reminiscing about an old, happy childhood memory. But in his case, life outside prison brought recollections of relationships back to the front burner as he said:

"Of course, he knew that seldom did anyone ever call back, so why leave? You could not make this former boiler technician nervous. He believed completely that choosing our company was the best option for the homeowner. His confusion at their reluctance was obvious on his face. He just could not understand why every single one of his customers didn't move forward. After all, he knew for certain that there was nothing that Weldon Long wouldn't do to honor his company's guarantee. If there was anything about our system that a customer didn't like we would take out the system and give them their money back," he said.

"We had a woman that got cancer. We refunded her money. Then we even let her keep the system. Another time we had a customer that got transferred out of town. We bought his system back. We would get these amazing letters all the time. It gave our salespeople so much confidence; they knew that they couldn't 'oversell' our guarantee. This salesman, that you might call *stylistic*, was just good at solving problems. He was the absolute best at building relationships and had nerves of steel. If that is *stylistic*, then I would hire people with his style of service all day."

Weldon seemed to be closing our conversation like a sale. He said, "The final thing as a salesman that I always said in the home was, 'Mr. Walker, this is the system that I'm going to recommend. Will you trust my recommendation?'"

Weldon continued to share what helped him turn his life around. From a life of such great losses came the unexpected **power of consistency**. From the power of consistency came a life redefined!

It should be obvious in reading about the life of Weldon Long why he had to choose to be vulnerable in order to accept his past mistakes and turn his life around. Now I offer a concluding question for you, the reader: "What would you say Brené Brown's *Power of Vulnerability* means in your life?" Think about how you would answer. I've shared some personal experiences with you of my own journey from divorce to loss of employment to a destination that I hope is not only humility but a fork in the road we all have to choose. Do we go left, and focus only on ourselves, meeting our selfish needs, or make a right turn and put others first? Vulnerability may be described as the willingness to not only listen to others' ideas but to solicit them. Not only to listen but to hear what they are saying. Not only to hear what they're suggesting but to find a way to make those things happen.

Vulnerability might be what we learn from life experiences, failures, disappointments, and even decisions of a great person like Weldon

Long. His story is real and profound. Did the excitement in his voice come from starting companies and selling them? Maybe. What I heard was his passion for life, his appreciation of people, his regrets, but also his forward thinking and his positive outlook on life. It was hard not to have the conversation loop back into his plans to digitize his training methods and his videos of an old prison cell that he planned to use to promote his next book. Weldon went to prison in the past, but he is thriving in the present. Do you personally know someone who went to prison or is now still in prison? Maybe the real vulnerability comes from our willingness to acknowledge our humanity and our failures, and to leverage that in our relationships. How do we do that? By watching the *Stylistic Salesperson* investing in relationships, and their focus on intentionally LISTENING to understand!

Weldon also told me about hiring a man in the halfway house he was in. Who else would hire him? Weldon trusted another prison inmate with the success of his first business. Is that vulnerability? Is it being like a former boiler technician who willingly establishes deep, meaningful relationships as you peel off the crustiness from his old Army sergeant mentality? What is *vulnerability* to you? Accepting the responsibility for causing my divorce made me teachable. I knew one thing, "Tomorrow I can choose differently."

# Chapter Ten

## "The Conversational Close"
## Keep the Doors Open

Peter Bulger hired me at Champion Windows before we ever met. How did he do that, you ask? Well it started when we had five telephone calls before I arrived in Cincinnati, Ohio for my first day at the corporate offices. It became obvious that selling was not just a job for Peter but his lifeblood. Selling makes him get up each morning and fills his emotional *cup of Joe*. His drug of choice is sugar. He's a dynamic, high energy guy. This chapter will give you a taste of the comprehensive stylistic training manual, *The Conversational Close*, offered in my consulting practice, Titan Global Group, LLC., from the basics to the *Linear Closing Clinic* that can be customized to fit your promotions, your process and your people.

Peter was clearly a *Stylistic Sales professional*, and during our telephone conversations it turned out that we shared similar experiences, successes, and approaches to sales. My challenge was putting together a new training program based on previous experiences but in concert with Peter's style.

Champion's Ten Step Program was close to what I had learned at Sears. Peter had worked for Sears thirty-five years earlier at Amre, a Sears subsidiary. Until 2001, Sears operated through subsidiaries such as Diamond Roofing, K-Designers, Spraytek, and of course,

Amre. Financial issues at Diamond and Amre resulted in ending long relationships with Sears. With the value of Amre at salvage prices, Peter and two principles bought it. They built a new company with cabinet refacing as their main product. Home Depot eventually bought them out and Peter was looking for another project. That new gig would turn out to be National Director of Sales as well as Regional Manager of the Central Region's Divisions for Champion Windows. That would turn out to be a bridge too far.

As a result of learning, developing, and training a new system, three of us, hired as national trainers, would be learning new linear closing skills. What I learned was to *keep the conversation going* to allow the customer to make a decision on a purchase. Due to professional ethics, I can't share exactly what our new system was, but what I can tell you is as follows:

What is the obstacle for most potential buyers? The price is too high! But how do they know it is too high? Based on what? For example, is the price of a Tesla too high? "How about a Lexus or a Honda? Okay then, how about a Kia, or let's go back in time to the Ford Pinto?"

When getting price objections, we're tempted to pitch harder. When confronted by a fair **retail price**, what do customers do? When they react emotionally, they may have talked to a neighbor about the vinyl windows he had installed at his home. They are better than the old ones and more energy efficient, for a surprisingly low price. Why is every purchase so often about price? We need to include "tomorrow's costs" of replacement when they fail in the overall price vs. value equation. If you buy a cheaper product, what's the life-service term expectancy? Half price often lasts half as long. Why is it when you sell to a retiring couple, they want to fix things "once and for all" and then quality seems to make sense?

Quoting an *ISPO News* article, January 2015, "*90% of all purchasing decisions are made subconsciously.*" Just like researching any product, there are facts. This leaves the burden on the sales professional to do the following:

Give a professional presentation; and

Let customers see, feel, and operate your product.

It is up to the sales manager to train their sales force how to walk customers through the price presentation process to help them make their best decision.

"The Conversational Close" isn't a hard close. There is no secret price on a piece of paper, only to be revealed when you ask for the sale. I've heard sales representatives at Champion and other companies say: **"Mr. Jones, if you *could* get our *best windows* priced like our *better windows*, *could* I earn your business today?"** What's wrong with that proposition? Nothing, if it meets the customer's needs and fits their budget. A win-win for everyone! But what if it doesn't?

When customers ask questions after they see the price, they're not really objecting to price at all. This is a **buying signal.** At this point, do you know what they really want to do? They want to buy from someone who CAN answer their questions. Don't give up now. You are 90% of the way there. What do you do then? Don't pressure. Don't challenge their objections just because you THOUGHT they heard everything you said for two hours. Don't be frustrated. They must like you or they would have already thanked you for coming and helped you carry your samples to your car. Keep the doors open to further conversation. Listen and ask questions to clarify their needs so you can meet them.

I remember when this first happened to me. The objection was, **"My father owns the home."**

Oh great, I just spent two hours presenting to someone who didn't even own the home. Why didn't I ask, "So how long have you owned this home?" Okay, do I just pack up my stuff, with my tail between my legs, and run home like in the *Tommy Boy* movie? Then a thought occurred to me, "Why not ask where his father lives?" Okay, I'll give that a try.

"Where does your father live?"

Just like when I waited and the lady with a clipboard taking notes said, "Okay, let's do it," this guy answers me, "He lives next door." Wow!

Obviously, the customer had an additional objection that I hadn't isolated with the Sears' *"Circle Close"* approach. He had to think about it because he had to talk to his father. The MONEY was coming from his dad. I hadn't isolated objections to just price. In fact, he hadn't objected to the price at all. My having continued the conversation was the key. I asked the man to call his father. We went next door. His father asked if his son thought the price was fair. He said, "Yes." That's all dad wanted to know. We wrote up the contract. But what really happened was we met his need. In a similar scenario, my friend, Dan, drove to one guy's father's office at lunch to close a sale.

While at Sears training others how to sell, not much time was spent on *how to close a sale*. I had Sears' reputation, the strength of their warranty, even *Kenmore, Craftsman* and *DieHard* behind me. Things have since changed. Today you can buy those products at multiple retailers, and consumers are savvy to price, product, and quality. So how do we close?

What if I had given my customers the lowest price I could and they still didn't purchase? At that point, would I know what the obstacle was? No. When you compete on price alone, you have nowhere to go. I know I said company reputation, warranty, guaranteed standards of installation, price, and financing are powerful tools in addition to features and benefits beyond the quality of the products. We had those at Sears and at Champion, but price can't be the only close.

At Sears we weren't prepared with any alternate closing approaches. Had we read a list of alternate closes? Had we memorized some of them? Did we know the *Ben Franklin* close, for example? Sure. Had it worked in every case? No. We had little faith in a list of sales closes that were not linked in a logical linear sequence. Sales management trained regimented presentations and memorized scripts to be delivered flawlessly, but we can't automate talent. Everyone has their style. You may have read many sales books that have quotes like:

"If you use power words they will buy from you."

*News Flash:* Even if you use all the power words, not everyone will buy. It takes more than price and power words. Do I read another book? Do I go to another selling seminar? Do I speak with a famous sales guru?

In the movie *Tommy Boy*, do you remember Chris Farley as he sat across the desk from the buyer? He next set a plastic toy car on fire. The potential client was furious. In this scene Farley memorialized every sales novice who then puts his tail between his legs and hurriedly leaves at the first objection. First, don't set a collector series toy on fire, but do find a way to stay almost until they throw you out. Okay, that example was funny because it was a bit over the top, but is that the answer?

That's not how my screenplay of *The Stylistic Salesperson* ends in my imagined closing scene. Maybe if we were in that scene we'd go back to the office and blame it on *The Leads.* "Hey boss, why don't I get the *Glengarry Glen Ross* leads?" We're new, so the superstars always get the best leads. I mean, why waste a good lead on rookies? This is where many salespeople fail to accept complete responsibility for their success. They can make a living, but can an average salesperson become good or even great with that attitude? "Is it the lead or is it me?" *Stylistic salespeople* are past that. **"It is us!"**

It's also not only training. I had one week of training on the paperwork and my classmate got one week of training on the product. In 2000, at American Home Improvements, that's all we got. The lead quality was not great. Often, they were telemarketing leads. All we would hear was the battle cry *"Go get-em!"* *Some win, some lose* was the explanation.

I didn't complain as most home improvement companies required you to get your own leads. But I'd never sold on full commission before. All I had was the responsibility I felt to support my family, including my ex-wife who was an invalid with a life-threatening condition, and the belief in me coming from my boss at Sears who said to me, "I think you can do this."

He wasn't the only one who believed in me. When I lost my job at *La Agencia de Orci*, the woman I was dating said, "Everything I need comes to me and everything always works out. Now you can come to Denver." I learned a lot that day as everything seemed to happen for a reason. That woman is now my wife.

Somehow, I succeeded. Looking back, I now know exactly how it all happened. When I was interviewed by Glenn L. Moore, Denver District Sales Manager, for my first real commission sales position at Sears Home Improvements, he had said, "I think you can do this." Before I realized it, I had taken the straight commission position on faith along with the desperate need to succeed. If it wasn't the training, the company, or the products, what was it? It was my way of communicating, my love of people, and a little bit of my theater background, my enjoyment of "being on stage" so to speak. It was my style and there was nobody exactly like me. It's the same with you. Each of us brings something unique, something *stylistic*, to each creative challenge we face in the world's most challenging career, **selling.**

Later, when I accepted my third District Sales Management position in Denver, my soon-to-be good friend Greg found himself in a similar situation. He had a $5,000 loan from his father to buy a used car to get him on his feet. I didn't know the HR screening system had initially rejected him, but he was persistent. I had no idea of the details of his life, but Greg came to our first Sears employment Open House. We had tried newspaper ads and job fairs that didn't work. For our open house, we invited people from a stack of resumés, who we'd never interviewed, who wanted to sell for Sears. Our management team was there so that applicants would see who they would be working for. I hired Greg and six others we met that night.

I don't know about you, but **it is more important to me who I work with than the product I sell**. If I believe in the company and respect the manager, I'm happy. I also believe you can learn a product, and you can train process, but to find *Stylistic Salespeople*, or *Ride the Horses and Feed the Lions*, managers must recognize their unique characteristics. I attribute the keys to my success in running three #1 rated districts as recognizing, recruiting, relating-to, and retaining *Stylistic Salespeople*.

What Peter taught me at Champion lifted me even higher than any accolade I've received before or since. At some point in a successful sales career, someone may think you can train others. If the timing is right, it will be when you decide to give back. It came in my second year at Sears.

My career at Sears ended in November 2014. In January 2015, the offer came at Champion. Tutored by Peter Bulger, I learned how to keep the conversation open, a process I've now titled "The Conversational Close." Peter taught four sequential, linear "Time" or "Urgency" closes, and seven other Sales closes to address objections (buying signals) related to money or affordability. I had never been given closing tools like that. In the powerful interpersonal-skilled world of *Stylistic Salespeople*, these closing techniques are trainable. You can train potential *thoroughbred*s; they are willing to learn. *Ride the Horses!* They will win, place and show!

## *Urgency and Affordability*

In this linear close process, if the first solution to a customer's concern regarding when to move forward with a project didn't satisfy them, then there was another solution for the customer to consider. Creativity and flexibility is required. But first you need to:

1.   Know the basic scripted closing conversations.
2.   Listen and address customer's objections with solutions.

One of the closes we used addressed any new issues following a previous discussion, and each would lead logically to the next customer concern. A linear process!

Scenario: You're very successful, either in sales or are a sales manager. You're with your customer and confronted by the first objection:

"We just have to think about it." "We never make a decision on the same day." "We need to get three bids," or the classic excuse, "We always sleep on major decisions like this."

Imagine someone trained you on all the sales "closes" you've ever read. Instead of using one to address each specific objection, you learned to present solutions in a linear sequence. You'd always have another close (*conversation*) ready to go, in case the first close (*approach*) didn't address concerns about *WHEN* to move forward, budget or *AFFORDABILITY*. You are never stumped. This isn't a *Second City* improvisational style. You respond to what customers say. Your conversations will be enhanced by knowing exactly what approach to use. How would that make you feel?

Show me that list again!

At this point you probably want to *cut to the chase*. "Just tell me how to find *The horses and the lions* and I'll go hire them. If you'll give me the list of characteristics of *The Stylistic Salespeople* you describe, I'll hire a whole ZOO of them and retire early." You should be a little impatient or intrigued at this point in the book. You could actually stop, leave the book with your HR people, insist they interview potential members of your sales team and wait to interview them. What's the common concern here? How do I explain simply how to find "natural" salespeople? At the end of this book, or even as you read it and decide to start looking at your job applicants more closely, or if you ask your HR personnel to be first focused on *like-ability* instead of background qualifications, you'll then, perhaps for the first time, start to see what I see. On the back cover of this book are the names of sixteen LinkedIn Influencers I interviewed. Most of those I interviewed may have hired or worked with one or two *Stylistic Salespeople* in their careers. Some of the companies like Franklin-Covey clearly have had a *people-first-focus* that attracted, inspired, retained, and managed these *Stylistic Salespeople* by *giving them the reins* so they could become *thoroughbreds.* That is why I have included their stories, experiences, quotes and comments in *Ride the Horses, Feed the Lions.*

The greatest teachers, the best salespeople, and the most effective managers teach by using stories. *Stylistic Salespeople live their stories.* An HR algorithm will filter key words and discover strong sales backgrounds **but won't find the horses or the lions.** We talk a lot in business today about disruptors. People are sometimes confused about the difference between innovation and disruption. I will be the first to admit that I want to disrupt the HR process of hiring salespeople, since by doing this we innovate HR approaches to hiring.

If we want to be the Michael Jordan of sales executives or managers, we have to study Phil Jackson and how he trained and managed Michael Jordan to be selfless enough to lift the team to an unheard-of NBA record we now call *the three-peat.* And they did it twice! **Can we?**

I'm not sure if the sixteen LinkedIn executives I interviewed had ever been asked, "Who is the best salesperson you ever knew, ever worked with, or who ever worked for you?" After describing their favorite sales superstar, I asked, "What made them different, so persistent, so successful, what were they like and, at the end of the day, what made them tick?"

**Here's the list again:**

## *Characteristics of a Stylistic Salesperson*

1.  They are **creative!** They only need your guidance on policy. They are problem solvers.
2.  You can't **make** them; you **find** them. This is the best part of your journey. Training new people to become like robots is simply *not* fun, for you or them.
3.  They are **people-people**. They are naturally sincere, authentic, warm and **charismatic**. For them each appointment is like a first date.
4.  They sell with **integrity**, honesty, are concerned about the customer's needs more than their own, and they feel they cannot be dishonest and succeed.
5.  They need to be **motivated,** not managed. How would you manage Michael Jordan? Take an interest in them so they will "get you."
6.  The need for **recognition** is different for each person. The challenge is how to reach them. In this sense each manager must be stylistic too.
7.  Want to **adopt them** or invite them for dinner? These are my tests. I hire on this basis when looking for a superstar. Eyes wide open? Yes!
8.  You can't find these characteristics on their **resumé.** I admit that I never read resumés when hiring a salesperson. I look and listen for who they really are.
9.  They're **happy** by nature. **50%** of how we handle rejection is how we are raised. **10%** of events are out of our control, but **40%** is our choice!
10. They want to **help** people. This is an intangible. Look for it. You don't have to push someone who **pulls others up**. They'll help you if you establish a relationship with them.

Know these *thoroughbred*s personally; don't rein them in right out of the gate. Let them set their own pace. Be on their team so they're on yours. Like most things, learning how to manage *Stylistic Salespeople* is on-the-job training. Each person is like a book with something unique on each page. Don't rush. Listen to stories they tell. Watch, learn, have fun! **Note to Sales Managers**: They want you to get to know them!

What about the *lions*? They're the one-in-a-thousand who sell millions! They're salespeople operating outside of the box procedurally, yet they drive tremendous sales revenue. You don't train them. FEED them and learn from them!

There are many purposes for reading this book. I am boldly sharing many things that propelled me from discovering that I loved to sell to the point where I wanted to help others to be successful. Not only successful at sales or at making an income, but successful in life.

"It wasn't you, Bill." Remember that? I think one of the basic desires of human beings is to be first, to do something that people say "can't be done." At that point we become unique, we're recognized, and we start to have *self-confidence* and a *self-worth* that makes up for all the failures we have had along the way.

Throughout my journey, I found out a great deal about what made me enjoy my work and my life more. All I had to do was LISTEN to Zig Ziglar as he gave his **KEY** to everyone: helping others was his secret to success. The same could be shared with all teenagers. "Listen to your parents" is generally good advice but not every person had the kind of parents who inspired them to be *greater than they were*. Some parents have actually been heard to say, *"You won't amount to nothin'."* As a sales manager, you'll sometimes be the parent they never had, the encouragement they need!

The above list of characteristics typify the *horses and lions* that I refer to as *Stylistic Salespeople*. Here you find the list placed halfway on your journey through the profound stories of great salespeople by mentors like Zig Ziglar, Tom Hopkins, Brian Tracy, Dale Carnegie, Jeffrey Gitomer, and Stephen R. Covey. What's your challenge? Isn't it basically to *close the sale* after all customer objections? Yes, but it's also for you as a sales executive to be able to find great salespeople with natural people-skills, abilities, and the discipline to become great. Will you teach them they have to pressure the customer? No. Keep the conversation open. Don't close any doors. Don't give customers a reason to send you packing. *The Conversational Close* approach takes trainees from *BASICS* to *BELIEF*, arming them with conversations covering objections from time *(urgency)* to affordability. Remember, they did call you. No matter what objection, what matters to serious customers is a universal value equation: "Is it worth it and can I afford it?"

# Chapter Eleven

## Poor to Average, Average to Good, Good to Great

Ever read the management book *Built to Last,* Successful Habits of Visionary Companies by authors James C. Collins and Jerry I. Porras? This catapulted James's perceptive tome *Good to Great* into the front row in what I proudly call *The Theater of Business Organizational Change Agents™.* Paul Minors' blog article posted July 7, 2014 provides a short summary:

"James C. Collins outlines a model for turning a good, average or even mediocre company into a great one. The book includes a useful model which brings the theory together in meaningful and memorable ways. Bringing together disciplined people, using disciplined thought and action, companies can build up and break through barriers that hold them back from greatness. James Collins and his research team put together a list of *'good to great'* compared to a [control group] of companies, in order to determine what separates the elite from the rest."

In *Good to Great,* James C. Collins's book speaks to managers and executives about gaining momentum while fostering a new excellence in management. He describes how companies transition from mediocre or good to great companies, or how they can fail to make that critical transition. His book should be read by upper middle managers who are in a position to have direct influence in their executive teams.

Why do we care about *Good to Great*? The "good" companies were not those we'd describe as average. And none of the readers of *Ride the Horses, Feed the Lions* will think of themselves or their companies and sales teams as "average" or perhaps even "good." But some of the companies cited in *Good to Great* could have avoided falling from retail grace by focusing on the sales team and growing top line revenues, not just on cost containment. Accountants and CFOs seldom embrace sales organizations. Business is not a game, but even to win games, recruiting and retaining talent is the secret.

Here are some companies James C. Collins studied in preparing to write his book, *Good to Great*: Abbott Laboratories, Circuit City Stores, Fannie Mae, Gillette Company, Kimberly-Clark, Kroger, Nucor, Philip Morris, Pitney Bowes, Walgreens and Wells Fargo.

Similarly, Peter Strohkorb, author of *The OneTEAM Method: How Sales+Marketing Collaboration Boosts Big Business, Smarketing™*, points to the lack of cooperation between sales and marketing as the enemy.

Let me introduce you to some interesting new concepts that will help us understand what James C. Collins outlined in his book. Concept #1 - *"Poor to Gone."* Concept #2 – *"Average to Good."* And then of course the obvious, #3 - *"Good to Great."*

*"Poor to Gone"* is introduced here because when it comes to the sales world there will always be some recruits who will find out sales is not for them. Dealing with that reality is a sales manager's job. I'm not talking about the GE program of releasing the bottom ten percent every year, fostered by Jack Welch when he was CEO. We need to keep a bench of average salespeople to maintain our business while we recruit *horses and lions*. It takes time to recruit, hire, train, and motivate salespeople in an effort to achieve acceptable productivity. In order to manage our resources and meet revenue targets, however, we will need to release low producers.

In an interview with Monica Pritchard, VP of Sales, Marketing and Product Development at Quality Edge in Walker, Michigan about performance standards, she shared her disdain for typical performance review processes utilized by HR departments in many corporations today. Terms like distinguished, excellent, good, or fair are used subjectively while others use numbers or percentages. She pointed to examples of managers having too many employees in each rating category or performance level, altering ratings. In short order, executives or HR appointees tell that manager to re-balance their employee rating results to match the HR bell curve.

Monica has tried to abolish the process. She stated, "Since I can't change the fact that others cannot see past the process and the need for change, I focus on...a partnership with the individual employee and me [and what areas they] need to put a little more effort around, going forward. I believe all managers should be continuously talking to and *coaching up their people*, rather than once or twice a year."

Monica shared a story of a struggling salesperson who applied to work for Quality Edge. She hired a man with no experience in the industry because she loved his attitude. In the beginning there were some issues with his performance and he wasn't catching on as quickly as she had hoped.

"About a month prior to our next interview, I'd traveled with him to meet a customer out of town. While we shared a meal that evening, before the sales appointment...the customer contacted the young salesman, inviting us to his home to visit with him and his wife." Monica said, "I love meeting customers the night before because it gets the *meet and greet* out of the way so we can get right to work the next day. So I immediately agreed to the invitation, 'Let's go meet them,' I responded enthusiastically."

They drove to the customer's home to find that he'd converted a portion of it into a cigar lounge. Unable to endure the smoke, Monica busied herself talking with other guests on the patio while the salesman spoke with his client and shared stories along with a long Cuban cigar. Eventually her new hire and his customer came out to the patio and she saw, firsthand, the relationship he had built with his client. Taking him aside she said:

"What impresses me is your prospects want to meet with you. It is clear they want to figure out a way to do business with you because of who you are. Your way with people made him want to do business with you. That quality is hard to find."

Monica summarized her perspective on this rookie salesperson in just one sentence:

"When our meetings were all done and we left the client's home, I said to my salesman, 'You may not have the experience, and you may not yet be up to par, but customers love you.'"

Her message is also mine. We seldom find that a *Stylistic Salesperson*'s **profound interpersonal skills** show up on their resumé. You can train a *thoroughbred* horse to win a race, but you have to find the *lions*. Perhaps sales managers can convert persistently poor performing salespeople to be average or good by getting them to write down lofty personal goals, you know the kind where if you actually accomplished them, siblings and friends from high school who didn't think much of you would be astounded. When I say *"lofty personal goals,"* I do **not** mean business goals. I mean accomplishing personal goals even poor performers can't deny. As they do, it may give them *something to look forward to* when they go home after work. This was an idea I had after reading an MBA thesis by Michelle Bellas and Colin Collard. I wanted to help my average salespeople believe in themselves. I decided to take a chance on implementing some of their theories with a twist. More on this soon.

Why would you read about my approach to managing or motivating poor to become at least average and either retaining them or separating them, if they didn't respond? Because they are part of our challenge as sales managers. As we grow our sales organizations, some of our "sales team" who usually could "get a base hit" will stay on the bench and we don't know why. We can't just fire them or stop giving them any leads. We depend on that "bench" while we are making "trades" and getting "draft choices" to build our team of the future. We are sales managers, mentors and sales gurus with the wisdom to make it happen. If you feel at times like I have felt, struggling to treat each member of the team as an individual while trying to maintain a relationship with a superstar, maybe you have asked yourself,

"Where's the how-to book focusing on Poor to Average and Average to Good? Help!"

In the next chapter, I offer a rather surprising answer.

## *Recruiting Quality People*

"It is the journey along the path to achievement
that excites the adventurer."
William Dilworth Hatch

Two sources of motivation, or what I call performance energy on a sales team, come from leveraging the influence of *Stylistic Salespeople* who achieve certain levels of performance. They set new goals and write them down. "How high is up?" they wonder and plan to reach their next level of achievement. We have examples around us of individuals who accomplish physical and intellectual achievements no one thought were possible. They amazingly end up being acknowledged as a part of history as legends.

As sales managers we have two basic goals. First, find quality people. Second, improve the productivity of those currently in our organizations.

The quickest return will come from improving our existing teams. They're already trained. They know products and processes. By soliciting the support of our top performers to help average salespeople succeed, we are doing two things. First, we obviously provide mentors for those *thoroughbreds-in-embryo*. But, second, we are establishing a relationship between the manager and the best salespeople we manage. That's the motivation. It isn't always easy. Everyone needs to feel they're of value to their supervisor, their spouse, their parents and even their God. We may wonder, *What's in it for us?* If we are able to harness the power and influence of these sales **mavericks** over our team, we'll begin to see the Ten Characteristics of those we respectfully refer to as **Stylistic Salespeople.**

Soon the *Stylistic Salesperson's* behaviors, disciplines and positive interpersonal communication skills show up as your team emulates the salesperson. The challenge for sales managers is to establish a relationship with *horses and lions* that motivates them to positively influence our teams. The payback for them? Flexibility, respect from management, space, encouragement and empowerment in the very best definition of this overused phrase, "can achieve." The payback for us? The entire team begins to consistently demonstrate persistence, self-confidence and, finally, their drive to be the best. A desire to help others may also emerge in the process. It's *Zig Ziglar's message*: If you want to achieve your desired success [paraphrasing here] help others achieve theirs.

Perhaps the best outcome of your efforts as sales managers is not just in your company but in your sales force taking responsibility for their family, those they are accountable to, and their desire to succeed personally and financially. Now you have improved the lives of an entire community. Time well spent.

With patience and rigorous discipline, long hours, and an uncertain financial outcome, rejections and emotional demands in a sales career add up, and may eventually bring any salesperson to the point of physical exhaustion or even a breaking point. Wake-up call? Unless we motivate salespeople to have a goal other than a career focused on money, we can lose them. Better said, they can lose themselves. How do we do this when not everyone is a sports star with amazing accomplishments and astounding physical feats, and few of us seem to be naturally blessed with multiple God-given physical talents? I will cover this soon.

Sports teams will scout high school, junior college, and college stars, recruit and train them. In that process a coach or team executive will make a trade to put a veteran in the locker room. Shouldn't our process be similar if we want to recruit those NFL, NBA or World Series Baseball-quality salespeople? Why is our HR algorithm's screening process often failing to recognize the "key qualities" in the very *thoroughbred* racehorses and the somewhat wild *lion*s we all need? Why aren't we seeing them being referred to hiring decision-makers? What team would draft Michael when 15-year-old Jordan was on Laney High School's JV basketball team? Would some NBA Scout have read Michael's *resumé* only to ultimately *take a pass* on him:

"He's not tall enough, fast enough, or skilled enough."

Who would have imagined his growth spurt or development that happened after that? What changed in Michael to cause him to desire being the best? Was it a giant 42" vertical leap for him to set that as his goal? If we could clone what drove his belief in himself and his resulting work ethic, we could find the **gold** in all of us. Do we often leave too much of our recruiting to some of our human resource personnel? Have any of them ever sold on commission? Been B2B account executives? Sat across from a client who said "I have to think about it" and wondered how to motivate them to move forward? Then how can they sense—or almost smell—the fever that we might call desire so rare in potential *thoroughbreds* so they set up an interview? Indeed, when do our HR people ask themselves:

"Would I invite them over to my home for a barbeque?"

Roberto, a contact on LinkedIn who read my post about this upcoming book, shared his frustration:

"Another book on sales. People buy from those they like and trust. Why don't you write about that?"

What he didn't realize from my note sending him to my webpage, www.WilliamDHatch.com, was that his frustration mirrors my own:

"Why don't we realize that people buy from those they like and trust?"

Indeed it is the reason I decided to write *Ride the Horses, Feed the Lions.*

Is it past time for a *Crusade to Humanize Selling*? Or just in time? Who we recruit is the game changer! Okay, what do we look for? Who do we find if we personally interview so few candidates through the HR resumé process that we miss those **golden nuggets** Matt Kelly talked about?

Shawn Moon of Franklin-Covey spoke of one of the best sales professionals he ever hired. His description of this person sends all hiring managers a reality check:

He never would have been sent from HR to me for an interview. He never would've passed the tests." So is our current process of *"resumé to algorithm to key words to initial scheduling interviews"* really working to feed our sales organization? Are we intentionally looking for *thoroughbreds* or does our technology only "play it safe" while we are missing the Michael Jordans in embryo? If we disrupt and change our HR process to put the priority on casting a wider net and triple our interviews to filter more by "gut feel" and interpersonal skills, where do we find the *horses,* and who is caging their *lions*? We need some junior-varsity sales legends!

Can we trust HR professionals to interview using the List of Ten Characteristics of Stylistic Salespeople?

If we do, that is when we go back to the resumé, filtering key words and experiences, things like discipline, as many I interviewed identified as being a key to excellence. What we look for next is perhaps the greatest sales challenge of all: **Consistency**. Perhaps we should all read Weldon Long's book, *The Power of Consistency.*

"Can you go *four-for-four* the next day, the next week or the next year?"

"When will your next *three-peat* be, or for that matter your first one?"

We all look up to someone like Michael Jordan. We see the level of pride in his excellence. But even he had to find reasons to always improve. It had to be more than just the feeling, the thrill of winning. Jordan was known to practice long after the other team members ended their practice. He never stopped bettering himself. He was motivated to do his best every time. What I am trying to say is sales managers who want to *Ride the Horses and Feed the Lions* should take a page out of coach Phil Jackson's book so your team will say about you what Michael Jordan said when offered $25 million for one year to play for coach Jeff Van Gundy of the New York Knicks in 1996:

"My coach is everything."

Jordan even told Spike Lee, "I don't know what kind of coach Van Gundy is. I know Phil" (*READJACK*; 22 May, 2016).

A great manager must unearth sources of motivation unique to each salesperson similar to the interaction between coaches and athletes. Each person has different needs. Let's step out of our comfort zone. Taking them out to dinner every now and then isn't enough. Relationships take an investment of time. Your time!

Perhaps Steve Booz, a B2B building materials marketing executive, put it best:

"Based on Hersey-Blanchard Situational Leadership Theory, if you have a superstar, it's up to you as the manager to recognize [their] unique skills and figure out how you should treat them differently. I look for people who show passion for what they'd do if they worked for me."

Steve Booz, VP New Product Development and Management, Royal Building Products (Philadelphia)

www.linkedin.com/in/stevebooz

By now we all should accept that attitude is important. In fact, it is critical to us obtaining any success. The next key challenge is how to harness it, how to build ourselves up and strengthen our resolve to better the lives of others and not just our own. We need a higher purpose. "What's in it for me" is more effective in our lives when it is defined by the inspiring results of helping others to achieve their goals. To do that, we have to believe in something besides ourselves. Ask yourself, "How do I stay positive in the face of adversity?" I'm not pulling any punches. This means something to me. Why write this book? What is my motivation? What's in it for me? Maybe it is that I can't wait any longer. Maybe I hope the message will lift some burdens off the backs of the average sales executive by defining how to find *horses and lions*. Maybe even to enlighten Geoffrey Riddle's sales executives that come into town once a year to go with him on a sales call:

"Hello, he sells **every time**, but they still rate him low based on how closely he adheres to their process. He's a *Stylistic Salesperson*! You need to learn from him!" He told me he wants to buy a copy of this book and send one to every one of those people who have come into town to enlighten him. Monica Pritchard would probably say, "A low score on our annual review does nothing but discourage us."

If management retains an "arm's distance" in the way they relate to their sales teams, nothing changes. It is NOT the process that inspires or motivates a salesperson, it is encouraging them and extending them the flexibility to be authentic, invest time in relationships with their clients and thereby earn their trust. Life for me as a sales professional wasn't about money. People are what made sales fun for me. That's what makes all the long hours worth it. If it is the same for you, then get ready to *ride some horses*.

# Chapter Twelve

## "The 97 Club"

© William D. Hatch

I briefly referred to this in a previous chapter regarding the power of setting and writing down lofty *personal* goals and its potential to change salespeople from *poor to average*, *average to good,* and *good to great*. What I'll share with you now is a true life experience I had when addressing this challenge within my own sales team. Join me on a journey through a phenomenal experience I have chosen to call *The 97 Club*. You may soon be able to learn all the details, from start to finish, of our meetings in a book by the same name.

I am excited to share why my experiment with *The 97 Club* may be significant. It raises the philosophical question, "Why don't people write down goals?" Even more important was, "Why didn't I?" As you read this brief synopsis of our 16-week experiment, I believe that you'll find we have discovered part of the answer to "Why are some people phenomenally successful, while with similar opportunities, training, and management, some never reach a sense of fulfillment in whatever career they choose or obtain financial security?"

*The 97 Club* was unlike any business meeting. The ten salespeople who volunteered to meet once a week, early in the morning on the same day of our three-hour sales meeting, would gather to encourage each other to set and achieve *lofty personal goals.* In my case, by doing this I was challenging the normal *Doubting Thomas* response from the average salesperson as well as myself. "What difference will it make?" This wasn't only a personal challenge for me, it was a professional one. I was stumped. How could I transfer my enthusiasm about writing down goals if I wasn't convinced it would make any difference? We become somewhat jaded about the idea of setting sales goals when our managers "bark" about it every week. Would these meetings be any different?

### *Would there be any Sales Agenda in The 97 Club meetings? No! There would be a personal agenda!*

As Brené Brown writes in *Daring Greatly*, a characteristic of the greatest managers is being vulnerable or, in other words, teachable. Believe me, I was vulnerable here. I never thought that writing down goals would make any difference, but the Harvard Study (described below) gave me reason to question my belief that all my success came from my talents, abilities and hard work, not whether I wrote down goals. One day after expressing frustration about not being able to transfer the enthusiasm and discipline of writing down sales goals to my team, Greg Bickelhaupt sent me *Resolutions to Reality* by Michelle Bellas, MA and Colin Collard, MA. As I started to read it I was clearly judgmental. Without any facts, without testing their theory, I assumed my writing down goals wouldn't work. Ego and pride whispered that in my ears. It reminded me of when I was a salesman and I was advised one day to make a photo album of kitchens I sold. The advice came from someone I would call one of the *horses* that I'm referring to in the book. He suggested specifically I include in the album all my before and after pictures so people could visualize what their new kitchen might look like. I didn't believe it would make any difference, but I finally did it a year later. As I thought back to that event, I questioned myself,

"Was Harvard's study actually correct?"

The study I am referring to was conducted at Harvard between 1979 and 1989. In the study, graduates of the MBA program were asked,

"Have you set clear written goals for your future and made plans to accomplish them?"

The eye-opening statistics regarding their answers were:

Only 3% had written goals and plans.

13% had goals but not in writing.

84% had no specific goals at all.

**10 years later Harvard interviewed the same class members and found:**

Those 13% who had some goals but never wrote them down were earning on average twice as much as the 84% of the MBA graduates with no specific goals. The 3% who had clear, written goals were earning on average 10 times as much as all the other 97% of graduates all together. The only difference between groups was the clarity of the goals they had and that they memorialized them by writing them down.

"Oh brother, maybe there is something to this after all," I squirmed. Statistics quoted above are taken from an August 18, 2010 article by Mike Morrison.

## *Vulnerability Needed, Bill? Yes!*

Accepting a bit more vulnerability as a manager, I had to test it out myself. I would see if it worked. When I suggested to my team of thirty salespeople my idea of coming in an hour early with me, once a week, before our weekly sales meeting, I waited for their reaction. The regular meeting was already three hours. Attendance at *The 97 Club* would be totally voluntary. Would anyone come? I listened for groans. For some reason, no one groaned. I was shocked. Were they seriously considering it? I added the tried and true incentive: A free lunch! We always had snacks like donuts and bagels for our weekly meeting but seldom did we have lunch. As an inducement, I had sandwich meats, mayonnaise, mustard, bread, soda, and potato chips for all *97 Club* members who came.

Ten of the thirty sales representatives came voluntarily. Of course we had lunch together. Was this like the *"If you build it they will come"* phenomenon from the 1989 movie *Field of Dreams?*

As we started meeting, we became aware how hard it was to set, let alone to verbalize, three crazy, inspirational, lofty personal goals that would rock our world. We'd tried everything with sales goals, but nothing had worked. It never occurred to me to write down lofty personal goals.

I read the statistics again: "84% had no specific goals and 13% had goals but hadn't committed them to paper. The remaining 3% had clear written goals and the plans to accomplish them." I wanted to believe writing down goals actually makes a difference, but I'd have to prove it to myself. At our first meeting of *The 97 Club,* I told the ten members of my sales team who came:

"I believe that having goals, planning, executing plans, and working together as a team in business or in life makes a difference. I'm sorry to admit it but I'm not sure if writing down these goals makes any difference at all. If you're willing, together, we will test Harvard's theory of writing down goals and prove it one way or the other. Are you with me?"

Then, to their surprise, I explained that it would not be about business goals and there would be no agenda. We would try this experiment setting **personal** goals. I got complete buy-in from the group of ten. I was shocked. Preparing for each meeting, I created a PowerPoint slide presentation to pitch the idea of *"Setting Lofty Personal Goals."* Would it work? Could ten average salespeople change behaviors? Would they actually write down three goals, visualize them, and hopefully achieve them? Would my doing this, right along with them, validate the process?

### *Was this Personal for Me? Yes very personal!*

To approach this challenge, I thought, "I first have to convince myself." Greg, one of my salespeople who didn't like selling, rose to be ranked sixth nationally out of 1500 Sears sales consultants his second year. Having since moved away, his accomplishments were still legendary in the Denver office. I explained to the ten who came that Greg had sent me a pamphlet about setting goals that was sixty pages long with forms and fill-in-the-blank questions. Words impulsively blurted out of my mouth:

"Oh great," I admitted saying to myself, "I'm not reading that whole thing. How could I get out of this now?" I had begun the experiment. "Okay, I will read a few pages as we go along," I was committed.

After just three pages I got caught up in its inspiring content and I had a hard time disagreeing with what Bellas and Collard had written. As I mentioned previously, the premise of the Harvard Study was that "writing down goals makes a difference." The 3% of MBA students who believed it also made specific plans to accomplish their goals. They were the most successful MBA grads in the Harvard study, so it was clearly worth trying.

If 3% *are* the highly successful ones, maybe *The 97 Club* for us, the other 97%, will have a benefit for all of our average sales teams. My purpose in a PowerPoint presentation each week was to generate an open dialog. I wanted open discussions and a process that would result in blatant, honest communication. This would not be a *12-step-program* to admit we were *workalcoholics* like *Glengarry Glen Ross*; it was a *Leap of Faith* program.

We say selling is an art. Perhaps we spend too much time following authors who try to turn selling into a science. Consumers buy from people they like and trust. Portraits require paint. Salespeople are the painters looking to you for encouragement as they progress in their sales skills. Selling is the art of investing in personal relationships.

© Mark Skovron. Used with permission.

## "The Jury of my Mind" by Mark Skovron

I recently had a chance to speak with Mark Skovron, a renowned CEO, business coach, marketing and branding expert, business leader, thought generator and author. He's MaxGroup Business Solution's journalist in the Phoenix, Arizona area with whom I connected on LinkedIn. He agreed to an interview with me during the time I was doing research for the book. One thing about him that caught my attention was the profound way he processed knowledge and how he filtered out any negative outside input. He stated the following:

"You have to be *'at cause'* when you express opinions. First of all, they may not be the truth. Whenever I think about things I share, I bring them before *'The Jury of my Mind.'* Then I ask myself:

**"'Is this [something in] which I hear the Truth?'"**

I shared with him my experiment, *The 97 Club*. I said I felt I'd failed when one salesperson quit after the eighth of sixteen meetings. He never set a goal, he never wrote one down; he couldn't do it. Then Mark noted,

"I'm not saying I'm right in this particular case but what I'm going to say is you may have done as much for the man who quit as you did for the rest of the members of your '*97 Club.*"

Mark was right. Later I met the guy who had not only quit *The 97 Club* but quit our company. He was happier installing bathrooms. In the process of trying to set goals I felt he had failed, but did he? **What was his original goal? He never shared any goals with us, but he had decided!** *The 97 Club* process was effective for him after all.

Mark shared his own story of a troubled upbringing in which finally his grandparents came to his rescue, positioning him for great success. We shared private things, painful things, previously unspoken things. Mark said:

"It made me write as an *outlet*. I poured [my] emotions and my deepest feelings into books and screenplays. The answer for me was to heal myself and rise above it all. As a child, I was only worth fourteen cents, which was the cost of a bullet to take my life, my abusive father said."

Mark's sincerity, his very private words from this man who wanted to contribute to better mankind, impressed me deeply. He went on to share,

"I've always written down goals starting in high school."

Here was a validation that I was on the right track. He reinforced my belief that average folks may become great ones if they can resolve tragic personal issues in life.

"If these burdens remain unresolved they hold us back from achievement," Mark said. "If we overcome them, it's as if doors to greatness fly open. I know God is doing it."

That had been my conclusion as well. His words seemed to ring true to me, especially about unresolved personal issues. That would be the test for *The 97 Club*. Could we believe we could do great things? Could we, in a private way, make a goal to resolve some of the personal issues holding us back? Mark was prophetic!

I shared with Mark a sales comparison of all ten sales representatives after we completed our sixteen weeks together in *The 97 Club*. Sales performance results were never my goal but I was curious. I hadn't spoken with Mark prior to our meetings, so I didn't have his frame of reference, but the numbers were staggering. I will share them with you later in the book. Suffice to say that setting lofty personal goals and addressing issues in the lives of the ten sales representatives over a sixteen-week period had impacted not only their personal lives but it also improved their professional outcomes!

### January 31, 2014
### First Meeting of The 97 Club

I hoped we could go from the single anecdotal Harvard Study's results and have each of the ten original members become part of the 3% who wrote down goals and become as highly successful as the Harvard MBA students had become. Would my club members see themselves that way? Would writing down goals, along with a plan to achieve them, make a difference?

I told myself, don't be tempted to set goals about sales or income, and no "I want to be a millionaire" or "retire early at 40." It can't be about that. These must be almost unattainable lofty *personal* goals. For *my three lofty personal goals* I chose: Taking a cruise on Royal Caribbean's largest cruise ship at the time, Allure of the Seas, certainly "over-the-moon" at the time. I knew we couldn't afford it, but it was lofty and it was personal. Second, a family reunion with my divorced and divided family, in which many of my children weren't speaking to me much at the time. This was a lofty goal for sure. My third goal was to finish the first book I wrote in 2012 and get it published. That is still a work in progress; *Ride the Horses, Feed the Lions* had to come first.

### Mini Vision Boards clipped to your Car Visor?

In the *Resolutions to Reality* instructions was a follow-up requirement to place an image, picture or photo representing each of three goals on a piece of stiff white paper (light card stock or 100 lb. paper), folded in half, and laminate it on a 4" x 8" mini vision board. Then we were to somehow attach that laminated sheet to our car visor. I used two alligator clips. Michelle Bellas and Colin Collard suggested this imagery would *bake-the-goal-setting-cake* to remind us of our goals. Would it make a difference subconsciously? Was I done? It sure got my attention. My images were of a cruise ship, of a family gathered at a reunion, and the cover of a 400+ page book that I wrote in 2012 but is waiting to be published.

Why didn't I ask the sixteen LinkedIn CEOs, thought leaders, best-selling authors and successful business coaches I interviewed if they wrote down goals? I don't know. I now knew Mark Skovron did. During the first part of our interview about *Ride the Horses, Feed the Lions*, I spelled out my plan for *The 97 Club* step-by-step to get his feedback. Even passionate writers who believe strongly in the purpose of the book they intend to publish to the world still need validation, and I was getting it. I quickly realized as we spoke that Mark was one of the best examples of the premise that Bellas and Collard outlined in their thesis. He had always set goals from the time he was young, and had written them down. His business influence worldwide demonstrated the impact of this discipline. The message? Write down goals!

One principle in *Resolutions to Reality* surprisingly suggested "it [isn't] accomplishing the goals that [is] most enjoyable," as explained in this Bellas and Collard quote:

"Beyond actually accomplishing the goal, it is...[the] small steps along the way to accomplishing your goals that will be most rewarding."

In other words, it is the "doing" and not "reaching our goals" that would be emotionally fulfilling.

## *Meetings of The 97 Club*

*The 97 Club* met, not very secretly, in an unused regional manager's office in the warehouse of Denver's Sears Home Improvements. I'm embarrassed to say that throughout this process I was skeptical as to whether writing down goals would make any difference. I pridefully pondered how I'd achieved anything before if my approach didn't already work as well as it could have. Where would I be today, however, if I had followed the discipline so many great leaders had? What if I had written down goals?

Something unique had already started to occur in *The 97 Club* meetings. By writing down goals together it focused me more on my sales team as individuals. The personal connections we had made initially seemed to increase. Was this an unintended consequence or did I just not see loyalty resulting from it? Managers often live life separate from their teams. I know I did. I had been externally gregarious and yet private. Life was changing!

I'm going to share with you exactly what happened to me. My work as a District Sales Manager, with $18 to $25 million in annual sales in three Districts that I ran, training and motivating 25-40 commission sales representatives, took all my time. It was a six-day-a-week commitment. I got texts all hours of the day and night. My sincere statement to salespeople was,

"You only need me when you need me. Contact me, my cell phone is the way I can stealthily meet your needs while you are with the customer. After you leave their home, is too late to help. Text me, I will respond."

And they did, every day...all day. What started to happen to me was what I hoped was occurring with the other club members as well. We worked so many long hours that sometimes we don't have a life outside of sales. That is a problem in itself. But, without any prompting, I began to work on one of my goals. One day it might be thinking about the cruise. Another day, I might rewrite a page or two in my book, editing or checking spelling and grammar. I was excited. I actually began to look forward to being at home. I mean, I always was happy to be home with my wife, don't get me wrong, but now I had something else besides WORK to do when I got home. The mini vision board that I had clipped to my visor was subconsciously reminding me I had goals.

The first thing I started to do was read my book over again. I edited it multiple times. I took 125 pages of *The Prodigal Parent's* 432 pages and reworked it as a companion syllabus to my *Moby-Dick-sized* treatment on the subject of forgiveness. Tough subject? Yes, very personal but needed. The resulting 325-page book is now titled *Forgive, The Third Great Commandment*, which draws from my life experiences and that of others. How would I ever finish it or even publish it? It's still a reminder I see daily on my car visor. Publishing *Ride the Horses, Feed the Lions* soon became my first priority. *Forgive* now became goal #4 instead.

As for my goal of a 2016 family reunion, to gather my children and my ex-wife, that did not happen exactly. I'd wanted to heal wounds caused by divorce. In deciding to call extended family members, we had a successful four-generation reunion, including siblings and children, along with grandchildren and great grandchildren, at Bear Lake, Utah. My own family is reunion is still a lofty goal! In the past couple years, however, relationships have been improving greatly. As I look back on the success of our extended family reunion, what I didn't realize was there were extended family members who needed it too.

After the first of the sixteen weekly meetings of *The 97 Club* was held on the last week of January of 2014, unusual things began to affect me. It was hard to deny that the small accomplishments of the goals I had chosen were giving me the greatest enjoyment. Since then, my eyes always glance at the pictures of my goals every time I am in my car. I'm continually reminded of what I wrote down and why I should be working on them. As I accomplished one goal I added another. You've got to try this yourself.

## The Last Meeting of The 97 Club

Our last meeting of *The 97 Club* was on May 24, 2014. Before I give you the *unexpected professional results* of this experiment, I want to put my personal goals into some context. Halloween night, 2014, two days before my last day at Sears Home Improvements, I decided to look at what's called a *90-day-tickler*. We didn't live in Florida, so we weren't on the list for local *last minute cruisers*. But this site is where anyone can see special deals. On the list that Halloween night was Royal Caribbean's new *Allure of the Seas* listed as having a sale with $399 and $599 per person rates and $799 per person for an *outside cabin*. Wow! My wife and I couldn't believe it. Excited? Yes!

A week or so before this discovery, Sears had announced a national reorganization of Home Improvement's management structure. My boss's regional position was eliminated and he stepped down to take my District Sales Manager job. Sound familiar? Has this happened to you too? Patronizingly he said I could be a salesperson again if I wanted but, ironically, I decided to take a second Sears early retirement. Like John Elway of our Denver Broncos, I decided to leave at the peak of my Sears career. To celebrate, for lack of a better word, my wife and I sat down on Halloween night, took out the credit card and booked a cruise! An unexpected cruise was the perfect *we-just-got-fired gift* for the two of us.

I never expected that in *The 97 Club* process of selecting goals, writing them down, placing a laminated paper on my car visor billboard and seeing my goals every day would take me from *Resolutions to Reality*. It did. *The Allure of the Seas* had never been on my 90-day Tickler list before. There it was. Bingo! Goal #1 was done! A year later Sears changed the organization again to the previous structure, forcing out my former boss. Change is a part of business and life. It was time to set a new goal, oh...and to write it down!

## *Back to The 97 Club*

Did the ten salespeople who had signed up to attend realize the real potential of writing down goals? Would it make a difference like the Harvard Study examples of successful people?

"Lofty personal goals" meant we got personal. In meetings we sometimes shared openly what was going on in our lives as we made weekly progress on putting our three goals in writing. All of us spent time thinking about and writing goals. Not everyone was ready with three goals right away, but we took it seriously.

Remember the guy who never wrote down a goal, who after eight weeks left Sears? He never *bought into* sales training or the whole idea of *The 97 Club*. He didn't believe writing down goals would make any difference. Maybe he never believed in himself. His *horse* was symbolically tied to a watering trough while he was dying of thirst in a desert of indecision. He refused to drink. What was holding him back? Did we fail or had we succeeded in his case? Not everyone wants to be a salesperson. Installing bathrooms was his gig.

## *From Poor to Gone?*

Unfortunately, this is part of the job. I never worried about losing poor salespeople. If I motivated, encouraged, and trained, and they refused to set goals, they just left. I never had to fire salespeople who tried, who believed in themselves, the company, our product and the future. If they took 100% responsibility for their success, they progressed and ultimately succeeded.

What made *The 97 Club* so unique? Our club meetings evolved like launching a ship off the docks without knowing all the thought and work that went into it beforehand. We were average people but when we shared our three goals, something else happened I never expected. I'll give you an example. One day a club member shared one of his goals was to build a world record-breaking pyrotechnic fireworks unit. Just one big bang high up in the air. Who was I to question his selection? Another member happened to be a pyrotechnic expert and offered to help him. They decided to work together on it! These two guys got more excited about working together than after any motivational speeches on selling. You had to be there. After this, supporting each other became a core principle of *The 97 Club*. A team spirit began to develop. We would help each other accomplish our goals. Remember, no sales goals would be part of *The 97 Club*. They got pressured enough in sales meetings. After all, this was a home improvement company!

Instead, we got to know each other. We were comfortable sharing our goals with each other. I allowed myself to become sort of *Brené-Brown vulnerable* during meetings. I opened up about my divorce and how it impacted my whole family and my lofty goal of a family reunion. Admitting the divorce was my fault was not easy, but unexpectedly it put all the members of *The 97 Club* on the same playing field. This was me as vulnerable as I'd ever been and soon it would be the encouragement one man needed to reconnect with his family too.

Gus Carlson had been estranged from his siblings for years. He had not seen or visited his sister for decades. It weighed on him with heavy pain. He didn't say anything about it in our meetings but I could sense something was wrong. His performance was average to poor and he seemed to be okay with just getting by. Nothing anyone did seemed to light a fire under him. I insisted Gus call *one hundred former Sears customers* to set appointments to see if he could help them with any Home Improvement they might need. I gave him a script and made giving him any future new leads *conditional* upon him making the calls. He didn't reach them all, but he was able to set three appointments and got one sale from his efforts, which led to $1300 in commissions. In a subsequent meeting I recognized his success by sharing this example with the other salespeople. No matter how you sliced it, the hardest thing at Sears was to get sales professionals to cold-call potential customers. No one likes cold-calling. I don't. But these previous customers were more like warm leads.

While sharing Gus's success, I asked,

"Who would be willing to call former customers if I paid you $13 a call?"

I was speaking metaphorically. Was I going to pay $13 per call? No. That was an example of the commission that came to with Gus from one $15,000 sale. Wait for it! I queried the group again:

"Would you make 100 calls if I paid you $13 a call?" Lots of hands went up. Then I asked Gus again. He said,

"Sure, why not?"

I reminded him of the one hundred phone calls he'd made before it resulted in a sale. I emphasized the positive impact on customers who rarely get **thank you calls**. Then when I explained the process Gus had gone through to get the $1300 in commissions from the 100 calls he made to set up appointments, their hands went down, one by one. Putting in the work first and having faith in the outcome isn't most salespeople's "strong suit." In golf, you never know which shot will be a hole-in-one, but you take them. Michael Jordan was given the ball and failed to sink the game winning shot 300 times, but he kept shouldering that responsibility. We've all heard, "You will miss 100% of the shots you don't take." What is the message? You can only succeed by reaching out, by taking a chance at making the shot, setting goals and persisting until you accomplish them, and having confidence in yourself, your products and your company. "Take your best shot!"

At each *97 Club* weekly meeting, everyone would report back on the progress they had made on their personal goals. It took weeks for some members to write down three goals and put the mini vision boards on their car visors. In meetings I'd encourage them to **buddy-up** just like on sales appointments when we'd send two sales consultants out together.

I never required anyone to talk at the meetings, Usually silent, Gus was finally ready to talk in one meeting of *The 97 Club*. He started slowly but firmly.

"Last weekend I reunited with my estranged sister. I decided today was time to share my story. Taking the bull by the horns I called her," Gus said.

He suggested they get together up at their family cabin the next weekend. All it took was one phone call. How many years had she waited for that call? The result was a huge success. Gus and his sister had one great conversation which led to another. I could see it on Gus's face immediately. He had a much happier disposition than I had ever seen before in the five years he had worked for me.

At the beginning of our first meeting, I had explained that I had no agenda. It wasn't about setting sales goals. *Been there done that.* This was our adventure, our experiment to see if writing down goals would make any difference in our lives. It would be months before I even wondered if Gus's income had changed because of what was obviously a positive change of attitude. I would find that out later. But his life surely had changed.

Remember my discussion about actively listening to our customers with the intent of getting to know them without any agenda? I believe turning a stranger into a friend, whether you make a sale or not, will allow you to have a sales career for the rest of your life. It's the person-to-person connections that make sales the best vocation in the world. It certainly was for me and I wanted my sales team to discover it could be for them too.

I intentionally, repeatedly told my new hires when they came back from their first sale:

"If after two or three hours with complete strangers you met for the first time in your Sears appointment they want to adopt you or introduce you to their daughter or son, if you are young and single, or want to invite you over for the **barbeque** on Saturday, you're exactly what I'm looking for."

The power of personality, listening skills, and taking an interest in the customer's life are key behavioral *"markers"* that I look for when seeking out a new hire. I can also tell by their responses if they have a pedigree worthy of being developed into a *thoroughbred,* and will win, place or show for me. Only if you are looking will your next *Stylistic Salesperson* be sitting across the desk at an interview. Review the list of characteristics common to these superstars and start the process.

One of the realities for those attending *The 97 Club* is some sales team members had a hard time following the advice I shared from *Resolutions to Reality* by Michelle Bellas and Colin Collard about implementing a program and embracing the discipline of setting and writing down goals. Why? Here's a quote I recently heard:

"The only people we don't listen to are family and friends who know us best."

On the other hand, I noticed fewer complaints about their leads. That was a big plus! *The 97 Club* members began telling other salespeople what a great time they were having in the meetings and how it helped them. Their sales would also improve over the course of the sixteen-week program. Some attitude changes were simply amazing.

"Wait," you might be thinking, "I'm a high powered executive, is this author really asking me to start some club and be vulnerable just to get my team to write down goals? I'm not comfortable doing that."

Answering your question with a question, "What are you doing now to be vulnerable and approachable in order to connect with the people *you are responsible for?*" Notice I *did not* say who you *manage,* leaving the door open to your being creative in how to improve your personal relationships. From a manager's perspective, Brené Brown's book *Daring Greatly* can open you up to the idea. For me, I didn't have a *device,* if I can use it to explain my next thought, to extend my *approachable self* on a more personal basis. *The 97 Club* became my non-public venue to experiment. So...the answer is yes. Reconfigure the principles we experienced as we met on a weekly non-business basis any way that fits you best. Don't just golf, have drinks, go home and say you're now somehow vulnerable, approachable and have connected with your people. They are waiting in the office every day. How will you become more of a servant leader, the greatest type of leader of all?

### *"To Create a World Class Sales Team, You Must Learn to... Ride the Horses, Feed the Lions."*

What's the difference between the mediocre performer and a strong achiever? Is it that we can train and motivate them instead of believing *Stylistic Sales* techniques cannot be transferred from one person to another? What can be modeled is the investment in relationships all *Stylistic Salespeople* make. Closing the gap so sales anchors, *the ones who somehow stay around because you can't seem to replace them*, go from poor to average, average to good, and good to great can also be implemented by any sales manager. Set and write down at least three lofty personal goals. You will be subconsciously exposed to them visually in the car with the pictures on your visor. If you work from home, put your mini vision board up on the wall above you. If your job has you flying, then adhere what you would clip on your car visor to the cover of your laptop. What if someone at work saw your goals? They might ask you about your *97 Club* approach to goal setting and might follow your example. Is this something new? Haven't you read about this before? No one benefits from reading as much as doing. Do it.

Concert pianists, sports figures and Olympians know how much work it takes to be the best at something they're passionate about and they're willing to put in the work that it takes to succeed. Great achievers already know who the best performer in their field is and know them by name. Sales professionals can greatly improve their performance by studying the techniques and interpersonal skills of those they might call *Stylistic Salespeople*. They all set goals and write them down. I didn't, but I do now. They are disciplined, knowledgeable, and competitive. Everyone must develop their own style. Remember Zach, whose uncle asked him to ride with him on sales calls? He knew. He had to be his authentic-self and leverage his interpersonal skills to succeed.

Sir Roger Gilbert Bannister, a physician and middle-distance athlete, ran the first sub-four-minute mile at the 1952 Olympics held in Helsinki,

Finland. Prior to his success, it was widely accepted by doctors that it was physically impossible for a human being to run a mile in under four minutes. After Roger had achieved his goal, many athletes would soon equal and surpass his record. It just took someone to show that it could be done. Then others had the courage to try. By believing in himself, Roger became another example that setting a goal could result in an astonishing victory, the victory over fear and self-doubt. He believed he could do it, and did.

After my conversation with Mark Skovron I discovered *Living Your Dream*, an article he wrote along with Jeff Peltin, his business partner. I ran across it when I did a Google Image search for a picture of Mark to put in this book. Paraphrasing Mark in the article, "Who you are on the internet is who you really who are," the title of their article, *Living Your Dream*, simply says **belief comes from within**. Mark was right on!

## *Belief Comes From Within!*
## *The Moving Van Miracle—A story from my childhood*

One of the factors in Zig Ziglar's success was inspiring audiences. Don't worry, we're not taking you to church, but in junior high school I had an experience that relates to belief in someone greater than yourself. We lived in Syracuse, NY until I was thirteen. There, I felt accepted; I was smart and I did well in school. In eighth grade we moved to Valley Forge, PA to what's called "The Main Line." People had money and there was a large dose of social snobbery I wasn't familiar with. Now I was the *new kid in school.*

We rode to Tredyffrin Easttown Junior High School on the bus for thirty to forty minutes each day. On our bus there was a social practice they called "a cut." What it was really was bullying. Today it known to be an alarming emotional scar for many students. It was for me. It was different than a kid in the 1950s saying *"Your mother wears Army boots."* That phrase came from women in WWII working on assembly lines. Tanks, airplanes and munitions for the war were largely manufactured by women, which opened more opportunities for women in the workforce. Today bullying has become an epidemic.

---

**BUSINESS**

# Living Your Dream

*Entrepreneurs and investors around the world look to the experts for advice when starting new business ventures.*

In today's ever changing economic climate leaving your business plans to chance can turn the American Dream into a nightmare. For most people, owning a successful business that could provide for their family would be the hallmark of their life. Perhaps you are one of the numerous men and women alike who have spent many hours daydreaming about how to make this happen and the rewards that will be bestowed upon you when it does. Finally the day comes to turn those dreams into reality. Excitement fills your very soul as you quit your job and take your life savings to set out to conquer the world. This is the life, no more punching a time clock, no boss to take orders from, new business cards with your name as the "Owner." YES! You're living your dream.

Then after months of long hours, expense and struggle it's time to write more checks but there is a slight problem, there is no more money. The life savings have vanished. This is when the nightmare begins and you start second guessing yourself. Did I really negotiate the best deal? Now that I own one, what if I don't like running a restaurant? Why can't I find any decent help? How did I spend my life savings so fast? Why didn't I do more planning and research to find out what the upcoming trends were going to be? Why didn't I seek help from a business expert?

Wouldn't it be wise to get the answers to those questions and many more before making a career change and investing your life savings? Wouldn't it be great to see your dream come true? Well, it can when you call on the experts to help you choose the business that's right for you. Find out what the next economic explosions are going to be before they happen and put yourself in front of them. Keep your life savings and let Mark Skovron and Jeff Peltin do the work and research for you.

Mark Skovron and Jeff Peltin are the creators and owners of Maximum Achievement Group, Inc. "MaxGroup" is a marketing, training and consulting enterprise, which specializes in helping entrepreneurs, find the business that is the best fit for them.

Mark and Jeff are passionate to teach what they have learned. Imagine the leverage of having an expert work along side of you to create the perfect business model, which taps into the power of the largest industries in the world. By using a proven turn-key business system, you have the opportunity to capitalize on several markets creating a significant residual income stream.

Mark and Jeff are accustomed to success in business. Both have an accomplished background in sales, sales management and as vice presidents for some of the country's best-known brands. As business partners they have also owned and operated a large and successful financial services business.

Actively involved in personal training and development technologies for decades, Mark is one of the worlds leading authorities on success and achievement. Having reached thousands of people, Mark is one of the most sought-after speakers and mentors in business today.

Jeff's accomplishments have landed him on stages across the country as well. Through a very unique life evaluation process, Jeff teaches how to get and stay on mission. His passion is in helping others become personally and financially free.

The opportunity is yours to see why many of Mark and Jeff's protégés are among some of the most successful people in business today. All across the country they have helped others establish multi-million dollar enterprises.

The real essence of entrepreneurship is the ability to spot an opportunity and the willingness to go after it. Action will always be the precurser to success. Mark and Jeff are available for a personal discussion of what is possible. They can be reached at: (727)667-4300, or you may send an email to Mark@MarkSkovron.com.

**Mark Skovron and Jeff Peltin**

Photo by www.ChristineReynolds.com

Used with permission.

Watch a short film at YouTube:
https://www.youtube.com/watch?v=6xygfp_RX2Q
Back at Valley Forge, bullying happened every day. Popular kids criticized younger kids about their clothes or their haircut to make them cry. It started on the bus. Criticism, like a rumor, passed from one kid to another. In my 8th grade class, five boys picked on me, knocking my books to the floor or slapping my head if I got a haircut. Would I break down? My dad taught me to *turn the other cheek.* I was running out of cheeks.

My confidence was devastated. One day when I came home, I got out my Boy Scout knife, opened the blade, and stabbed my pillow dozens of times as if it were the abusive boys. My mother said, "Bill, this will help you understand people." She sewed the cuts in my pillow, never saying another word. The next year four of the boys moved away. The fifth was in a different class. Why did I call this my Moving Van Miracle? They moved!

## Belief comes from within!

*The 97 Club* didn't focus on belief in our company, products or our services. It came down to members believing in themselves. Let's just review any Home Improvement career's realities for a moment. Selling can be a lonely life. Rejection, long hours, late nights, and driving over 40,000 miles each year. I wish I could insert an original cartoon by Liz Climo, an illustrator for *The Simpsons.* Have you already discovered her utterly cute world? It would feature a salesman in the Denver area who drove seven hours in each direction to the southwestern Colorado Mountains for one appointment. The caption would be: "This is the Life!"

One salesman asked for far-away leads because statistically the close rate was double the district average. Another one drove one of those vans you can practically live in and took his dog with him, never complaining about the 70,000 miles he drove one year. Selling can be discouraging. Remaining positive can be arduous. There are personal matters to deal with that may happen, like divorce. As sales managers what can you do to make this career worth it for your sales team? Why should they stay, year after year? They interview for a sales position perhaps initially because of income potential. They accept an offer because of company values. They stay because of you.

Let me share a page out of my retirement speech given to Sears Denver District on November 2, 2014. I had recently recruited some new hires not aware of me retiring, including two women sitting in the front row in our meeting room. They had great faith in me and it was reciprocal. As I began to deliver my Sears Eulogy, I spoke directly to those two women:

"I don't like leaving you both in the early stages of your mentoring. I have thought about what I could leave with you that might make a difference in your success here."

One by one I talked about the influence and impact on my life that each of the mentors, supervisors, co-workers and members of our sales team had on my fourteen years Sears Home Improvement Division. I had the privilege of working in three District Offices: San Francisco, CA; Washington DC; and finally Denver, CO. What was my bottom line? It's the people that matter. If those I worked with finally got it, now I could say goodbye.

Why was it important to leave my Sears team a message of substance? Why not just announce that I was retiring and thank them for their support? Because that wasn't my style and would not represent who I was inside. I had crafted the presentation with about 40 slides to give them an example of my career and of the many ups and downs they may experience. Some of the slides included personal messages that might inspire their loyalty to the company that I loved. Each one of the influences of my mentors was part of my legacy.

I shared the words of Glenn L. Moore who hired me as they echoed in my memory of sitting in his office for the interview:

**"I think you can do this."**

My overall message to the salespeople in my office would be to "believe in yourself, in your family, in your company and the products and services you offer. You must believe in something and someone bigger than yourself to be truly successful in life. Belief comes from within!"

Part of my legacy would also be include comments about experiences I had with the ten sales consultants who took a chance on me and came every week for sixteen weeks to sit in a former Regional Manager's office in the warehouse. They had volunteered not knowing why or what would come next. They knew me. That's all.

## The Rest of the Story

At this point, you probably want to know if *The 97 Club* and setting lofty personal goals impacted the sales production of these initial members. What's the bottom line?

## Summary of Professional sales results after The 97 Club meetings

Compared to their "Percentage to Par"—the Sears District's Average Sales Closing Rate
(*This is defined as how many sales you make as a percentage of the appointments you ran.*)

Here are the before and after results of eight of the ten *97 Club* members who completed sixteen weeks of meetings:

Fred 80.6% to **96%** (of par)
Steve 72.9% to **99%** (of par)
Humberto 87.7% to **100%** (at par)
G.W. 59.4% to **107.5%** (over par)
Mark 62.9% to **114.3%** (over par)
Gus 94.7% to **162.1%** (over par)
Chris 102.6% to **162.3%** (over par)
David 80.9% to **172.8%** (over par)

I have to admit I was more surprised at the results than anyone. And I never told anyone at Sears, including these salespeople. While it was not my objective, their writing down lofty personal goals had actually improved their sales performance. While this is not a double-blind study of 1000 sales people who attended *The 97 Club* meetings all around the world, it is an anecdotal sample. This was a real test with real people. Our personal lives greatly influence success in our professional lives. When we get them both in order, life is good!

It appears that the journey from "Poor to Average and Average to Good" can be shorter when we address some of our unresolved personal issues. Anecdotal evidence is all that *The 97 Club* experience is at this point, but is there enough data presented here that you might start your own experiment. Choose three lofty personal goals, write them down, make a mini vision board and clip it to the visor of your car. Your adventure will then begin.

It did for Carole who I connected with on LinkedIn on March 13, 2016 asking if she would read a first draft of *The 97 Club* and write a review with her experiences for me. I got a note from her early in November 2018, just before this book went to publication. She told me that reading *The 97 Club* had been an amazing experience. Unexpected great things had happened in her life as a result of setting and writing down goals. Her final comment was this:

"My little mini vision board is still clipped to my car visor. I have met the man of my dreams as well."

## *Three Goal Setting Principles*

Principle #1 – Make your three goals personal. Write them down. Select three images representing each one. Place the three photos and laminate them onto a 4"x 8" piece of 100 lb. white paper. If you are in your car a lot then fasten your mini vision board to your car visor with alligator clips. If you work from home and don't spend much time in the car, create a larger "vision board" in your home office so you see it daily. If you fly instead of drive for work, then adhere a mini vision board to the top of your laptop or the front of your iPad.

Principle #2 – The enjoyment of this process of setting and writing down goals doesn't necessarily come from the accomplishment of goals but rather it comes from your progress along the way (Bellas and Collard).

Principle #3 – Help others accomplish their goals. One unexpected result of *The 97 Club* was the interest club members had in helping each other accomplish their goals. It was something they could share outside of work. It became a core value.

**Note:** If you have nothing fun to look forward to outside of your job when you come home you will never really enjoy life regardless of how hard you work, how much you make, how many awards you win or the millions you win in a lottery. Look at those in Hollywood who say, *"I don't have time for relationships."*

"Do you work to live or live to work?" is a meaningful, famous phrase. I always worked to live and provide for my family. In doing so I always enjoyed the new challenges that came my way. My wife and children were what I looked forward to coming home to. Now that my children have grown, setting and writing down goals gives me something to look forward to.

### My Own 3 Lofty Personal Goals - Update

**Goal #1** – A Cruise on Royal Caribbean's "Allure of the Seas."
I unexpectedly retired early from Sears on October 31, 2014. Sears reorganization? Bah Humbug! Well, as planned I had clipped a laminated mini vision board of three goals on my car visor from March

to October, 2014. On Halloween night I decided to look at the *90-day tickler* of last minute cruises. In moments, my wife and I got out our credit card and charged a Royal Caribbean cruise. ***Bingo! Goal #1 accomplished!***

**Goal #2** – Get one of my books published!

Never retire, but if you do, write a book. It shouldn't be a book about your life. Make it a subject you are passionate about. Don't worry. Your life story and experiences will end up in any nonfiction book you write.

© William D. Hatch

I found that writing has become a creative outlet for me on a scale I never imagined. In my case, I started writing a self-help book titled *The Prodigal Parent* on July 19, 2012. I completed a first draft of 432 pages on October 19, 2012.

I had written lyrics, composed music, performed live on stage, and sung before thousands of people in theaters not very far from New York City, but I'd never written a book. I went on to write five as well as a screenplay. Getting my *Ride the Horses, Feed the Lions* ready for publication by the end of 2018 has been a labor of love and that includes five other people: Carrie, Steve, Leya, Margaret, and Mario, a book editor in Los Angeles. I have been helped by many including those who have read the book, agreed to interviews, and offered stories, comments and quotes as well as accolades to be added to this book.

Finally, out of the blue, Ben Gay III, a sales legend over the last 40 years in the era of Zig Ziglar, Brian Tracy, Tom Hopkins and others has written a foreword to this book.

With three *The 97 Club* icons on my car visor I was now motivated to *think* of my goals subconsciously—another intangible result of writing them down.

Roll back the clock. Keep in mind that I was completely skeptical about writing down goals. I had read a few pages in *Resolutions to Reality* by Michelle Bellas and Colin Collard, thanks to my close friend, Greg, who had sent it to me. The substance in the principles they outlined in those first few pages were so deep and powerful I stopped there. The main reason I had doubted the premise of writing down goals was that none of my own efforts had succeeded in motivating my sales team to actually write down their goals. Nothing worked. We tried everything. And during my career I had never written down goals. I didn't want to be President of the United States someday. I didn't **plan** to become a millionaire or need to write that down. Maybe that's why it didn't happen. Actually, I wouldn't mind being a millionaire someday but that is just an issue of PRIDE. Just like Frank Sinatra said, we all seem to want to "do it *our* way."

I decided the only way I could change the goal setting behavioral patterns of others was by changing my own first. I had to believe that writing down goals would make a potent difference in my own behavior. I would write down my goals right along with my salesmen. Together, we became charter members of *The 97 Club!*

## *My adventure as a writer began in 2012*

A friend of mine, a well respect psychologist, suggested my first book was too long, so I separated out 125 pages into its own syllabus. Now, *The Prodigal Parent* profiles thirty-three stories of people who forgave parents so they could be released from the many emotional burdens their parents had caused. That came from *Forgive—The Third Great Commandment*. It delivers critical messages of why to forgive. Regardless of the circumstances, we must forgive. Does that mean we have to associate with those who haven't changed their ways? That's a personal choice.

Life has a business bottom line and a personal bottom line. I learned the business bottom line by setting and writing down goals from meeting together in *The 97 Club*. Resolving issues in our personal lives will lead to greater success professionally. The personal bottom line I learned from writing my first book helped me to see that as we withhold forgiveness it's withheld from us and we are the ones left to carry burdens of the past, not those who perpetrate crimes, abuse, abandonment or breach of trust. "Let it go," the message of the song from the Disney movie "Frozen," is the only answer. Forgive and let go of what you've been carrying for years.

## *"That's what my parents should do."*

Let me share another story with you. I was in a lawyer's office discussing an employment case when the associate legal counsel asked me what I was doing this weekend. I told her I was working on my book. She asked me what it was about. Then I stopped and asked her, "Why is it so hard to forgive our parents?"

She paused, tipped her head back and said nothing for what seemed like a long time. Then she began to relate a story about her *prodigal parents*, who never really valued her. I could see the pain in her face and the sincerity in her eyes. I told her some of my children still wouldn't speak to me after the divorce. It was pains from her parents' divorce, losing the joys of their wonderful family life, that devastated her the most. That was my case too. After I told her that my divorce was my fault and I was trying very hard to reach out to my children, my ex-wife, and close but now distant family, she said, "That's what my parents should do! There is so much pain in these cases, pain for both children and parents."

My second book became the one to retain the title *The Prodigal Parent*—thirty-three stories of forgiveness. I was never able to include stories of *parental prodigalism*™ in their own lives, as I have coined the term. After hearing this young female associate counsel so burdened with the pain of her broken relationship with her parents, I asked myself the question all prodigal parents want someone to answer for them as they turn their lives around and want to mend broken fences: "Where is the road back home?"

Goal #2 now became publishing *Ride the Horses, Feed the Lions.*

At this writing, this book has not only attracted the interest of an agent but a publisher. I signed a book deal July 9th, 2018 and the website went up for pre-sales in October. Shipments will start in February, 2019. It took writing three other books and putting updates and articles about them on LinkedIn to attract interest in this being published. Sometime next year *The 97 Club* will be published and within two years there will be a version *Ride the Horses, Feed the Lions* in Spanish. I have to say that this is pretty exciting. As Michelle Bellas and Colin Collard suggested, progress made along the way motivates you! It's not the destination but the journey. Only when I became immersed in setting multiple goals did I realize the importance of that statement. It is absolutely true. **Goal #2 accomplished!**

**Goal #3 – A Family Reunion!** This goal was something no one who has been divorced might choose or imagine would be possible. In my opinion, divorce doesn't bring happiness to either party. It may separate one party from the other legally and reduce a threat, especially cases of abuse or emotionally destructive behaviors. For that reason, divorce could open doors to a brighter future. Eighteen years after my divorce my family was no closer to getting together than any other time since the divorce. Each year the estrangement and separation seemed to grow. Why set a goal to have a family reunion? That's crazy and unrealistic, right? I wanted it because my divorce was the most profoundly devastating event that negatively impacted my personal life and my family's lives, and continues to do so. It is always on my mind.

My attempts to get my family together in the past had not been successful. Thinking about what I could do to lay the foundation to make it happen in the future, I proposed a bigger family reunion of all my siblings, their children and grandchildren. I discovered organizing a reunion is difficult. The logistics? Profound! Getting almost one hundred people in the same place for two or three days? Where do we hold it? How will everyone be able to take time off to come? How can it be affordable for the young families with little children? What about

FAMILY

food? My head was spinning. Then Champion Windows restructured and suddenly I had time on my hands. Financial problems caused 35 managers to be let go, including me. Good news? It's all in how you perceive changes in life.

What I found is you just choose a date and start communicating, collecting deposits on a five-condo unit and get "off to the races." I chose the last three days of the Fourth of July week, July 8-10, 2016. Ironically, that was the same weekend of our last family reunion in 2005. The location? Bear Lake in Utah, allowing travel by car for some. I did invite my children, my siblings, their children, grandchildren and the great-grandchildren. It was not the family reunion I had originally envisioned but at least it would be a reunion of sorts. The final results? All my siblings and many of their children and grandchildren came. One of my sons, his wife and three of my grandchildren came. The biggest question, "Where do you put 100 people in one place?" worked out. Water sports were available for the families. Two big wedding tents made eating together easy and friendly. Everyone tested the Bear Lake ice cream providers to see which one had the best raspberry flavor.

They made us ice cream and we made some memories. Many doors opened to friendships across four generations.

"Whether you think you can, or you think you can't—you're right." Henry Ford. ***Goal #3 accomplished!***

Would this family gathering have happened if I had not experienced *The 97 Club*? No, without question. My commitment to set goals, write them down and memorialize them visually on a mini vision board clipped to my car visor all made them happen. Did I stop setting goals after three? No!

The three most recent goals clipped onto my car visor now include:

1 - An award-winning Screenplay/TV mini-series
2 - A walk on the Red Carpet
3 – A New York Times Best Selling book

Since *Ride the Horses, Feed the Lions* became a reality I ventured to New York in July 2018 having become a candidate to attend the International Model and Talent Association auditions after taking acting, cold read and runway classes at the John Casablancas Agency, a division of MTM International. I came away from IMTA NY 2018 with five "Excellence in Acting" awards and won "Best Male Adult Singer" after facing two, then sixteen, and finally seventy-two judges. Twelve model and talent agencies expressed an interest in working with me and so far I've recently signed with two agencies in Los Angeles, one in New York and one in Tampa, Florida. I've been approached by a casting director to help get a book published that she edited as well as a Hollywood actress who, after spending a day with me in New York, said she'd like to be in a film with me someday. To make the last six months complete I was also interviewed by Fallon *"Fal"* Adams, editor of *Hollywood Weekly Magazine*, resulting in placement of a two-page editorial in the October 2018 Emmy Awards edition. What's my bottom line? Never retire. Life is too exciting to close the doors to the future. Oh...and please WRITE *your* BOOK!

**New Goal #1:** Work on a screenplay with Thomas M. Collins, who was recognized by *Sports Illustrated* in the 1980s and 1990s as the #1 or #2 sports agent. He represented Kareem Abdul-Jabbar, George Foreman,

Ralph Sampson, Wayne Tisdale and many more. The screenplay is completed now but because of length it has been converted into a thirteen-episode TV mini-series. We have two professionals in the entertainment industry, one in New York and one in Denver, who will read the TV pilot script—Episode One. Meanwhile, Tom and I will be working on a second TV series. After WGAw registration of that logline and synopsis, as we did with the TV pilot script, an executive producer in Los Angeles has agreed to allow an informal "pitch" of the concept. She likes getting in on the ground floor. We will soon also be working on a children's book about the life of Alec Cabacungan whose Shriners Children's Hospital TV commercials have raised over $350 million nationwide. He has a rare brittle bone disease and had broken 60 bones by age fifteen. This project is intended to help Alec with medical bills that will stop being covered when he reaches adulthood.

# Chapter Thirteen

## Selling with Integrity

Right after World War II, when our soldiers came home they wanted to forget everything about the pain of war. They hoped their sweethearts were waiting for them, wanted to get married and have a bucket of kids. They also wanted to buy a house, a piece of land and a have little bit of peace.

The economy began to expand. Notably, from 1928 to 1954, Sears Roebuck & Co. was headed by a man called General Robert E. Wood who became president and later CEO. While this isn't a book about Sears, after having spent a combined forty years working in almost every capacity, Sears' history becomes more interesting to me. At that time, Sears and Montgomery Ward were about the same size, but a strategic decision General Wood supported would make all the difference. Sears noticed that, as men returned from the war, suburbs began to pop up all across the country, beginning as small settlements and soon becoming commercialized with retail stores.

By moving Sears to the suburbs, retailers provided needed goods and services and Sears grew to over eight hundred stores, doubling the size of Montgomery Ward. Sears became an icon, a part of American life, Thus the tagline, "Sears, where America shops." A Sears catalog, which preceded the internet and Amazon.com, was found in every home. In rural areas a Sears catalog was the internet. Once read it was never discarded.

The Sears Wish Book was the favorite of every child as they circled items they wanted for Christmas. Smart parents took a peek at what their children circled before shopping. Growing up in Syracuse, New York, I remember holding my mother's hand as we walked into a local Sears store. The top of the sales counters were above my head so I must have been four or five. The jewelry cases were filled with glitter and glam. There was always a smell of popcorn in the store and a key shop out in the parking lot. History is heritage and Sears' is almost gone.

That was the setting for the times we lived in. Little did any of us know about needing life insurance or how much aluminum siding would be sold and installed with post-war surpluses of so many materials. Now, as I'm writing, I remember we had army blankets when I was growing up, as I supposed everyone did.

I remember watching *Tin Men*, a funny movie written and directed by Barry Levinson, when I started at American Home Improvements, Sears' subsidiary. The trickery they used wasn't what I'd ever do. I also remember powerful scenes capturing the essence of what I feared becoming. In one, Richard Dreyfuss as BB stood outside a woman's home, reminding me of one of the homes in my neighborhood in upstate New York. The home was set way back into the property, yielding the right-of-way to a large yard, shrubs, bushes, and azaleas planted by the sidewalk and as far as you could see. At his side, Danny DeVito as Ernest Tilley waited for his buddy to start their "sales con." BB Babowsky had a Brownie camera by Kodak on a tripod stand. He stood there, looking through the lens at the house. They were veteran aluminum siding salesmen waiting for the homeowner to notice them. Ernest engaged BB in conversation just to make everything appear legitimate.

We didn't lock our doors in those days, and often sat on the front porch. If someone strange came into our neighborhood or approached the door, everyone knew about it. Soon, the lady of the house came out the door shouting, "What are you doing on my lawn?" Ernest and BB stood quietly, not responding, just looking in the camera then at her house. As BB questioned Ernest to delay any conversation with the woman, who stood with a stern look on her face, the "sales con" was well underway.

"That house will be perfect, right?"

Before she could tell them to get off her lawn, they explained they were working on a *LIFE Magazine* story. They had customers down the street who had bought new aluminum siding and they needed a perfect "before" picture of another house just like theirs.

"You see, Mrs. Brown, we need a great picture of a 'before house' for our article, so people can see how good the siding makes another house look, compared to one like yours."

While these slimy, slick salesmen gave good salespeople a bad name back then, we still see some poor salespeople losing the trust of consumers today. Almost all of us have stories about being cheated or not being treated right by a salesperson. There was no question I wouldn't be a salesman if I had to sell like that. The funniest part in the movie *Tin Men* for me comes when the woman realizes her house will be in *LIFE Magazine* for everyone to see. Some lady down the street will have the photo of her beautiful home with aluminum siding and her house will be the **junker**. We see the lady's face flush as she tries to convince the *Tin Men* to let her be the one with aluminum siding. They pretend to struggle with the idea. As they planned from the start, she takes the bait. Her husband comes home, sees her point and the look on her face and the contract is signed. *Tin Men!*

Sales managers should reinforce the reality that great salespeople never need to manipulate, lie, mislead, cheat, or be dishonest with people. If that is the way any manager made sales, then this chapter is for them first. Each of us can sell and make a great income with integrity and have a clear conscience, if we do three things:

First – Work for a reputable company that stands behind it products, workmanship, and warrantees.

Second – Sell products or services for a company you can believe in. You won't have to lie and create a bigger lie to cover the first. You will sleep well at night. Just be Honest!

Third – Make friends. If you feel you have no people-skills or been told you're not a people-person, then you shouldn't be in sales, at least not in residential sales. If you don't enjoy talking to and meeting new people, perhaps a desk job is more appropriate for you. Being dishonest will not keep anyone in sales for long. You can make money for a little while but you won't be successful. Make friends, not excuses.

*Tin Men* fits this discussion about integrity quite well, but other stories I will share can play a role too. Integrity, you may notice, is not a term that is spoken often. It may be that money is the pursuit of so many that the way it is acquired is sort of an "the ends justify the means" philosophy today.

### *The John Wesley Callison Story—"Settling?"*

In late 1964, Johnny Callison achieved a .300 batting average as the playoffs approached. He promptly asked the coach to bench him the last game of the season to guarantee the record, and the coach agreed. Johnny never batted .300 again. Was it the right message to send to the rest of the team? Would you do that?

Okay, the Phillies had thirteen games left in the season, were up 6½ games in their National League Division and headed for a guaranteed page in the record books. The previous year, their record was a forgettable 47 wins and 107 losses. For those who remember the old "Whiz Kids" of Philadelphia, that era was ending. But things were remarkably different this year. Youth had become more seasoned and the sweet smell of victory was in the air. It was obvious to baseball fans that all the Phillies had to do was win one of their remaining thirteen games in order to be a *shoo-in* for the World Series. But the most unplanned, unexpected, unheard of thing happened next.

The Phillies stumbled into a ten-game losing streak. Earlier in the fall season, in a single game, Callison had hit three home runs. But with Callison choosing to be benched, some confidence had gone out of his team.

"Just let Callison do it," cried the fans.

Every player has to want to win for you to be a winning coach in baseball, on the football field and in sales. It's too easy for salespeople to look at selling without a team focus. In sales we only succeed as a team. In sports as in sales, coaches do NOT look to recruit someone who will "settle" just to preserve their record. If we include our clients and customers on our team we won't settle for less than the best sales experience for them. We can't be "all about us" in any organization. Selflessness means "taking one for the customer" and the team.

In the Washington, DC and Denver Districts, I initiated a new system of sales plaques on the wall. Each salesperson's plaque had record numbers on it representing the best performance in their best sales month since that person had worked for Sears Home Improvements. It took a lot of research for me to document it. I actually used wooden kitchen cabinet doors with an arched shape, looking like award plaques. Placing a white card-stock overlay, I computer-printed the best record sales volume, dollars sold per appointment run, and average dollars sold per appointment that month. My idea? "Beat your best month!"

Recognition plays an important role in relationships, family and in any of our personal interactions. It most certainly is critical in sales management. Ask yourself this question:

"When was the last time you were publicly or privately recognized for your work?" Been a long time? The *"madness in my method"* came from a very human tendency to forget our accomplishments and therefore "who we are." We become what we've done with our lives and how we've impacted other's lives. Sometimes in life others forget what we've achieved, sacrificed, whose lives we've influenced, perhaps children we raised or difficulties we faced. It's easy to have a sales slump like in baseball. We don't know exactly what's happening, but we are not hitting like we used to. We wonder what's happened. The plaques helped my team not forget.

"Is it me, the leads, maybe the new boss doesn't respect me? Have I lost my edge? What do I do?"

With plaques on the wall starting with at least $90,000 in sales in a month, a salesperson's first best month was their record. In fact, on the wall above these plaques in Washington DC, I put the words "Capitol Records" like the record company. I even used black CDs like an actual small vinyl 45 RPM record common in the 1950s. What was the method in my madness? When any salesperson had a tough month or was obviously struggling, and they came to a weekly meeting, there staring them in the face was their best month ever! Their record sales plaque was something they couldn't deny. We all need to remember **who we are** and **who we've been** so we can know **who we can become**. Well, that *was* your record, your actual black vinyl-looking record.

This isn't about beating the best salesperson on the team. It's about beating your own record. What's magic about a baseball player batting

.300 in a game? Anyone who plays baseball knows how hard that is. What about doing that for a whole season? Callison apparently did with a pitcher throwing a baseball at 95 miles per hour.

Comparing Sears Home Improvements to baseball, if you sell 3 of 10 one-call-close appointments in a commission sales environment, you are superb. But can you beat your record? In my world, if you met the challenge of having a sales month better than your first best, your black CD would be replaced with a gold CD. If you then beat your gold sales record, your CD went PLATINUM, just like in the music industry. Most salespeople going *PLATINUM* became managers.

**It worked!** The Capitol Record plaques increased morale on a consistent basis. Try something like this!

## *One More Touch of Baseball Nostalgia—The World Series*

I grew up in upstate New York where devotion to the Yankees was *an assumption*. It was almost required. I'd constantly hear people say, "Are you from New York? Then you are a Yankees fan, right?"

I remember the Milwaukee Braves playing the untarnished New York Yankees in the 1957 World Series when I was in elementary school. Warren Spawn, the legendary pitcher, was on the mound for Milwaukee. The series went the full seven games, and my teacher let us listen to the final game instead of our normal curriculum that day. Even in the strict, *slap-on-the-wrist* discipline of New York State's educational system in the '50s, my memories of my two teachers, sisters both called Miss Orr, were fond. They were seldom fun as they taught correct curvature of the hand when writing longhand or the multiplication tables or when putting us in math groups, but that one time when we got to listen to the World Series shows a type of flexibility sales managers can use.

Sales can't be all work and no play, nor can it be all about play. While some managers may try to manage by *"all play all the time"* or always go out for drinks with their team, eventually life screams for a balance. Make sure you play with your team—in moderation. You'll see them more as individuals, learning what makes them tick, quicker than just in sales meetings. You may find some behaviors that *die* hard, revealing a lack of discipline. You may hear words of criticism otherwise hidden from you. Passive-aggressive sales consultants may blurt out what they really feel about you under the influence of too much alcohol, or out in the parking lot, far out of earshot. While this is not new to you and me as managers, it is a reminder to be sure to play—in moderation—and to have your ears to the ground.

### *What does Manage with Integrity mean to you?*

In a chapter titled "Selling with Integrity," shouldn't we also discuss "Managing with Integrity"? Since sales management is all about people, *Managing with Integrity* produces sales professionals who *Sell with Integrity*. You always want that. While any example is powerful, your honesty becomes a stock you can invest in that gives you a consistent guaranteed return. At Sears Home Improvements, we had customers who believed the *over-promising salesperson* who declared "Nothing ever goes wrong! But if it does, Sears covers everything." That made sales easy, and did not require anything of that salesperson. If you haven't run into an *over-promiser*, you will.

These *over-promisers* are not *Stylistic Salespeople*, they are the "Slick Sammys" who will sell at first, then move on to the next company who hasn't figured them out yet, then the next, leaving you with costly problems, destroying your profitability and reputation. Some salespeople will do anything to get a sale. What they never realize is that when we pay customers to settle issues unrelated to product failure it costs us $20 in new sales to offset the loss of every dollar we spend. When we manage and sell with integrity, we always need to under-promise and over-deliver!

*Managing with Integrity* means training all our salespeople to *Sell with Integrity*. If we are sales professionals who sell in that way, then our example and reputation and the reputation of our company will precede us. Set an example.

Charlie Brown is quoted crying out in one Peanuts cartoon by Charles M. Schultz,

"There is no heavier burden than a great potential."

Great managers don't give up on the potential growth of those they hire. While we may not see the potential in some we initially hire, we can really succeed by finding and recruiting *Stylistic Salespeople.* That is why your battle cry could soon be "*Ride the Horses, Feed the Lions!*"

There's only room on racetracks for *thoroughbreds*; *plow horses* need not apply. And there is a reason we put *lions* in cages. We can't train *lions*, we just FEED them. We don't need kittens on the team, but some may be small *lion cubs*. The management challenge is how to motivate each part of the sales team in ways that maximize performance while utilizing the *horses and lions* to grow the team. Invest in relationships. Build loyalty. That is the key! Not one *highly successful executive* I worked for ever put the "reins" on me.

When I was working in the corporate marketing department in the Sears Tower I had a mentor at the VP level who allowed me to operate on my own direction, if I felt it was right. I grew confident in my abilities and accomplished many things some said "couldn't be done." The exceptions in my Sears retail career came in the field, in stores and regional offices where *middle managers* tried to control and micromanage me. Trust? These middle managers simply lost out on what I could offer. They felt they were being good managers, but just like an overly controlling person in a relationship they judged me based on their own limitations. Tightening the reins on *thoroughbreds* and forcing them to *do things your way* results in salespeople who may hit a sales target for you once but miss their true potential. You may never see them *gallop at their full stride.*

One such person stands out in my mind as someone who manipulated loyalty, demanded obedience, and restricted my district's potential. This senior manager was convinced I was not training our team correctly. Little by little, he worked his way into some of my meetings. He taught that there was a specific structure in how the words were used in the sales process and they couldn't vary. He was convinced if we outlined every step into smaller steps, like diagramming sentences in English class in junior high school, we would excel. By the way, he *was* once a high school English teacher. He never ran three #1 rated Districts like I had, which was a record in the company, but he knew best. As I watched this Regional Vice President try to surreptitiously force additional structured steps on my team, he made everyone feel uncomfortable.

"Hey boss, not everyone learns or comprehends the way you teach or comprehends your suggestions." He'd forgotten that things weren't the same as when he sold; technology changes, business product lines are added. This manager was the same one pushing the twenty-seven page script salespeople nationally had to memorize, but he was *sure* of what he was doing. Many great salespeople struggled. Then even more changes in the Sears sales scripts came down from headquarters. That drove my *Stylistic Salespeople* crazy. Theirs wasn't the way he sold, nor the way he approached customers. This executive's approach to selling resulted in a rote delivery of each and every little step. We had to change the way every manager had trained us to sell. He also undermined my authority. Never do that. Empower, Support and Validate!

Why do we keep trying to claim selling is a science and put everyone in a box? "Do it my way" is the highway to mediocrity. Watch them leave! They will.

What happened next? Well, we did what he wanted while he was the boss. When he wasn't looking over my shoulder, behind the scenes there was unrest. Why should everyone change to this highly scripted, prohibitively structured, inflexible way of selling?

In *THE BLOG*, July 25, 2015 article by Joanne Lang, she says "*The 7 Habits of Highly Effective People*" by Dr. Stephen R. Covey is my favorite book. Habit #5's message, '*Seek First to Understand, Then to be Understood*' teaches us that people form opinions based on experiences, unless they see things from another person's perspective. Two people can see the same thing from completely different viewpoints because of their understanding 'autobiographically.'"

Even now, when you read the quote, "*Seek first to understand, then to be understood,*" everyone knows it's true. We write, speak, and lead from a perspective of our own life experiences. In my mind, a manager who says "*You must first understand how I think. We all think the same don't we?*" is wrong! Even if we speak the same language, we comprehend the meanings of what people say based on HOW they say it.

Why didn't this executive know how to work with people? He was working with some superstars, but unwittingly turned them into *plow horses* and many left, even those we thought were loyal to him. Watch for red flags. We cannot lose superstars because we think we have all the answers. Using the term *Mr. Know-it-All* is accurate in describing those who manage as if their way is the only way. Don't lose a *Stylistic Salesperson*, a golden nugget, a *rainmaker*, as Matt Kelly calls them.

## *Do they Grow on Trees?*

I recently spoke with Clint Geog, Divisional VP Sears Home Services, and asked him to describe what a *Stylistic Salesperson* looks like. He perked up and trumpeted key characteristics he saw in his best performers. Then he began to explain exactly what he looks for when hiring salespeople:

"It was funny as I thought, 'are *Stylistic Salespeople* made or do we make them? Do they follow a process, or don't they follow a process? What do they look like, what makes them tick?'" He continued, "I think, during the interview process, what I look for is one thing only. I look for a *personable* person. In sales I care less about what their skill set is at this point, what they did in the past or what they've accomplished. I want to know one thing, 'Do I like them?' Everyone says that [they are a people-person, but] it comes down to who you have led and what the legacy is you left whether you're a people-person or not. It shows up in how you manage and interact. When I'm talking to a candidate, I ask myself, '**Do I like this person?** Is this a person that I like?'

"If I like this person then I want to listen to them. I listen in order to give them an opportunity to tell me **why** they want to work for me. And when it comes to how they sell I want to know if they will listen to what the customer has to say to understand why they say it. They have to be personable. As a new hire, if a salesperson is doing a good job, portraying a good company image, treating people correctly, never doing anything immoral or unethical, following company policies while **not** overpromising, and bringing in additional business, I wouldn't give them a lead I paid for at first. There's a reason why. Even If they sell me, tell a good story and look good on paper, I need to know how they'll go about their business because of the detailed sales process they will be trained to deliver."

Notice he wants to observe how they sell, not just who they are.

"Do I like this person" comes first for Clint, then an HR-like examination process. Even then he wants to watch how they conduct business before he retains them as a member of his team. While recruiting is where we start to build our sales teams, retention is the real challenge. That's where our management skills show.

Reflecting on the comments of many of those I have spoken with, I thought again to use a sports analogy when it comes to retention and motivation. There is one proven sports training process similar to what Clint described.

When a new hire or a veteran is struggling, try going back to basics. It will work for most people. If it doesn't work, try sending them to the minors to get more *at bats*. See what happens. If they have their own style but it isn't working, some coaches will have struggling players coach other hitters so they learn from teaching, from correcting others' weaknesses. When they see themselves through others' challenges it allows them to correct their own skills by observation. Then we can put them back in the lineup. In sales it's often the same. We often put a struggling salesperson with a veteran to ride along with or we have them ride with a rookie. Often in a slump we forget all we have learned, we may short-cut the process, stop listening-on-purpose. If we put them with a new hire, they will almost always do their best sales presentation to impress the rookie. In doing that they may rediscover the style that made them so successful before.

A hitting coach would say, *"square up your shoulders and extend your arms."* Going back to the basics could get them back in the lineup. I often had two salespeople, whether rookies or veterans or struggling performers, ride together, not with a manager this time. After they returned to basic sales disciplines, after some time back in the lineup, they began to hit consistently.

In Clint's example, managers should be comfortable recommending that players approach the plate and address the ball in a way natural to them, in other words "in their style." Everyone has a style, but they still must produce results. Soon they regain their confidence to be their *authentic self*, the key to their past successes.

When the boss believes in you and takes an interest in you, and tries to make you successful, you'll do whatever it takes to prove you can still *do it*. Great managers do things behind the scenes to help salespeople succeed.

"My dad is a carpenter, but he swings a hammer in the weirdest way I have ever seen," Clint Geog said. "We are all unique in some way."

"Jim Furyk holds a record for the lowest [best] score of fifty-eight in any round of championship golf in PGA history. It occurred, amazingly, in the last round of the 2016 Travelers Championship, but if you watch, he swings a golf club differently than anyone I have ever seen," Clint remarked.

Clint explains his bottom line as a manager when he was Terminix International's Divisional VP from 2011–2015, what we might describe as his *style*, in one short sentence:

"If you're selling differently than the Terminix 6-Step process, but you're successful, I like you and I'll look for what I can learn from you to share with my team." He got the message about the *horses and the lions.*

Clint Geog, Divisional VP, Sears Home Services.
https://www.linkedin.com/in/clintgeog

## *The Clipboard in Review*
### *"She sat with a Clipboard Taking Notes. What would you do?"*

As a Field Sales Manager my normal sales presentation in a home was two to three hours. I looked at it as if I was *punching a time card*. Not that I was bored or was a robot, doing the same thing, telling the same jokes and stories like Robert, previously related in an earlier chapter. I had learned what worked for me. My approach was respectful and I was always interested to get to know the person behind the door when I rang it.

Remember my story of visiting a woman whose business was in her home? In 2003 it wasn't as common to work in your home as it is today. This savvy woman sat respectfully for my presentation with clipboard in hand.

"She must have the clipboard to take notes on my presentation," I thought.

My impression was this was never going to be a sale. It would be easy to lose hope or confidence at that point. What do I do? "Just keep on rolling," the little voice in my head whispered, and so I did.

In those early days of my development as a salesperson and field manager, I'd never experienced this before. The clipboard was a tool of *my* trade. I took measurements, wrote paperwork, but in this case she acted as if she was taking notes at a meeting or just getting an estimate.

"Well I'm already here, so I will just do my job. I'm a professional!" I thought to myself.

This is how we distinguish between creative *Stylistic Salespeople* and what many call a *headhunter*. A headhunter runs leads and spends just enough time to judge if they think customers are serious or have credit. If the answer is yes, then they will put in the effort to get the sale. If not, they'll leave. A *Stylistic Salesperson* always believes they can get the sale. I would train my sales team with the attitude, "*Punch your time card. Do your job. Be professional. Ask questions, listen, solve problems and don't judge!*"

## "If I use Power Words, Will They Buy?"

Let me share my own personal perspective on whether selling is an art or a science. The temptation to say selling is a science is thinking that there's a magic bullet. There are really no power words that, if you say them, customers will somehow become mesmerized and want to buy from you. If you never say *contract* and always say *work order*, believe me they will still know you want them to buy tonight. Don't think that by leaning back in your chair trying to mirror the way a customer is sitting or how he folds his arms they will say to themselves, "He gets me."

Don't expect them to say, "You know, you sit just like me. You talk with the same accent. You have the same interests I've had all my life. I'll buy from you." It is not about the glass of water you asked for or the way you complimented their yard work. Trust must be deserved! The road leading to trust has a foundation of authenticity, sincerity, being yourself, and investing in personal relationships.

Don't get me wrong, hints, ideas and advice from famous sales writers have great value. I hope mine do too. The sales processes most successful sales professionals use are worth reading about in order to "tweak" your own approach to selling. The power, however, is not just in the books we read but in *testing out* what they recommend to see if they fit our style, our approach, our personality. Books can inspire us, and I hope mine inspires you, but the purpose of this book is to challenge you to *test out* the ten characteristics identifying the interpersonal skill sets of those I refer to, using myself as an example, as *Stylistic Salespeople* so that we might recognize, recruit, relate-to and retain those we describe as natural, personable, authentic or, as the title suggests, *the horses and the lions.*

I recall something that Clint Geog said near the end of our interview that says it all:

"Today, customers seldom find a salesperson they trust, are comfortable with and can say to themselves, 'I like that salesperson.'"

Success starts with *active listening* and grows when we take the time to get to know customers before we enter their home, present a product, or ask for the sale. It's not just making sure *we sit down in the kitchen* as the proper place to talk about ideas or design a kitchen, as I loved to do. It may not just come from the power of setting goals, writing them down, keeping them in front of us visually, and enjoying the process of moving ahead to accomplish them. I learned that there is great power in doing those things myself. The success we achieve may also not be rooted in positive "self-talk" and attitude adjustments, in listening to audio books on CD or MP3 or other streaming technology in the car, or even the support we receive at home or from others. Yet these all play a role. With the time and emotional demands a commission sales career places on *Stylistic Salespeople*, the bottom-line reason for their amazing success is ***"They love interacting with people!"***

## *A Stylistic Salesperson, a former CIA Agent or a Closer?*

I learned an interesting lesson from one of the super salespeople in Denver. He was quite the character! He was also quite distinctive with a shiny, bald head and the appearance of a retired CIA agent. In fact, that was the rumor in the office. After weekly meetings, we talked about whether anyone knew if Vince was his real name. Was he former CIA? How many *contract hits* had he processed? Had he killed spies and been on covert missions? This was the stuff that kept the idle minds of salespeople occupied after a long sales meeting.

Vince was one of the best sales producers in the office when I started at Sears. He regularly turned in over $100,000 in sales each month. To put things in perspective, the Denver office's territory covered all of Wyoming, all of Colorado, and half of Nebraska, requiring a lot of travel. Vince loved going to remote areas. Few companies offered services to Grand Junction, Colorado; Shoshone, Wyoming; or Grand Island, Nebraska. But Vince would bring Home Improvements to their doorstep. He was, however, what we called the "classic headhunter."

Managers know the difference between a headhunter and the unique and authentic characteristics of a *Stylistic Salesperson* and their incredible people-skills. A headhunter-type wastes sales leads we pay for instead of maximizing each appointment. I'll compare Vince to Zach, who was described previously as a *Stylistic Salesperson*. The average salesperson was given two or three leads a day. One year, Zach was very ill and ran only 175 appointments or about 1/2 an appointment a day. But he still sold $1 million. *Stylistic Salespeople* like Zach earn and deserve people's trust. Headhunters only ask, "What's in it for me?"

Vince would run about forty appointments a month. After spending only thirty minutes with the majority of those appointments, he decided if they were serious or price shopping. If they were ready to make a decision he would stay. He challenged the person directly, not something we taught him. Maybe it was his CIA training! If they were not ready, he thanked them, left his phone number for them to call when they wanted to sit down, never intending to return. Headhunters will quickly kill your office with that kind of attitude. It is like a disease that will spread to the rest of the team. A headhunter isn't a *horse* or a *lion*. The *Stylistic Salesperson* sees a customer as a challenge rather than a pest and does the full job even if a sale isn't imminent, even if it takes hours!

### *Abraham Lincoln, Goldie Hawn, a Grammy Winner, a Biker Woman or a Sleepover?*

Ready for another story about Vince, Mr. CIA? One day he had a Sears appointment in Grand Junction, CO, with a woman who obviously loved motorcycles, playing pool, and grew up back when body art was called tattoos, and wasn't as common as today. After he made the presentation he thought he had convinced her to buy.

"Vince," she said, "I'm not going to 'make a decision' today." Vince paused. He explained that to come back he would have to drive 4½ hours to Denver and back to Grand Junction, or he had to pay for a hotel and come back tomorrow. Then a smile curled on the side of her mouth as she challenged him to a game of pool. Vince caught the quirky grimace on her face as she racked up pool balls and chalked her cue. Vince knew he could *take her,* but she was obviously a *hustler.* Vince responded,

"Let's make it a real game. If I win you sign a contract. If not I drive to back Denver and lose a night's sleep."

It was obvious he had told the story before about having to drive home four hours. She chuckled and a *match game* began. The problem was she didn't know Vince was that good. Before long he could see the bet had been a great investment. The look on her face told him that. When it was all over Vince helped her pick up the heavy leather pool table cover, neatly folded, and replace it on the pool table. That was the least he could do. He didn't gloat, he just sat back down with her at the kitchen table and he pulled out the contract paperwork.

The final Score? Vince: <u>1</u> vs. the Biker woman: <u>0.</u> Vince got that $30,000 sale! *Don't mess with the CIA!*

A career in sales is often described as a career of telling stories. How well do your salespeople utilize a story as a teaching tool with their customers? Perhaps that's a criterion for who we should hire.

Okay, one more Vince story. This is about a couple in Grand Junction. Since Vince was high pressure, never wasting a chance to close a sale, it would become apparent this religious couple wasn't Vince's style. At the end of his presentation he asked for the sale. This time they said,

"We need to pray about it. It's a major decision. We need to sleep on it. Can we let you know in the morning?"

Vince thought for a moment. He looked around the room and down the hallway and said,

"By any chance do you have a guest room?"

Somewhat stunned, the husband sputtered, "Yes we do."

Vince responded exactly as if he had planned it. Had he done this before?

"It's about a four hour drive back home. If I make a sale the company pays the hotel. If not, we pay for the hotel ourselves. If I can just sleep tonight in your guest room, in the morning I'll take you to the best breakfast in Grand Junction. If you buy the siding, that will be great. If not, I'll drive *all the way back* to Denver."

As Vince looked at the couple with his *puppy eyes* you could see little wheels in their minds begin turning. Their obvious fear of this bald-headed man took over. They thought for a moment whether they really needed to sleep on it. In a New York minute they prayed about it.

They signed the contracts!

### *It's the people you meet!*

I was on a sales call in Fort Collins, Colorado. It started out like any other appointment. I was just doing my job as I drove two hours from my home in Littleton, Colorado to the office and then to the customer's home. Little did I know what I was about to experience with this man whose wife who was eight years younger. At his life stage, the age difference played a role in this story. We sat down together, casually, and I spent twenty to thirty minutes "warming up." The first step of Sears Ten Step Selling Plan was always my favorite part. You just never knew who you were going to meet. I love the *people part* of selling. All of a sudden his wife blurted,

"Okay, tell him. Tell him the story. I know you want to, go ahead."

Her husband seemed to flinch, a bit embarrassed at her frontal approach. He obviously loved telling his stories and it wasn't the first time for her.

I sat there for a moment wondering what that was all about. I felt like I'd walked in on a sporting event during a TV timeout with soda in my hands while a vendor barked in the aisle, "Get your popcorn here...."

The husband began his story. He was currently 80 years old but his father was 84 years old when he was born! He was conceived when his father was 84 years old. I repeated that for effect because I didn't get it the first time I heard him say it. Wait! Is this "his story" or rather, *history*?

I did some quick math, and deciphered that this man's father had been born about 1840. As his story continued he shocked me saying Abraham Lincoln had commissioned his father, at age 18, to West Point. This man, at a Sears kitchen appointment, opened the windows of history and gave me a glimpse of what our 16th President was like. He continued as if that wasn't startling enough.

"Two years later, Lincoln went to check on my father to see how he was doing."

What a story! What a thrill for me. The people I met were priceless. Instead of my stories helping us to connect on a personal basis, this time it was theirs. This was one of many personal experiences that helped me have a real love for people through the art of selling. Listening was the key. That will never change. Stories like these validate the reason I have come to believe that commission selling can be the best career in the world.

## *It wasn't the skiing at Vail, Colorado!*

Here's a story, from one of our Denver window installers. He called our District Production Manager to tell him about installing a six-foot glass sliding patio door at the Russell residence. He drove in heavy snow and got his truck up the steep driveway. Then, using a dolly and a ramp, he maneuvered the patio door to the back side of the house. It was to be installed just off the deck where the luxurious family room opened out to reveal the most breathtaking view he could imagine. He walked up to the front door, rang the bell and waited. Who answered the door? Goldie Hawn! It was the home of Goldie Hawn and Kurt Russell! The installer was beyond excited. You couldn't keep his feet on the ground. On the phone on way home he kept saying to Russ Boyack, his boss, over and over again,

"I love this job. I love this job! Goldie Hawn and Kurt Russell bought a patio door. I love this job."

Selling is about the people you meet! It certainly was for him. Kurt and Goldie trusted Sears. Who else would they call in Colorado that would drive to Vail and install a patio door at no extra charge?

In another Sears assignment, I had transferred to the Gaithersburg, Maryland office as sales manager of the Washington DC District. The DC Office covered the Washington Capitol District, half of the state of Virginia, and Maryland, except the Baltimore area. It was big, and we traveled a lot of miles. The DC District had the highest staffing budget for kitchen salespeople and I could tell their revenue had not yet peaked. I wanted that opportunity. I loved selling kitchens and training others how to close a kitchen remodeling or cabinet refacing sale in a three-hour, *same-day* visit. What we did every day is a one-call close, clearly the PhD of selling.

When I first arrived at my new assignment as District Sales Manager in the DC office, I was trying not to step on any toes. There was already a kitchen Sales Manager there and it was separate from the heating and air conditioning team, which led the nation. Steve, the General Manager, was an HVAC expert. He really didn't need me, or so I thought, but I had been recommended to him by the District Sales Manager in Chicago and was escaping an uncomfortable political situation I had unwittingly caused for Jim Brown, VP General Manager of Sears Home Improvement while I was in San Francisco, which has since been resolved and we are now friends. He was actually one of the first to pre-order a copy of *Ride the Horses, Feed the Lions*. **Thanks Jim!**

Anyway, it was a bit awkward being the 2nd kitchen District Manager in the Washington D.C. District so I decided to do *ride-alongs* to get to know our current kitchen remodeling and cabinet refacing sales team. What I learned selling kitchens in Denver and as District Sales Manager in San Francisco seemed to quickly inspire and encourage Washington DC District's interior product sales team. Wow! People-skills! Sales began to explode.

Along with the powerful HVAC sales team's reputation and performance during the summers, we were positioned to accelerate our national reputation. We were on our way to the top! Soon we hired more salespeople faster than I could train them, so I had to run some appointments myself.

One appointment took me to a small, one story brick home right in the center of DC. It was a beautiful African-American woman's childhood home where she had grown up. After her mother passed away she decided to remodel the kitchen. I had a great time just being myself, a *Stylistic Salesperson*, and I did what I normally would do. I got to know her! She had fun helping design the kitchen for her childhood home. It wasn't a surprise when she signed the paperwork for a $25,000 kitchen remodel. As we completed the paperwork we talked. Soon I found out about her upbringing and her family. Then she told me that while we were sitting right there in her mother's home, she should have been in Los Angeles getting the Grammy she won! When she wasn't on tour singing she would be living in that home. Why did she choose to be in DC that night? It tells you a little bit about what was important to her in life. It told me even more about her character. Family values!

Selling is hard. The hours are long. Each day on commission you start out at zero, but the fuel in my fire came from time I spent with people like her! Why are stories relevant to our discussion of management style?

When we are hiring sales professionals the real question, if you are getting this message, can be:

"How can we recognize, recruit, relate-to, and retain *Stylistic Salespeople*?" Is it to share with new hires that the best part of this career is the people you meet? Yes! Is it that selling is more about relating to those we eventually want to sell to by teaching the importance of LISTENING? Yes! The critical role that people-skills plays becomes clear when investing in relationships. It is about the importance of earning and deserving trust? Yes, all of the above. It is my purpose to convey the role that a love for people plays in a person's sales success.

This is not just another sales book as Roberto on LinkedIn feared when I sent him a picture of the book's front cover. Peter Strohkorb of Smarketing™ fame defined it as "One Man's Crusade to Humanize Selling."

I hope you enjoyed these stories. They were not likely ever to have come from great sales movies like *Glengarry Glen Ross* or *Death of a Salesman*, but stories about great people will light a *Stylistic Salesperson*'s fire!

Another thing about these *Stylistic Salespeople, lions, super-achievers, thoroughbred racehorses,* or whoever you may call your *superstars*, is often they will find it difficult to teach us exactly what they do. When you find them, hire them to be part of your sales team. If we *seek first to understand* what they are made of and how they sell millions, we will not only learn from them but we will demonstrate that we value them and we will not lose them.

## The Ken Kops Story

One more story. One thing that experience teaches us is "very little in life is coincidental, and the people we meet teach us important life lessons." I met such a man while managing the Washington, DC office in Gaithersburg, Maryland. Ken Kops was clearly a man of integrity, truly a *Stylistic Salesperson*, and a genius. I met his loving wife, Judi, at a dinner. It was easy to see she was his rock and he was hers. Ken was an example that people talk about but fail to emulate. He was a solid performer. He loved to sell Sears Cabinet Refacing. We had Kitchen Remodeling product design software, but it was "not his thing." I could still count on Ken closing at an acceptable rate, if not distinguishing himself at times. He was reliable, honest, a veritable corporate Boy Scout. He was my kind of guy. I would eventually discover his integrity was based on his personal religious beliefs.

One day, Ken came into my office, barely an open space off the warehouse near where we kept samples. As we sat down, obviously having something serious on his mind, Ken hesitated but then began to speak. This strong but humble man started out uncharacteristically timid.

"I'm not sure if this will be okay with you, but I want to discuss it anyway. My back is becoming a real problem and I don't think I can be running two appointments a day. The samples are just too heavy.

I'm not as young as I used to be." He smiled but got serious. He was obviously creative as he began to share his proposal. "Bill, I have an idea."

Ken had been a radio announcer back in the 1970s. He was known as B.J. Crocker, or *"BJ the DJ"* on Wisconsin radio. He was part of the "On-Air" staff and at the same time was program director in Colby, Wisconsin. He had worked as a program director at station WKAU-Kaukauna and then at 95.5 WIFC, a Top 40 (CHR) radio station in Wausau. He had sold baseball season tickets for the Minnesota Twins and seemingly had done a thousand other things. I heard history ring in his voice as he spoke with his radio voice and I imagined his play by play.

*"This is Ken live from Minneapolis. It's the Twins versus the Yankees. The pitcher seems nervous and the fans are going wild. It's another beautiful day and the home team's winning game is nine innings away."*

Ken went on to present his solution for the physical situation he now found himself in.

"Bill, I'd like to run one Sears refacing lead a day, come to the office, call 25 or 30 Sears customers and set up my own appointments." He paused, not worrying about my reaction, but hoping this could work for him.

What Ken suggested to me was intriguing. We had an area in the back of the office for administrative assistants, and a storage area full of kitchen, window, siding, and door samples. One room was double the size of the other with two heavy fireproof-grade metal doors. As we talked he suggested we clear out that area and get him a phone. He would make his calls where it was soundproof and private. I agreed easily and at times even listened with my ear to the door as his warm, booming radio voice captured the interest of former customers.

I wasn't going to kill the golden goose. Those heavy, soundproof metal doors allowed Ken to do his thing where no one would be bothered. Whenever you opened the door, you would see Ken sitting there. You could almost imagine a vintage silver-grooved radio microphone on his desk, waiting for *"BJ the DJ"* to sound the clarion call, or imagine he was announcing the third inning of a Twins game.

"Harmon Killebrew is up to bat here folks. Here it comes fans...the pitch is now on its way. Oh my...." And with a few imaginary thundering whisper-claps, we could see dreams of the past as Ken's eyes lit up. You could almost see the home run fly over the left field fence.

Harmon Clayton Killebrew, Jr. (1936–2011), nicknamed "The Killer" and "Hammerin' Harmon," was an American professional baseball first baseman, third baseman, and left fielder. During his long twenty-two-year career in Major League Baseball (MLB), primarily with the Minnesota Twins, Killebrew was a prolific power hitter. At the time of retirement, he was fourth all-time. He was second to Babe Ruth in the American League (AL) in home runs, an AL career leader in home runs by a right-handed batter. In 1984 he was inducted into the National Baseball Hall of Fame (Wikipedia).

Down the hall from our main office was a long narrow closet lined with file cabinets. Each file cabinet drawer had a month's worth of lead sheets with folders for each day and a summary page showing last names, some other information, and a lead number to identify that appointment. Sears *owned* the leads until one year after the original date. It meant that when you went back to the customer you would still get your full 10% commission. If customers didn't buy on a year-old previous appointment, Ken could earn an additional 5% on each sale. I suggested that Ken first call those customers who hadn't purchased. He started this exciting experiment the next day. Calling two hours a day he set nineteen appointments that first month. This golden goose began to lay some pretty golden eggs!

Ken ran one Sears lead a day, closing 20% of those I assigned to him, but he closed 40% of those he'd called and set himself. He didn't have to run as many appointments. In a year he had sales of $750,000 from setting his own appointments. To make the same commission the usual way at the normal commission rate he needed $1.25 million in sales. Plato was often credited with the phrase "necessity is the mother of invention." Plato would have stood in the shadows of this *Stylistic Salesperson* if he had gone into commission sales. Creative? Yes.

I watched as other salespeople reacted to Ken's story. The average salesperson whined and balked, even among this great Washington, DC staff. Few if any wanted to do what amounted to working harder. In other words, the weak salespeople refused to even try. They hated cold-calling customers even when I made the point that these were really warm leads.

"Look, somebody already went out there. Why would they buy if I went back out again?" was the belief.

"Thanks for making my point," I said in a sales meeting. "Ask yourself, Ken called back and found out some of them hadn't bought from anyone else in over a year after we came to their home the first time. What does that tell you? They set another appointment with Ken. Why? Well, here's the answer, in my opinion. They wanted to buy from Sears but something wasn't right at the time. Maybe it was who we sent to their home. Maybe it was financial. "What is your closing percent?" I asked them, point blank.

"Is it 40% like Ken's on leads he is setting himself?"

A hush fell over the room. Did they volunteer to make calls? Not one. Were they *horses or lions?* No.

When I shared Ken's amazing success setting his own leads, no one else asked to make phone calls. Denver District salespeople would be the same way two years later. I told everyone the Ken Kops story. Your *Stylistic Salesperson* sets an example. I spoke of John Conner who went from Achiever to Super-Achiever at Champion Home Exteriors in Cincinnati. He also set an example. We just need to get the others to follow.

Hire the *horses and the lions*! They'll make you successful. You will grow as a manager as you learn to love your customers and the salespeople you meet, mentor, mold and motivate. If you let the potential *thoroughbreds* take the reins after your training you will enjoy investing in those relationships and they'll become more loyal to you. It works both ways. Maybe managers should ask salespeople one by one,

"Would I be the kind of person you would invite over for a barbeque?" While it might be humbling, it might give you an idea of how they perceive you, and it might give them an idea how they can change to be more likeable, trustworthy and a people-person. We can all teach our process to almost anyone. If they show up, work hard and take total responsibility for their career, they can become good salespeople. But you will find, by referring to the list of the characteristics of *Stylistic Salespeople* included at the beginning, middle and end of this book,

"To create a World Class Sales Team...you must learn to *Ride the Horses, Feed the Lions!*"

# Chapter Fourteen

## The Challenger Sale vs. The Stylistic Salesperson

"The Challenger" described in the book *The Challenger Sale* by Brent Adamson and Matthew Dixon created some significant discussion in the sales community. They claim traditional selling styles they identify as *The Hard Worker, The Relationship Builder, The Lone Wolf* and *The Problem Solver* underperform compared to *The Challenger* type of salesperson. On its face this statement may openly provoke sales executives to question their entire career of sales successes and even their achievements in managing salespeople.

Until we take a closer look at the three characteristics identified by Adamson and Dixon uniquely describing someone they are calling *"The Challenger Salesperson,"* you might be intimidated into huddling the executive sales management team and suggest a total *retooling* of your sales process. What Adamson and Dixon describe here is not a type of salesperson you can now look to recruit. They're describing a sales process they discovered that some top salespeople use to close a sale. Let me suggest as you read "The Challenger Sale vs. The Stylistic Salesperson" that we do a little statistical check and review the caveats stated up front. I challenged myself to ask if *Stylistic Salespeople* don't already have the characteristics discussed. Do they already approach selling in these key categorized ways or in an equally effective manner? Are we simply using different terms? I think so.

The inferences seem staggering. Here's a summary of statistics directly from *The Challenger Sale*:

- 40% of high sales performers primarily used a *Challenger* approach.
- High performers were more than twice as likely to use a *Challenger* approach.
- More than 50% of all-star performers fit the *Challenger* profile in complex sales.
- Only 7% of top performers took a *relationship-building approach* (worst group).

## *Let's look at their Disclaimers and Caveats*

We should note the *Challenger approach* **only worked better among** [*the 40% of*] **high performers.** Among average performers, all profiles were *roughly as successful* as one another. This would lead someone to question the selling style of the other **60%** of high performing superstars in any company that do not use the Challenger approach.

Are they saying the only high performing methodology is *the Challenger approach?* Maybe they are. Is it true? **No.** Referring to *vital characteristics,* Adamson and Dixon admit, "The Challenger Sale" is common to only **40% of high performers**," but they don't identify sales styles of the other **60%** *of all high performers.* **Why?** Perhaps they never discovered them. While the statistics support the process described as *The Challenger Sale* being what 40% of high performers use, they leave us to speculate what makes the other 60% successful.

My first question: "Do Challenger Salespeople spend time building relationships?"

In 2011, "Success Mindset" interviews with Adamson and Dixon by Jill Konrath were titled,

"What the *'Challenger Sales Rep Profile'* does that others won't."

I will directly quote Matthew Dixon answering one of the clarifying questions:

**Jill**: Can you define the Challenger style in more depth? What kinds of things will Challengers do, others won't?

**Dixon:** They teach the customer during the sales interaction. They share new ideas for making money or saving money the customers themselves had not even realized existed. This is a very different type of sales conversation than what most reps deliver.

## *"What facts are initially missing here, from my perspective?"*

**My Review:** Listed below are *three types* of successful salespeople. Whether they become *High Performers* depends on a number of factors. Weldon Long and I agree that many larger companies with big training budgets use a sales process that's too complex. Too much detail! By simplifying their process, Weldon has succeeded in lifting sales performance and opening doors to greater success by all types of sales professionals in a number of companies. Comparing four types of salespeople outlined by Adamson and Dixon, let's compare *Challengers* with those they call *"The Problem Solver."* While they critique this type of salesperson, you may contrast each to other types of salespeople and high performers, starting with those who I might even call *"The know-it-alls."*

**Type #1: The Problem Solver:** Dixon identifies this type of salesperson as "highly detail oriented. Reliable! Responds to Stakeholders! Ensures all problems are solved!" Sounds like a B2B rather than general or residential in-home sales category. Product and process takes the lead over people-skills. The Problem Solver appears to be the *"know-it-all type"* of salesperson, sharing information *as if they have an encyclopedia* in their brain. They know everything about the product. One man I knew wouldn't let customers buy until he *unloaded* every piece of information about the product. I described him as "putting the last nail in the coffin." Some people will buy based on your knowledge. *Stylistic Salespeople* command a great deal of product knowledge.

**My Review:** A problem solver seems to share not just new ideas about product, but would most certainly share new ideas for saving money, such as in cases of any energy efficient purchases. A problem solver selling insurance or an investment banker or securities trader would certainly be *up to date*. Real estate salespeople, those selling securities or insurance products demonstrate a basic discipline of sharing new ideas for "*making or saving money customers themselves had not even realized existed.*" In today's internet-savvy world, product technology races so fast, but I still believe customers aren't as knowledgeable as trained salespeople.

**Dixon:** [*The Challengers*] tailor those insights to different types of customers and stakeholders they're engaging. This is obviously a **select for** skill in a world where complex sales demand more and more of a consensus in order to get *the sale* done [*emphasis added*].

**My Review:** After twenty-four years of experience in the field and Chicago Sears Tower and Hoffman Estates corporate retail as well as fourteen years of management at Sears Home Improvements and as a national sales trainer at Champion Windows in Cincinnati, sixteen interviews with LinkedIn executives like Franklin-Covey's Shawn Moon taught me some things. Speaking with these reputable sales trainers, keynote speakers, and a cadre of highly successful middle managers leads me to suggest that "***Tailoring of insights shared with B2B clients or in-home customers***" referred to as unique to **The Challenger Sale** process is actually a common sales practice.

For example, Chad Rawlins identified some clients as *Commanders.* Other salespeople study clients in order to recognize *Hartman Personality Profiles*, described previously. These practices are not unique to *The Challenger Salesperson.* Today's sales training seminars and books replete with *sales analysis doctrine* suggest that if you don't know what personality type your customer is you may not be able to sell to them. Others preach that if you say certain words to clients, as I have also mentioned before, you will fail to close the sale. *The Stylistic Salesperson* possesses natural interpersonal skills. Dixon and Adamson, however, identify groups taking *a relationship-building approach* as the worst performers.

**Dixon:** Nearly 40% of *Challengers* are high performers. *Relationship Builders* are [only] 7% of high performers.

Based on their statements, let me counter with four challenges of my own:

1 - Is a **"select for skillset"** in today's complex sales world unique to *The Challenger Salesperson*? **No!**

2 - Is a group taking *a relationship-building approach* devoid of every key skill set they identify? **No!**

"The Success Mindset" interview of Adamson and Dixon by Jill Konrath continues:

**Question:** What percent of *Challengers* not building relationships are high performers? Answer: **40%.**

3 - If the *Challenger* type of *high performer,* with identifiable approaches and disciplines, would add to their skill set that of the *Relationship Builder*, what would happen? Would it add to or decrease their performance?

In our discussion, Chad Rawlins pointed out how important it is for him to "pivot" in sales presentations once he determines if his customer or client is "an empathizer," or when he identifies them as a blue, white, red, or yellow as identified in the Hartmann Personality Profiles. Chad also outlined categories of learning styles of his customers as being important in order to solve problems and provide solutions. That probably came from one popular theory, the VARK model. It identifies four primary types of learners: visual, auditory, reading/writing, and kinesthetic.

The conflict continues between high performers, *Stylistic Salespeople* who build relationships, and Challengers.

When I was in Elementary School in upstate New York, I learned in class and never needed to do the homework teachers assigned. If you learn by reading books you are called a "reading/writing" learner.

Chad is an analytical *Stylistic Salesperson*. If he's also a *Relationship Builder* does it mean he doesn't "tailor those insights to different types of customers," the **select for skill** mentioned in The Challenger Sale? **No!**

In my interview with Chad he referred to his respect for *The 21 Irrefutable Laws of Leadership*, a book by John C. Maxwell, where one principle is described simply as **"follow them and they will follow you."**

Maxwell teaches salespeople to categorize each type of customer or client. Is that *Stylistic* or *Challenger?* Perhaps Dixon and Adamson encountered the 40% of high performers who read Maxwell's book. Maxwell points out a simple statement very similar to the one made in the book "The Challenger Sale"

Maxwell explains: "In B2B situations, salespeople size up prospects and adjust or *pivot*, responding to how customers present themselves."

*Challengers* use the **"select for"** skill. Chad, a *high performer*, pivots. A mere conflict in terms?


4 - Is this **"select for"** skill only exhibited in the 40% of high performers Dixon and Adamson refer to as *The Challenger Sales Rep*, account executive, or C-Suite presenter? **No!**

I'll quote again as Brent Adamson and Matthew Dixon contrast *relationship builders* with *Challengers.*

**Type #2: The Relationship Builder:** *Relationship Builders* focus on developing strong personal and professional relationships and advocate [for this] across the *customer organization.* They are generous with their time and tend to *acquiesce* to what the customer wants, *resolving* tensions in commercial relationships.

**Challenger: *They take control of the sale.*** This isn't about being *pushy or aggressive*, rather it's about being assertive around everything from the insights they share to the way they negotiate on pricing. This is absolutely critical when dealing with highly risk-averse customers who are content with the status quo.

Again this is not unique to *The Challenger Salesperson. Stylistic Salespeople* are highly interpersonally skilled professionals with needed skills for *today's complex world of selling.* Some customers will have deeper conversations with someone they "like or trust" but not necessarily more product knowledge or tailored technical updates. They may think *risk-aversely* too, but connections built by *authentic* sales professionals with interpersonal skill sets are as effective as those who think they **take control of the sale.** Their approach involves active listening, empathy, and taking interest in the customer. *The Stylistic Salesperson* will close sales *The Challenger* may not. Perhaps Dixon and Adamson can take a cue from those who build relationships. Learning from high performers means including those who have all these characteristics and connect with their clients on a personal basis. If it is only process that you think works to generate and deserve customer and employee loyalty, ask them. Respect, validation, vulnerability and investing in personal relationships = "We like you, we trust you, we buy from you."

Nothing in the world can take the place of persistence. Talent will not; nothing is more common than unsuccessful men with talent. Genius will not; unrewarded genius is almost a proverb. Education will not; the world is full of educated derelicts. The slogan "Press On" has solved and always will solve the problems of the human race. —Calvin Coolidge

*The Challenger Sale* by Adamson and Dixon identifies two types of salespeople who might also match the skill sets needed to be able to take control of the sale:

**The Hard Worker:** Doesn't give up. Self-motivated. Interested in feedback and personal development.

**The Lone Wolf:** Follows own instincts. Self-assured. Delivers results but difficult to manage.

**My Review:** *Stylistic Salespeople* are persistent salespeople. They are self-motivated and pursue personal growth. The challenge for management is to establish relationships with these *thoroughbreds* so feedback comes across as constructive. *Stylistic Salespeople* ask questions to know how to solve problems and concerns until the customer can decide to move forward. They follow their instincts and are creative. They listen to validate their clients and to get to know them on a personal basis. They often repeat back what a customer has said to show they heard them. Some customers need a strong, assertive salesperson. There are non-invasive interpersonal ways to provide the emotional support a client needs without being controlling. **Hard work beats talent. Persist!**

The interview continues:

**Jill:** You talk about the death of *relationship selling*. Is it truly dead?

**Adamson:** At the end of the day, *Challengers* are the ones who build stronger customer relationships because they build relationships founded on business value, not just like-ability.

**My Review:** When is a relationship not based on like-ability? Can anyone tell me about a close relationship based on business value and not like-ability? I suppose, tongue-in-cheek, after a divorce where one party escapes with a financial windfall and the other decides not to contest it, they've *built a relationship founded on business values, not just like-ability.* Frankly, I'm not sure what Adamson and Dixon describe here is even possible. But let's pursue it for a minute. What would it look like? B2B comes to mind, where a client contracts with a service provider at a rate that conveys great business value. The ongoing purchases provide profits to both parties involved and then, as Adamson then explains, *Challengers* are the ones who build stronger customer relationships because they build relationships founded on business value, not just like-ability.

Think for a moment about any B2B clients you do business with that you haven't gone golfing with, have never invited to dinner or for drinks after a meeting, and haven't given tickets to a sporting event as a thank you. Can you think of one? Are they still your client or did you lose to a competitor providing business value? Price? Business relationships are founded on business value. What company doesn't want to provide that? Then why does one salesperson with a B2B client do better than the one you just let go? *Stylistic Salespeople* have both business value and like-ability. Period!

In my opinion what we need to do in business is not to classify "types" of salespeople or come up with new sales genres. We need to recognize, recruit, relate-to, and retain *thoroughbred horses and lions* as follows: Would you invite them to your barbeque? Would you buy from them? Will clients like them? Would you trust them in your home, with your children? After the resumé *screams* "hire me," let these be your "gut feel" tests.

I applaud the research in Adamson and Dixon's book, *The Challenger Sale.* Without such efforts we fail to identify selling styles we can learn from. (My comparative reviews quote some content from *Success Mindset* by Jill Konrath interviewing Brent Adamson and Matthew Dixon in 2011.)

# Chapter Fifteen

## "The Fabian Effect"
### *"Here is some good news for anyone who wants to get into sales."*

As a sales manager, imagine you interview someone who has no idea why they want a job in sales. Even if someone you hire has never sold before, there is some good news. There are many types of salespeople who can be successful. No single type will close every sale. No one can. We know that. But you don't have to sell to more than one out of four customers, if the sale is big enough, in order to make a good living. At Sears Home Improvements my average sale was around $8,000. Two or three good sales a week, that don't cancel, can make life comfortable. You can earn six figures if you're likeable. Not everyone's style needs to be completely changed.

This is an important concept to remember for managers who think their way of selling is the right way. That assumption, when it is put into action, can be fatal to your career. Selling and managing others can really be fun if you enjoy people. We need to be flexible enough to recognize and acknowledge that if our salespeople do things a little differently they still are of great value.

Structure is important, don't get me wrong, but we shouldn't force the square, *stylistic* pegs into round holes. You will still catch some *gold dust* in the bottom of the pan, but you may miss some *gold nuggets*.

While this book's intended *target audience* is sales managers and sales executives, you'll find many salespeople will recognize the value of it, will also enjoy the read, and may be inspired to be more natural, authentic, sincere and personable as they approach their clients.

As a result of better understanding *Stylistic Salespeople*, my purpose also includes inspiring managers to rescue them. What do I mean? By recognizing *Stylistic Salespeople* in the interview process, you'll find some who left "micromanagers." If you have one and didn't realize it before, you will finally understand who they really are. By you recruiting, relating-to, and retaining *the horses* and feeding *the lions*, you'll put people first, as if they were your clients, because they are!

Why should you do this? First, you solve any problem of high turnover in your team without creating another problem, the loss of potential revenue growth. Will this be a challenge? Yes. Will you benefit too? Yes. Are you ready yet? You have to know that I'm sincerely reaching out, asking you to consider this concept.

The bottom line is that as sales managers we shouldn't just get rid of a *Stylistic Salesperson* because we can't manage them or they don't do things exactly the way we want. If we do, we'll never learn what they know and we won't retain the impact of the sales potential they represent. No one *closes* like your top salespeople. Do they have their own style? Yes! Does your team wish they all made the money they do? Can you learn things from *Stylistic Salespeople* to help the team? Accept the challenge! Recognize, recruit, relate-to and retain them.

What if you do hear someone whine, "He's way off the reservation!" and you will. That's one way you can identify top performers who may be *Stylistic Sales professionals*, by the envy. Your team may think you support them at the expense of other successful salespeople. If they do, step back and take another look at what we call *parking lot politicking*—manipulation by weaker salespeople to undermine your style of management. It is easier for them to complain than perform, excel or achieve. It's easier to talk than to sell. Talk, talk, talk!

There are people who complain "it's the leads." Then there's "If I got appointments that *super-duper, teacher's-pet* Tom runs, I would get his paycheck." If you're in sales and your company pays for leads you assign to salespeople and they whine, try this:

During one meeting, I guess I was frustrated hearing never-ending complaints. I addressed the subject directly. "If anyone thinks that Tom is the one that gets the good leads, then stand up and explain to me how I can tell what a good lead looks like. If you can help me with that, I most assuredly will give to Tom, who is the best salesperson in our District, the GOOD LEADS. In the meantime, I would like to offer anyone a chance to assign the leads. You can pick two leads first for yourself, any two, but no complaints if you don't sell them." When I became a field sales manager in Denver in 2002, Glenn Moore, my District Sales Manager, gave me the same chance to pick my own leads. That may be where the rumor comes from that Field Sales Managers get to pick their leads. Not fair, right? After a few days, these leads didn't pan out, and I asked Glenn to assign me my leads. Then I started selling again.

"Come on, pick your leads. Oh, and after you pick your two leads, you assign the rest of the leads for the team."

Dead SILENCE. There were no volunteers. Have you had this situation on your team? Confront it directly.

## Who Stylistic Salespeople are not!

Tim Wackel was rated #1 out of a ten-thousand-person sales organization, and has been a sales trainer, keynote speaker, consultant and is a former Director of Sales with Docent. Tim is founder and president of *The Wackel Group*, a consulting firm dedicated to helping organizations find, win, and keep customers for life. Located in the Dallas, Texas area, clients now hire Tim to coach managers and salespeople to succeed in business and in life. His list of clients includes Allstate, BMC Software, Cisco, Fossil, Hewlett Packard, Integrys Energy Services, Philips Medical Systems, Price Waterhouse Coopers, Raytheon, Red Hat, Toshiba, Wells Fargo, and some professional trade associations. He is also a member of the American Society for Training and Development and also holds a professional membership in the National Speakers Association.

Tim mentioned a *Stylistic Salesperson* he worked with for ten years who lives in Cincinnati. Even today, they connect whenever that salesman is in the Dallas area. To say they became friends is an understatement. "Yeah," Tim said, "we're still good friends." I thought it was interesting to hear him say that during our interview for this book, since some managers shy away from close relationships with their employees. Tim continued,

"He's coming to Dallas next week and we're going golfing. This went beyond just a manager-employee kind of relationship. I always make time to see him."

Tim is a fascinating guy. As I listened to his story online at LinkedIn—and I suggest you do too—it was like he was writing *The Stylistic Salesperson*, the book's original title, for me. I'll share Tim with you now—a *Stylistic Salesperson* in the flesh. He's a *LION* as in *"Ride the Horses, Feed the Lions."* He started out his sales career most assuredly as a *colt* but had the pedigree of a *thoroughbred*. First a word about *colts*.

Tim's first employer encouraged him to take a position in technical sales. At first, he wasn't interested. The more he imagined sales being *showing up late, going home early, playing golf every Thursday afternoon*, he decided to try it.

After a year of showing up late, leaving early, playing golf every Thursday, most people asked him how much he sold that first year:

*"You probably didn't sell a lot, right?"*

"The truth be known *I sold a ton*," Tim replied. "I sold my skis, my stereo, and then my motorcycle."

Quite a story! So how did he transition into the *lion* he ultimately became? Tim had started out intending to have a career as an electrical engineer, and found selling was harder than he expected.

"In the world today, selling is more like engineering and is very challenging for one to master. What's selling all about?

"First, it's about going to a client already understanding their problems. Second, it's figuring out the obstacles. Finally, the best part of selling is designing solutions that make people happy professionally as well as personally."

For Tim, a member of the American Society for Training and Development, #1 of 15,000 salespeople, a corporate sales executive, corporate sales trainer and keynote speaker, the most fulfilling part for him is when he works alongside sales professionals, helping them to *be their very best.*

"I'm old school. I think in business today we need to be accessible to our people and our clients. People buy when they're ready to buy, not always when you're ready to sell. Whether you pick up the phone, chat via website or communicate by email, it's the connection with people that makes the difference between selling our products and selling motorcycles. Your new hires can have *more successful* sales careers if they reach out and *invest time developing relationships.*"

Tim Wackel, sales trainer, keynote speaker and executive coach
https://www.linkedin.com/in/timwackel

Note to Sales Managers: The key is establishing relationships with *Stylistic Salespeople* like Tim does. They are *thoroughbreds.* Don't just rein them in, assuming they need to be controlled. Let them *set their pace.* People on your sales team will be motivated by your example as you reach out to them too. They want you to get to know them personally. *Be on their team so they're on yours.* Many aspects of learning how to manage others, for me, has been on-the-job training. Each person is their own book with something to discover on each page. Don't rush it. Listen to the stories they tell. Watch and learn. Getting to know them is the fun part.

We've all heard the **"walk the walk"** explanation. This is more critical to your future success as a sales manager than even we might think. It's more important for sales managers to *saddle up and ride alongside their thoroughbreds* than just turning every salesperson into replicas of themselves.

### Is it the Words they Say?—Discussion Revisited

In a highly respected legendary book *The Art of Selling*, Tom Hopkins recommends using certain words in place of others to overcome any negative customer reactions. Tom suggests we substitute *total investment* for *cost or price*, and *initial investment or amount* in place of *down payment.* Everyone uses the word *contract.* Instead, he suggests using words like *paperwork, form, or agreement,* and instead of asking customers to *sign it,* Tom suggests the phrases *"all I need is your approval"* or *"all I need is your okay"* or *"all I need is you to authorize it."* Finally, he offers the conceptual terms like *own or acquire* instead of *buy* and *opportunity or transaction* instead of *deal.* Tom makes a point: *"Words matter."* This is *Tom's style.* He's a *Stylistic Salesperson.* Can we teach style? **Yes!**

Will words we use create sales success? Paraphrasing a study by UCLA Professor Emeritus of Psychology Albert Mehrabian, persuasion results **7**% from *words,* **38**% from what he calls *"vocal liking,"* and 55% from our *body language.* Non-verbal elements present listeners with important clues to a speaker's thoughts or feelings, substantiating or contradicting a speaker's words. At the end of the day, word choice may not be the final arbiter of a sale.

*Stylistic Salespeople* are authentic and natural in their use of language, which is one thing we like about them. When we are interviewing sales professionals, *Ride the Horses, Feed the Lions* specifically suggests seeking out individuals who contribute like Tim. Remember his message? "Your new hires can have *more successful* sales careers if they reach out and *invest time developing relationships."*

### *"An Interview Test for Candidates to fill out First"*

Today, HR personnel in sales organizations don't know how to identify *potential Stylistic Salespeople.* I am therefore suggesting we invert the hiring process. This will be a disruptive change, but it would be just for interviews of sales candidates before recommending them to a sales executive. What is the plan? HR should interview people to decide if *they like them* in order to measure *customer-like-ability.* This includes a "gut feel" about the *trust factor* human interaction senses and measures. The key qualities found in high performing salespeople will never show up on a resumé. HR algorithms can't determine it. Key words won't reveal it. No technical methodology today or in the future will be a substitute for human interaction in the new hire process. That is the best explanation of my "one man's crusade to humanize selling," as the subtitle of this book, provided by Peter Strohkorb of Smarketing® and the One Team Method™ fame, suggests is its mission.

HR professionals tasked with finding budding or accomplished sales superstars should look for people they would like to *spend time with after work* as the criteria, rather than a resumé they may be impressed by or someone who over-sells themselves well in an interview. We all have had interviews like that. If HR personnel sense they can trust the prospect enough to invite them into their own home, then they're getting closer. That is the talent pool you want to interview. Then look at the resumé. Customers don't read resumés before buying; they *buy into people they like and trust.* Would you trust the person you are interviewing for a key sales position? Spend time **interviewing** so you FIND *horses and lions*, instead of filtering algorithms for key words in resumés.

Will we accept some quirkiness in a *Stylistic Salesperson* in order to facilitate their success, without bending these *potential thoroughbreds or pedigreed lions* to our will? Is it our job to *break their spirit* or insist they utilize a regimented process that ultimately causes them to lose motivation to be themselves? Can't we be flexible? Can we learn *on-the-job* as managers? Can we recognize one who isn't yet outstanding but possesses all ten characteristics of the *Stylistic Salesperson?* Some of them are currently working under managers who refuse to open *the starting gates.*

Can we get to know who they are, connect with them, motivate them, and facilitate their positive influence on the rest of our sales team? Can we get close enough, perhaps even ride with them and try to learn how *they do it?*

Can we adopt this philosophy of finding the *diamond in the rough?* Think there is merit in searching for *horses to ride and lions to feed* who are the *Michael Jordans of selling?* They are out there.

What we can learn from people with stylistic characteristics, as previously outlined, is how they interact with people and how they listen with the intent to get to know the customer, not just to discover what we call in the industry their hot buttons, just to get a sale. *Listen on purpose!*

Here I include again the characteristics of *Stylistic Salespeople* that HR teams can use to seek them out, as well as an HR Test Module to use for initial Human Resource interviews. Yes...interviews, not recommendations to a sales executive to interview, not to set appointments for someone else to get a "gut feel" if they like them, but in the many more HR interviews that I recommend Sales VP's insist their Human Resource professionals do.

Included at the end of this book is a list of questions for our Human Resource professionals to use in interviews intended as conversation starters. The candidate fills it out before the interview then you have a casual discussion about anything but the job opportunity. Instead of a traditional interview approach, this allows you to get to know them personally. This isn't a test as much as it arms HR with the perspective of the potential interpersonal skills of a new hire using characteristics of a *Stylistic Salesperson* outlined in the book.

## *Characteristics of Stylistic Salespeople—Manager's Review*

1. They are **creative!** They only need your guidance on policy. They are problem solvers.
2. You can't **make** them; you **find** them. This is the best part of your journey. Training new people to become like robots is simply *not* fun, for you or them.
3. They are **people-people**. They are naturally sincere, authentic, warm and **charismatic.** For them each appointment is like a first date.
4. They sell with **integrity**, honesty, are concerned about the customer's needs more than their own, and they feel they cannot be dishonest and succeed.
5. They need to be **motivated,** not managed. How would you manage Michael Jordan? Take an interest in them so they will "get you."
6. The need for **recognition** is different for each person. The challenge is how to reach them. In this sense each manager must be stylistic too.
7. Want to **adopt them** or invite them for dinner? These are my tests. I hire on this basis when looking for a superstar. Shawn Moon, VP of strategic markets calls it Franklin-Covey's "Barbeque Factor."
8. You can't find these characteristics on their **resumé.** I have stated previously that I never read resumés when hiring a salesperson. I look and listen for who they really are.

9.  They're **happy** by nature. **50%** of how we handle rejection is how we are raised. **10%** of events are out of our control. But **40%** is our choice!
10. They want to **help** people. This is an intangible. Look for it. You don't have to push someone who **pulls others up**. They'll help you if you establish a relationship with them.

### Note to Sales Executives and Sales Managers:

Salespeople want you to get to know you! Especially get to know Stylistic Salespeople personally. Don't rein them in right out of the gate. Let them set their own pace. Be on their team so they're on yours. Like most things, learning to manage *Stylistic Salespeople* is *on-the-job training*. Each person is a book with something unique on each page. Don't rush. Listen to stories they tell. Watch, learn, have fun!

Who are the *lions*? They're the one-in-a-thousand who sell millions! They're salespeople operating outside of the box procedurally, yet they drive tremendous sales revenue. You don't train them. *FEED* them and learn from them! Know them personally. They're *thoroughbreds*.

I said, "**R**ecognize, **R**ecruit and **R**elate-to them."
Now how do we **R**etain *Stylistic Salespeople*?

Let's admit that in management of people or in sales training, we all want a formula that works every time. When raising children and dealing with a parental disaster, for example, we must remember that each child must be treated as an individual. It is the same with our sales force.

Do you like horse racing movies? Remember the scene from the movie *Seabiscuit* where horse trainer Tom Smith, played by Chris Cooper, was struggling to get this *thoroughbred* to respond to the starting bell that would begin the race? If the horse breaks out of the gate slowly it may lose to a veteran who is used to hearing that sound. *Thoroughbreds* have certain characteristics and quirks. Their potential is discovered **by the trainer**.

Katherine Blocksdorf's May 27, 2017 article *Meet the Thoroughbred, Not Just a Racehorse*, explains:

"There's no actual breed standard for *thoroughbreds* as there is for an Arabian or Morgan. Their primary purpose is racing at speed. *Thoroughbreds* come in every color including gray and more rarely roan. Many are very dark and plain. They are 'people' oriented. *Thoroughbreds* have been bred to be fast, athletic, and spirited."

https://www.thesprucepets.com/meet-the-*thoroughbred*-1886140

Are you getting the comparison with *Stylistic Salespeople* who begin as *thoroughbreds-in-embryo*?

I will first focus on the term "*spirited*" and perhaps call it "*skittish*," a term used in the movie *Seabiscuit*. As Tom Smith prepared *Seabiscuit* to be a champion racer, he was careful not break his spirit. See the comparison?

Those we call *Stylistic Salespeople* could sell for any company. To retain them, remember they need to be appreciated. We must be the support system they need. Each case will be different. In my interview with one anonymous sales manager, he explained he was once approached by what he called a *workhorse*. This salesman had worked loyally for fifteen years for a local company, but no one seemed to value or even notice him anymore.

One day he stopped by his sales manager's office to share his frustration. The manager wisely invited him in to discuss his feelings privately.

"They don't pay me enough to just be ignored here."

Was it just a raise he needed? the sales manager wondered. He didn't want to lose him.

"Follow me Ted," he said. "We're going down to the head office."

The sales manager wasn't actually going to battle to get him an increase in pay. They walked to the front desk where the admin team members were. He asked which one of the four was the best at their job. It seemed he caught them by surprise. Finally one raised her hand. With Ted by his side the sales manager calmly asked,

"Would you be willing to dedicate one hour each week to help support this key sales professional with whatever he needs, so he generates even more revenue for the company? It may be with paperwork or collecting a check or calling a customer for Ted."

Without blinking an eye, she said, "Yes, for sure."

After thanking her, the sales manager and Ted headed back toward his office. Before they got there, Ted stopped him in the hallway.

"No one has ever done anything for me. Why did you do it?"

The manager answered,

"You're important to us, Ted. I want you to succeed."

In order to attract superstars we must do four basic things: "Recognize, Recruit, Relate-to and Retain!"

RECOGNIZE: Look for those you enjoy talking to. Would you buy from them? Would you hang out with them after work? Remember *The Barbeque Factor*! Never stop looking everywhere you go. Remember, they are rare.

RECRUIT: Invert the HR process. Have human resources interview to find personable people who show evidence that they care about people. Look for natural interpersonal skills. Look for a person who you can sense is a creative problem solver. Challenge them. See if they can tell stories. Is HR looking for a people-person? **Yes.**

RELATE-TO: Establish a relationship, validate and them recognize Stylistic Salespeople privately or publicly, where appropriate, and leverage what you learn from them to strengthen your team. Learn what is so unique about them. How do they relate to others? What is it they do that can be shared with other salespeople? What can you learn to make you better at managing sales professionals? Relate to them as people. Value them.

RETAIN: Does your company stand behind its products, warranties, and services or do they cut corners? Is the management team ethical? Ask yourself, if you were a salesperson, would customers believe in you? Does the company mission inspire sales professionals to stay or do you lose talent, leaving you only average performers? Remember superstars can sell any product anywhere for any company. Become their support system!

## The Underdog and The Fabian Story
## *"The Fabian Effect"*

In a fascinating discussion Olivier Riviére, a LinkedIn Influencer and consultant from Levallois-Perret, Île-de-France, France, he explained those I called *the horses and the lions* simply:

"Stylistic Salespeople? They are all different!"

As he described his adventures recruiting people in sales, he referenced being an underdog. There were obviously some personal experiences he had earlier in his career that made him feel that way. When he said underdog....

I remembered how I felt when other successful salespeople in the Denver office, who were more structured in the way they gave their Sears sales presentation than I was, got promoted ahead of me. It really bothered me. I felt my selling style wasn't appreciated. Had my style held me back? "You're stylistic, Bill," they would say. "You can't train style." The whole underdog category wasn't something I had considered.

I decided not to pursue the discussion of why Olivier felt like an underdog since he seemed focused on discussing the issues related to sales professionals who have their own style. I did wonder if his reference was to managers he worked for holding him back, or to the sales process he had to work with being too structured. His comment intrigued me but in order to get his opinions on the subject I said, "Sometimes I feel like our industry's cumbersome sales processes or policies dehumanize salespeople."

Olivier agreed, globally, then reflected on his initial impression of my statement:

"I am wondering if this is a problem unique to the United States and sales techniques that are used there. We have this problem here in Europe as well, but much less" (Olivier works mainly in Germany and France).

I shared that the best salespeople I hired and trained were those not from my industry. The ones from my industry had already developed so many bad selling habits we had to *undo the damage.*

Olivier said, "I agree with this. It is a complex matter." I asked him who the best sales salesperson he had hired, worked for or worked with. Without hesitating he said, "Fabian."

"Fabian was the best software salesperson I've ever met. Salespeople are all different, but he was the best. As CEO of a German software company, I was sent to France to solve a subsidiary's marketing problem. One salesperson they hired bragged he was a great closer and was in the *Elite Club* at a former company but had never sold anything at the French subsidiary. In contrast, Fabian was very gentle, but if the company wanted something, he got it. He had a warm heart, making efforts to connect even with people who weren't pleasant. In eighteen months, Fabian generated 70% of the revenue."

After some polite chatter between us during his interview as part of the list of 16 LinkedIn "influencers" I had solicited, he closed with,

"Bill, as you shared with me your descriptions of the *Stylistic Salesperson,* it was incredible. It all fits, it's incredible!" **Horses and lions!**

Used with permission.

# Chapter Sixteen

## The True Story of
## "An Authentic Stylistic Salesperson"

### *Michael S. Wooten*

*"Life is what you make of it"* is a profound statement with a lot of wisdom in it. It's also the title of a novel written by Preeti Shenoy that's unintentionally referenced here. Since attitude is crucial in selling or any endeavor, when you fail, or perceive you're a failure at important things in life like marriage in cases of divorce, you wake up every morning wondering,

"What do I do now to turn my life around? Can I choose differently?"

It's not like Hollywood where you go into rehab, appear in a movie, and applause starts cascading over your past, washing it clean as if it never happened. Real change only happens when we let go of *self-defeating behaviors* and have a *sincere change of heart.* Quoting Michael Wooten,

"The man upstairs expects us to." I now share a story about one man who made such a choice.

Michael Wooten's life-long journey started in a small Tennessee town. After high school he followed the path of many in his town. He went to work in construction at a local power plant. Deciding he wanted more out of life, Michael's quest led him to the financial services industry, where he spent over thirty years in sales training, sales management, and recruiting as well as team building, leadership development and compliance. He was a salesman first and everything else seemed come almost naturally after that. Sounds as if some magic happened, but his success came because of the humble roots he built upon.

It all started with a chance encounter, when he discovered people were buying whole life instead of term insurance, which started Michael thinking.

Here's an excerpt from Michael Wooten's upcoming book, *The Magic of Compound Results*:

"The day that changed my life began much like any other day. I was waiting for the NFL football games to start when I noticed one of the small magazines in the newspaper featured an article, *'Getting the life you've always wanted.'* I didn't usually give those Sunday magazines a second glance, but growing concerns about my future caused this particular article to get my attention."

Earlier in his life, Michael had been happy to just have a car—any car—and the freedom it would afford him, but now it seemed that almost every car passing by him was newer and nicer than his was.

"How could that be? I had been content in my little house, on my quiet little street, no traffic to speak of and wonderful neighbors. Then it occurred to me that my neighborhood was never included in what was called the *'Street of Dreams,'* an annual competition sponsored by our local newspapers. The winning neighborhood always featured big, beautiful homes with swimming pools and had perfect landscaping. Somehow all of these homeowners had put themselves in a much different situation than I had."

Michael began to read the magazine article with great interest. The key point was "in order to have the life we really want, we first have to determine what it would cost." The author pointed out *we have to decide if we're willing to earn enough money to pay for it.* The article even included a worksheet to help determine the cost of the house you want, the car you want, the vacation you want, as well as education costs, hobbies, charitable contributions, etc.

Suddenly Michael had long since forgotten about the football games and was totally immersed in designing the life he wanted. When Michael finished the workbook he was pleasantly surprised to learn he could have that life for about $100,000 a year. That was a lot of money in those days, three times what he earned at the nuclear power plant, but it wasn't impossible.

"I'd known for some time that something was wrong—I just couldn't put my finger on what it was. Now it was perfectly clear. People who enjoyed a better lifestyle weren't better than me. I suspected they weren't smarter than me, either. They just made more money! So I was faced with a choice. In order to have the life that I wanted, I'd have to make a career change, or I could compromise, stay in my comfort zone and keep my job, but I would have to settle for less—much less than the life that I really wanted. As I thought about it, it really wasn't much of a decision at all. Although somewhat uneasy about doing something different, I was exhilarated by the possibility I could actually do more, have more, and become more than I dared to dream about before."

What Michael had was a dream with a clear focus, a purpose, and a real inspirational turning point. Now he could *allow* himself to work for what he wanted, not just what some might think he deserved. I mean, after all, he already had a good job working in a power plant. That wasn't going to go away. Some people might have seen him sitting on his old front porch swing in Tennessee dreaming and wondered what some small-town kid was wasting his time doing. Or, in a few decades, Michael could be sitting on that same old swing, on a sweet fall afternoon, looking at the leaves falling from native gumbo limbo trees, sucking on lemonade with his retirement set, without a care in the world. Michael reminisces,

"I guess it was different for a lot of us, but for me it has become like the dream that allows me to just keep on dreaming. Retirement's a state of mind, and it isn't located in Tennessee. Not for me."

My experience was similar. I had been recently divorced and yet family still came first for me. I came alive when I tried commission selling as a career where your income is up to you. I discovered I could make more money than I had in twelve years at Sears corporate. I realized what Michael had realized.

*"Selling can allow us to provide for our families financially,"* I thought. In Michael's world it meant that even the sky wasn't his limit. Selling would do far more for him as he began to help others. In my world, being able to make enough money to take care of the healthcare needs of my ex-wife, who was on intravenous feeding for over twenty years, helping my youngest son afford college and providing for the future would open doors to this woman who I would marry in 2002 after starting as a Home Improvements salesman with Sears in early 2000.

## Characteristics of World Class Salespeople

World Class salespeople have the qualities that you would expect of top performers. They work hard, manage their time well, and are the experts in their fields. They communicate utilizing their *better-than-average people-skills, having an unshakeable confidence in their ability to solve problems and find solutions.*

They are typically neither cocky nor arrogant, but make no mistake, the confidence they carry shows in their natural, authentic body language. You can't fake confidence. If it is real, it gives their clients every reason to trust them, believe in them, and then, ultimately, do business with them.

## Michael Wooten's amazing life story continues:

"It was said of the late David "Chip" Reese, Hall of Fame professional poker player, '*All he needed* was *a chip and a chair.*' World Class salespeople feel the same way. All they may need is an audience—an opportunity to get in front of prospective clients to tell their story. The belief they possess in themselves, their product, and their service is genuine—and it's contagious! They don't just *sell stuff*—anyone can do that. They solve problems. They understand what clients want more than anything else is someone who can make their life or business better. Then they go about getting it. They embrace the concept of *relationship-based selling vs. transactional selling.*"

## *An observation from this book's author:*

"Please note the paragraph above, ending with *"They embrace the concept* of *relationship-based selling vs. transactional selling"* was expressed by a man considered by many to be one of the greatest salespeople in the world.

In an article by Karin Schwartz posted November 11, 2011 on the website *Springboard*, she reflects on her assessment of *Relationship Selling vs. Transactional Selling.*

"If we've said it once, we have said it a thousand times: **Business is all about building relationships!** While we're not saying that a transactional approach to selling is ineffective, what we are saying is that it is not the most efficient way to make a sale. The main difference between building relationships and transactional selling is in the approach.

"**Transactional Selling:** This strategy is about short-term solutions. The sales rep is primarily concerned with the promotion and selling of the product with little or no emphasis on customer needs. This strategy, also known as traditional selling, is all about the single sale.

"**Relationship Selling:** This strategy is all about building long-term relationships. The sales rep gets to know his or her customer, their needs and their wants. Then and only then does the salesperson even think about trying to make a sale. Organizations that utilize a relationship-building approach to sales have a competitive edge over their rivals. Companies practicing relationship-selling continually see substantial growth in revenues and lower expenses, year after year.

This is because it is cheaper to keep an existing client than it is to establish new clients with each and every sale. It's been said that 80% of an organization's business comes from 20% of its customers, those satisfied customers who keep coming back for more. As you can see, a relationship-based sales strategy has a tremendous upside.

http: //springboardbizdev.com

Michael S. Wooten also adds his perspective on success in sales:

"For organizations whose primary objective is obtaining new clients and retaining them for an extended period, relationship-based selling, marketing, and customer service *is not optional.* It's required. Our existing clients can become a valuable source of new clients. Herein they produce a steady stream of revenue, income, and profit. Therefore, developing and maintaining relationships with open communication [and] keeping customers happy becomes the priority. I've pondered this question for some time:

"'Is it possible the internet has rendered salespeople obsolete?' Yes, I think so—especially when we're trying to compete with the internet in areas where it's strongest, as in information, pricing, etc. To be relevant, sales and marketing professionals should focus on the one thing they can do that the internet cannot, building a relationship with the customer."

Michael S. Wooten's devotion to helping others resulted in his leap from becoming a *thoroughbred* to being well respected as a World Class *lion.* Winners of the *Preakness, Belmont Stakes,* and *Kentucky Derby* are sired by equestrian royalty, but still need trainers. Like *Stylistic Salespeople,* sales *thoroughbreds* need trainers too. In my story of Zach's having Uncle Robert—a disciplined and high respected sales professional—as an example, mere sales heredity didn't create success, but it did reveal potential. If you want to be like Michael Wooten, it will require hard work. It did for him. He just had to know how much money he needed to achieve his dreams, then he put in the effort necessary to reach his goals.

In the upcoming book *The Magic of Compound Results,* that will relate Michael's story, he is akin to *Seabiscuit,* a racehorse without peer. If a *colt* becomes a trainable *stallion* and then develops into a *thoroughbred,* success is just a dream and a lot of perseverance away.

And yet the trainer, just like in the movie, is a key. In the case of Michael, his journey from *colt* to *stallion* to *thoroughbred* did not stop there. When he became a *lion* he became a trainer himself.

Michael's story continues:

"Desire without immediate, meaningful and massive action is the beginning of disappointment, regret and delusion. I made my decision that day and I then started to aggressively pursue various career and business opportunities. I wasn't sure what I wanted to do, but I was sure that whatever it was, it had to pay me at least $100,000 per year, and I'd have to enjoy doing it. A few months later I found an opportunity with an expanding company in a huge industry. I was ready, I recognized it, and I took immediate action. Perhaps I should repeat that part for you and really drive it home. ***I was ready because I was looking for it.*** I recognized it because it synced with exactly what I was looking for. I took immediate action because '*desire without immediate, meaningful and massive action is the beginning of disappointment, regret and delusion.'*"

His journey, my journey and your journey in life, "if traveled alone, pursued purely for *instant material gratification*, can leave a trail of broken promises, *fractured and lost trust* behind us. Success alone is simply loneliness. Something needs to change inside us," Michael reflected.

Less than eight years from the day he read that little newspaper magazine worksheet, his adventure began.

"Yes, I was earning about a half million dollars a year, driving a beautiful top-end Mercedes, living in a wonderful sixteen-thousand-square-foot home, enjoying some memorable vacations to remarkable locations like Hawaii, Mexico, Bermuda, and Europe, and traveling to places across the United States and around the world. Even though I couldn't have known it at the time, that day [I read the article] became a significant emotional event for me. I finally knew what I wanted. I knew that I would have to change to get it. And most importantly, I knew that I was ready and willing to make those changes."

He learned from experience that ***the day that changes your life*** begins with you making the decision to change! Michael explained:

"I began to master the achievement of almost any result I desired by following a very specific formula. This recipe for success has nothing to do with luck, background, color of your skin, your previous education, or even all your previous failures. During those eight years, on my way to accomplishing my dream life, I made it my chief mission to teach, coach, and mentor others to see if these results [from my very specific formula] could be duplicated. I was convinced they could, so how could I not share these invaluable life-changing principles?"

Michael succeeded, but not just because he was a *stylistic*, charismatic, inspired, and motivated salesperson who put people first. He cared about his customers more than he did about himself. He *listened-on-purpose* so he could find out their needs. Then he put his creative side to work to design solutions that made them happy in their personal and work lives. His life formula worked over and over. But again, it was time to make a decision.

"Hundreds, probably thousands took me up on my offer to mentor them for free," Michael remarked. "But very few followed the formula. Very few gave it enough time or had the discipline, so they justified giving up on their dreams with every excuse imaginable, never accepting responsibility themselves. But many more than a handful did [succeed]. Dozens have accomplished all they set out to do. *'Take responsibility.'* That lesson made me millions!"

Throughout those eight years, people he trained were able to quit underpaying jobs they hated, drive much better automobiles, and move to homes and neighborhoods that had been an unattainable dream before. They enrolled their children in private schools and donated money to worthwhile causes, effecting change for countless people. They showed Michael photos of family trips to beautiful exotic resorts that made him cry.

"I became obsessed with how many people I could help, how many I could teach, coach, and mentor, how many families I could impact in a profound and lasting way. It's clear all of this didn't occur just because of me. The value that people were experiencing was because they replicated **'the magic of compound results.'** Every time I'd sit down with their parents, perhaps even their relatives, in their beautiful, lush, professionally landscaped homes and spent time with them, I'd laugh, watching children squeal with delight, running and playing in their new home, in their new lifestyle. I so often would have to fight back the tears of joy. Those years and experiences, thankfully, didn't make me proud or haughty. Instead, they actually humbled me significantly as I began to realize that what I began eight years ago simply *as an answer to the question* of how to better my life just a little became a much bigger future."

Over thirty years of selling financial services with offices in more than a dozen states, tens of thousands of agents and sales representatives who needed an example to follow reported to Michael, someone to believe in, who had *done it...really done it.* No one pulled him off that old porch swing in that small town in Tennessee.

Michael summarizes: "When you have your own dream, is it real or just in your mind? You determine that, and not just by wondering out loud. You determine it by deciding. Deciding what you want out of life."

When you *get it*, like Michael Wooten, it still begins with a decision. What will you do to make your dreams come true? And after you make the decision to pursue a path of optimism with your glass more than half full, will it really matter if you sell insurance or, like your author loved, sell kitchens?

I myself rose from selling shoes to a distinguished Sears corporate career. Choices I made caused my divorce and initially threatened my career. Life isn't over when we fail. Mine wasn't either. One morning I awoke to the reality that I needed to accept my part in those failures, or *"take responsibility,"* as Michael Wooten said. Divorce divides all families and forgiveness is uncommon. Regardless of justifications or finger-pointing, the reality was I could have chosen differently. That morning as I awoke, I chose to accept my part in it. I thought taking accountability would add burdens, but it lifted them from me.

Michael says, "Whether you're aware or not, the collective outcome of your life is often determined by a handful of significant emotional events. Sometimes these are unmistakable. Some turn simple coincidences [*and I believe there are none*] into marvelous outcomes. Make no mistake about it, when the failures occur, if you're ready to take immediate action, you can alter your future and change the direction of your life forever."

And so I did Michael... like him, I made a decision in my own way, perhaps not of the same magnitude!

# Chapter Seventeen

## "Life in a Millennial Sales World"

Okay, you've joined me on my life journey as I discovered how to manage myself, *a Stylistic Salesperson,* and others like me who had their own style, operated a little outside-of-the-box, but sold elegantly.

"You can't teach style," all my supervisors would say. "Stick with the Ten Step process."

While some of my sales career successes were as "an individual contributor," the real question I first had to ask myself was, "Do I really want to manage people?" The answer may not be relevant if you, the reader, are already a sales manager, but perhaps it still is. The question may, in that case, be better put:

"Do you enjoy managing people now?"

There are different styles of sales managers. Some are process-driven, focused around quality control, efficiency, and return on an investment or hard cost-cutting to save your company money. But no sales manager can be successful without the people they're responsible for being able to succeed too. If being a sales manager is emotionally, financially or intellectually unfulfilling or, in other words, there's *nothing in it for you*, why do it? The same goes for those who work for you. If your management style doesn't give them an adequate return on your personal and professional investment, why immerse yourself in it, attempting to acquire management skills you don't currently have?

The answer is taking total responsibility for your success, as Michael Wooten described. Invest in personal relationships. Isn't that what you're being asked to do in *Ride the Horses, Feed the Lions,* to learn how to recognize, recruit, hire, train, motivate and retain *Stylistic Salespeople*? To connect with them, find out what makes them tick? The "honeymoon" between new sales managers and their salespeople will fade if they don't choose to manage in a way that improves both their life and the lives of others so they are more meaningful.

For *Stylistic Salespeople,* the enjoyment of selling can be a lifetime pursuit or can be shortened, derailed and discouraged by a micromanager or a manager's ego that doesn't allow input and "out of the box" ideas. That is the very definition of creativity. Old ideas or solutions, processes or products fade in the background when new technology or any younger generation comes along. Sales managers will soon inherit *millennials*, if we haven't already. If we don't know how to relate to them, where will our future sales force come from? They're the next generation of salespeople. Do they like selling? If selling's only about money, the game can be an endless merry-go-round of employee turnover. Millennials may head to the exit. Worse than that, they may not apply for a sales position in the first place. So what is the answer when we are looking for talent in the next decade? Let's get some current insights.

In a February 6, 2015 article, Roberta Matuson, a Forbes contributor, adds fuel to sales manager's fears: "Turned off by the profession's reputation for pushiness and cut-throat competition, millennials are overlooking sales, often a springboard to higher level management executive positions, as a viable career...."

A February 2015 Wall Street Journal article is titled "Bright Future in Sales? Millennials are Hesitant." Here the writer highlighted the difficulty employers [are] having persuading millennials to work in sales.

In a subsequent June 16, 2016 article by Catherine McIntire, *Canada Business,* she echoes a death knell:

"Workforces are changing, and sales tactics need to change too. Cold calls are on the wane—and your younger employees know it."

According to a July 17, 2017 *Brookings Data Now* article by Fred Dews, "Millennials will make up 75% of the workforce by 2025." That's not even a decade away. It means we must be able to recruit and hire millennial talent. What is our plan? Quoting a June 28, 2016 article in *Sales Hub* here are some millennial realities we will face:

"Millennials don't want to cold call because they hate *being sold*. They grew up in the digital age, where all information they could want is at their fingertips online—customers today don't need a salesperson giving them information. They grew up in a world where, as the buyer, they had all the control in the buying cycle—they don't want a salesperson pressuring them into a sale. Because of their age, they better understand how people actually want to buy today, which makes them uniquely qualified to sell to today's customers, who are just like them."

*Millennials* would never want to *model* high pressure salespeople if they pursue selling as a career. They wouldn't be focused on products, delivering a price-based message, followed by overpromising language just to get a sale. Karen Schwartz, quoted previously, described the *traditional sales approach* as transactional in focus as follows:

"This strategy is about short-term solutions. The sales rep is primarily concerned with the promotion and selling of the product with little or no emphasis on customer needs [and]...is all about the single sale."

Admittedly, because instant access to information presents an entirely different sales landscape than in an era of the high pressure transactional salesperson, Karen reprises her recommendation for Relationship Selling:

"While we're not saying that a transactional approach to selling is ineffective, what we are saying is it is not the most efficient way to make a sale. The main difference between building relationships and transactional selling is in the approach."

*"Emerging as the largest demographic in the workforce, millennials are no longer the leaders of tomorrow – they're the leaders of today!"*
LinkedIn article by Emily Ryan, Melbourne, Australia;
Marketing Manager *at Mentorloop; 11-23-18*

"While *millennials* already occupy influential positions and have presumably enjoyed satisfactory career trajectories, when surveyed many believed they would leave their current business before the end of 2020. And it wasn't a small amount of people. It revealed 44% of *millennials* say if given the choice, they would like to leave their current employer in the next two years.

Not many businesses would be prepared to lose more than 1 in 3 of their workers. It's fast becoming a significant amount of senior talent (and investment) potentially walking out the door. As *people-first* advocates, we have to stop and ask why? Where does the "loyalty challenge" come from? And how can we win over the next generation of leaders?

Many studies show that *millennials* simply live by a different set of values and culture relative to other generations. Often emerging are two "stand out themes" First, feeling under-utilized or under-challenged and in turn, not being developed into the leaders they want to be. The second, feeling that most businesses lack any ambition beyond profit—a gap in perception that no one can afford.

### *Three ways to win over the next generation of leaders:*

**1. Demonstrate purpose beyond profit**

We all know business needs to be more than money. But weaving these values into organizational culture can sometimes be overlooked, or implemented half-heartedly. Aiming to include your people in the organization's vision minimizes the gap between what they believe the purpose of business should be and what they perceive it to be currently. I've seen colleagues push away projects, campaigns and even roles that strongly conflict with their own beliefs. Aligning these by living and breathing your values can often be a path to retention.

**2. Create the "ideal" working environment**

When salary or other financial benefits are removed from the equation, work/life balance and opportunities to progress or take on leadership roles stand out. You don't need the budget of Google or Facebook to retain exceptional talent in this area. No amount of ping pong tables or filtered coffee will help either. Often, poor work/life balance, the desire for flexibility, and a conflict of values compound a perceived lack of leadership skill development and feelings of being overlooked. Striving to redefine these areas can shift perception and promote growth.

### 3. Support ambition and professional development

This is the big one. How to do it? You guessed it—encouraging mentorship. Whether you have a learning and development program in swing already, it can't go without its most cost-effective and long-term impactful brother, mentoring. Starting a mentoring program is easy with mentoring software—in fact it can take only minutes.

This bottom-up approach where your people drive your people-strategy works far better than a top-down strategy of pushing learning upon them. And we've seen this success across our beloved clients and beyond.

*In fact, those that are intending to stay with their organization for more than five years are more than twice as likely to have a mentor.*

We have observed that loyalty to an employer is driven by understanding and support of millennials' career and life ambitions, as well as providing opportunities to progress and become leaders. Having a mentor is incredibly powerful in this regard. Millennials receive thirty-three percent less mentoring than they would like. Are you confident your organization is in the majority? For long-term success, bridge the values gap to retain talent. Not sure where to start?

In a recent article posted by Beejoli Shah on March 21, 2018, from the blog ST^NDDESK, the surprising headline is right on point:

*"Millennial Relationships are Stronger than Ever— And it's Keeping them Healthy."*

"If the media is to be believed, when it comes to love and relationships, millennials are in a state of catastrophe. [In reality,] judging by the mental, physical, and spiritual benefits [they] are looking for in their everyday lives, [millennials] seem to be taking their partnerships far more seriously, finding them infinitely more fulfilling than any [past] generation. Defined by researchers at Northwestern, the phenomenon goes, 'when close partners affirm and support each other's ideal selves, they and [their] relationship benefit greatly.'

"While our goalposts are indeed moving what love and relationships looks like, there's no reason to believe they're moving backwards. In fact, the strongest relationships now are deeper and [more nuanced] than their generational predecessors."

What Beejoli Shah points out here is reassuring regarding the future of relationships, businesses, career paths and those involved in them that they respect the value of connecting on a personal basis as a core cultural life-value.

Here's more good news about sales careers millennials hear loudly and clearly in *Ride the Horses, Feed the Lions*... Attention millennials: "Welcome Home!"

I am not unique, but in the feedback I got from interviews with sales gurus and from managers working in the trenches, a people-person, investing in relationships, can thrive in a career in selling. I was obviously a *people-person*, my friends even told me so, but I didn't think I would like management. If I were to be a manager again today, what would my approach be? Would it be different? And, first of all, how would I approach recruiting, relating-to and retaining millennials? The answer is the same: *relate to them*.

## *"Relating-to Them"*
### *The 97 Club—reprised*

Nothing as a salesperson prepared me to manage up to forty commission career professionals. I felt I had great success for ten years as a Sales Manager running three #1 Districts coast to coast before I *made a decision*, as Michael Wooten would say, to accept total responsibility to "connect." Breaking down barriers of pride many executives have due to their accomplishments leads us to expect we executives should always be "in control." It was only after my daughter sent me a copy of *Daring Greatly* by Brené Brown that the message of vulnerability broke through. What did I decide to do?

At this point I want to reprise a few conclusions and discoveries I made deciding how to reach out to my sales team through *The 97 Club* meetings. Struggling with the challenge of treating each member of my team as an individual, as a person, not only did I have to implement company programs, I had to discover what motivated the new hires and veterans I trained and mentored. What concerned me most was those salespeople I couldn't seem to help improve.

What were the *personality differences* in poor performers, as compared to top sales performers? Was it a lack of motivation? It seemed like it to me. Was it they only thought of themselves as average and were satisfied with that? Did they lack training? We think we are good trainers or loving parents until we realize we seem to have disconnected, lost a connection or no longer have a relationship. I certainly did. I had to face this reality. Were average salespeople just not making an effort? Was it upbringing, was mediocrity an inbred attitude? What was missing? Was it me? What could I do to raise a poor performer to average? What would move an average salesperson to good?

When I first worked with my team in *The 97 Club* meetings I thought there was no magic bullet or scientific method to find what motivates people to excel, with or without my influence. It wasn't the product, their process or the company they worked for. There was no technique to hypnotize people in a way that will result in excellence. It's not putting on a show of overly enthusiastic sales meetings trying to be a cross between Zig Ziglar and Hollywood. It's a competitive world we face. If there was such a thing as a magic potion we could put in a bottle so our salespeople could take a swig every morning, it wouldn't require anything of us. We wouldn't have to change in any way. Soon after, a book would be written, and the secret would be out.

What makes the difference? What drives us to be the best we can be? I found two key differences during *The 97 Club* meetings. Surprisingly or perhaps obviously, the difference-maker turned out to be personal goal setting! But there was an interesting twist. It wasn't someone else needing to believe having lofty aspirations was the answer. It was me. It was me that needed to change. I was on the same emotional treadmill as my salespeople, and I needed to be more vulnerable and more caring to be able to connect with them.

The second *personality difference* was more about life and how we impact and influence one another. Indeed, the reality is that life is a person-to-person adventure. Our interpersonal skills, our personality, our love or disdain for people determines our life outcomes. It's the same for us as managers. We must accept that we will be doing this work right along with every member of our team, each day, in reality's trenches. One key to making our careers enjoyable lies in our comprehension of how to interact, listen and seek to understand others first before we expect to be understood. There is Stephen R. Covey's wisdom again.

Are we motivated to do it? Where does the juice come from? Managing and empowering others to excel takes all we have, just like raising, educating, and helping our own children through the maturing process. The motivation must come from our desire to help others. If we have no such desire, if it's just the money, soon it won't be fun anymore. After making millions, the successful Michael Wooten said,

"I became obsessed with how many people I could help, how many I could teach, coach, and mentor, how many families I could impact in a profound and lasting way."

## *Becoming Selfless*

In order to help changes happen in the lives of the ten members of *The 97 Club* who volunteered to come to our meetings every week not knowing what it would all be about, I had my work cut out for me. It wasn't just them. I knew I'd have to discover for myself the value of setting goals, writing them down and visualizing them. I had my own challenges. When we held our first meeting of *The 97 Club*, our Denver District had become average. Two years prior, we had been the #1 District in the company. What had changed? Had I forgotten how to motivate others? Probably not. Did I think I could believe in writing down goals? No! There are just three simple steps! Set three "personal" goals. Write them down. Create a small mobile vision board you can clip on the visor of your car. The major benefit in your membership In *The 97 Club* would only become real for me if our adventure ended in each of us discovering there was power in writing down goals.

Please note that I have chosen to share some of my personal life with you. I have done that intentionally. It's now part of my management and communication style. If those you work with believe you have no human flaws, they will never open up to you, especially when they need to. Be authentic. A day will come when one of your *lion's* stars is falling, they stop selling like they always have, and you can't figure out why. If you have no relationship with your superstar, you'll seldom find the cause. The rest of the sales team will pick up on it. Don't assume they are not having a problem with something personal in their lives. When one of the *lions* stops eating or a pedigreed *thoroughbred* comes up lame, it may have nothing to do with your management skills. Or it might. You might think at first, *"Lions* can't really be managed."

They are people, human beings who need to be a part of things, be of value, and most will want to help others. Managing needs to be personal. Don't run away from it. **Connect, relate and retain. It's on you!**

As I've mentioned, one of my three lofty personal goals was to have a reunion of my "divorced family." I had shared with *The 97 Club* members how my divorce had impacted my children. You may remember Gus from earlier in the book. Openly discussing my failures allowed Gus to address an issue with his family. He never told us a reunion with his family was one of his goals. It all started by meeting his sister one weekend. We heard about that from Gus in 2014 and were pleased. Then the shock of my career came when I saw his Christmas 2015 *Facebook* photo. It was of Gus with all and his siblings around a large dinner table. Every one of the six of them was smiling! I could see his twin brother at the other end of the table. The caption under the photo simply read:

### *"Together again for the first time since 1962."*

Life *at home* impacts our ability to be successful *at work*. While you can't sit down, interview your employees, and ask them if they have unresolved personal issues, having your own *The 97 Club* environment creates unique levels of loyalty and trust. The personal connection is subtle, even passive, yet authentic. By connecting, I experienced the unexpected, and you can too. I know it changed me more than anyone else.

As I looked back on the experience of *The 97 Club*, and particularly what happened in Gus's life, I came to a conclusion: "Average people are just great people who have an unresolved personal issue that's holding them back from the self-confidence and purpose in life needed to see their value."

## Would anyone start their own "97 Club" Chapter?

After reading the first draft of my upcoming book, Geoffrey Riddle wrote back to me on LinkedIn:

"*The 97 Club* is fantastic! Setting sales goals can be easily compared to what you're suggesting we do. With sales, goals are cut and dried. Numbers, numbers, numbers! However, the three personal goals require you to dig really deep, and it's uncomfortable. I'm a huge fan of author Brené Brown. I understand the vulnerability that she talks about. [That] is why I've avoided joining *The 97 Club*, because, reading the title, I'd thought I was already a member. Life's like a seesaw. We have business and personal goals. However, when an overwhelming amount of real emotion is attached to whatever goal you set, you may tend to shy away from the uncomfortable emotional ones. Thanks for '*making it all right.*'

"Before writing the review, I called up several friends, inviting them to get together to create our very own *The 97 Club*. Their enthusiasm was high. I'm positive I chose my club members correctly, and we will all be successful."

Geoffrey Riddle, speaker, sales professional and voice-over artist
https://www.linkedin.com/in/geoffrey-riddle-359284ba

## One More Personal Story—Another Dedication

This short but powerful family experience is about Calvin Shipley Hatch, my uncle, a sixty-year-old executive who planned to retire after a highly successful career at Proctor & Gamble in Cincinnati, Ohio.

One day, just before retirement, Proctor & Gamble's CEO came to speak with Cal. Looking forward to retirement, he was surprised when it was explained to him that a man who had been hired to manage Clorox had it on the brink of disaster after only six months. The new executive was known as a head-cutter, and didn't focus on how to grow sales, never got in the trenches with his people to gain their confidence. He cut costs, meaning layoffs. Morale was devastated. Sales were down dramatically. It was crunch time and he felt that Cal was the answer. He asked Cal to be the new President and CEO of Clorox Corporation. Cal considered it and carefully crafted his response. He said,

"I will do this if you will make sure you have a succession plan in place when I am sixty-five, so I can retire and be with my family. In the meantime, I will get to work."

That was the plan, and after assessing the state of the company, Cal did something interesting. He called a meeting of all the managers at Clorox. That was a challenge since Clorox Corporation was diversified, owning businesses from gas stations to restaurants, suppliers, and production facilities. Cal's request was perhaps more daunting than my goal to reunite my family, but he would accomplish it starting in a very *straightforward* way.

The meeting was held in a large warehouse not unlike a scene in the movie *Dave*, where Kevin Kline doubles for the sitting U.S. President at public events. In the movie, the scene took place in a large factory with blue collar workers the President wanted to connect with on a personal level. It would help his chances of being re-elected. Visualize Kevin Kline standing, attached to an apparatus controlling a huge piece of remote-operated equipment, wearing a sleeve-like contraption on his arms as he faced the machinery. He spread his own arms, opening the mechanical arms wide, and said, "I caught a fish that was this...big!" Laughter burst forth!

In his case, Cal wasn't pretending to be a new CEO. He was the CEO, but the factory chosen for the Clorox meeting truly was "that big!" Cal outlined the direction he wanted the company to take and the role that each manager would play. It might be interesting to know the details of the plan he outlined was not the important part of the meeting. The key difference was he demonstrated he was approachable by sharing his plans with every level of management. It sent a message. After the meeting, a man came up to Cal and said,

"You know, I have really been working hard. But now I realize that I was pulling in the exact opposite direction. Now that I know your goals, I'll be able to support your efforts."

# Chapter Eighteen

## Is There an Upside of Fear?—Weldon Long

There's nothing better than a story of a person's life. As you read about Weldon Long's story, imagine you were a salesperson sitting in your beat-up old car, waiting until two minutes before your next Sears Home Improvement appointment. You drove down the street and checked houses needing siding, windows or anything else we sell. Why two minutes? Because you walk up to knock on the door at the exact appointment time so the soldier, the corporate executive or the busy housewife will compliment you for being *exactly on time*.

*"Now don't ring that doorbell. Friends knock. Salesmen ring the bell."*

Playing Harold Hill in *The Music Man* helped me understand how difficult a traveling salesman's life can be. *FEAR* is part of professional selling. In an article, *The Only 5 Fears We All Share* by Carl Albrecht Ph.D., March 22, 2012, the author ranks three of the most common fears as follows:

#3: The Fear of being restricted or otherwise being negatively influenced by circumstances beyond our control. It also extends to our social interactions and relationships.

#4: The Fear of abandonment, rejection, not being wanted, respected, or valued by anyone.

#5: The Fear of humiliation, shame, or any mechanism of profound self-disapproval that threatens the loss of integrity of the self, of lovability, capability, and worthiness. Rejection!

Carl, what about fear of speaking in public? How could you miss the #1 Fear? Just push a six-year-old onto the stage from the wings for their only three speaking lines in the elementary school play and what will any child tell you they're afraid of? Speaking in front of an audience! **Hello?** Death and bodily injury or paralysis is the #1 fear on Carl's list. The #2 fear he lists is "Falling." That one was real for me at the top of Sears Tower. Despite Carl's list, the #1 fear for many is getting up and speaking in front of a group. In the theater, if someone forgets their lines, most people won't know what to do.

*"Improv"* wasn't invented by Chicago's *Second City* theater troupe. *Improv* is not on the "Top 5" list of things most of us dream of doing some day. Admit it. Selling is like *being on stage.* What if they don't buy? What if I don't make any money? I'm on commission. Selling is scary! Shouldn't we admit we have fears?

## FEAR!

F.E.A.R. is often said to be **F**alse **E**vidence **A**ppearing **R**eal. Let me add some detail to that. Fear is also *False Evidence of failing*, of a lack of self-worth, of being insignificant or being rejected, abandoned, divorced, broke and bankrupt, fired, going to prison or even getting an "F" on tests of life...*Appearing Real.* Maybe you have all heard that F.E.A.R. acronym before, but for Weldon Long, who you met previously in Chapter Nine, *The Power of Vulnerability*, evidence of fear wasn't appearing false to him as a child.

In his very first book, *The Upside of Fear*, Weldon's life story unfolds with little optimism. He would never say to you that as a child he stood on a park bench, enthusiastically shouting, "There is an *Upside of Fear.*"

Perhaps it impressed you how he turned an unimaginable upbringing, thirteen years in prison and six months knocking on doors while living in a halfway house, into a phenomenal success. I'll never forget the seemingly insignificant detail of a small company hiring him. With only a ninth-grade education and having no job experience, this ex-con was selling air conditioning. There are no coincidences, someone *reached out!*

Basketball wasn't Weldon's ticket *out of the hood*. In the shadows of his past, reflecting on his struggles while he'd been in prison, he'd say,

"Finding sales as my calling opened doors to my future. Sales! I love it!"

The *Upside of Fear* is the title of a book by Weldon Long, but a statement from my perspective that is somewhat an oxymoron, or is it? What's an **upside** of fear for managers, executives, leaders, and even talented *Stylistic Salespeople* who may read this book? What is the **upside** message in *Ride the Horses, Feed the Lions?*

The message is "our investment in relationships is *the power that lies beneath,* waiting to come to the surface in our interpersonal interactions with businesses and consumers, between managers and associates, and hopefully through relationships with employees and sales professionals."

The principles remain the same at all levels of our human connections, whether professional or personal. Fear almost always crosses *the brain to emotion barrier* in people. So what is the basis for the **real fears** we experience? Let's get down to a somewhat bedrock level in addressing this core question, using parenting as our example. As parents we aren't just employers, waiting until our employees retire at 18 years of age and leave the nest. (Today, humorously, it may be age 30.) In a marriage relationship, while raising children, admittedly our biggest fear is failure. My heart would send me an instant message: "How can I allow myself to fail to support my family? What if I fail in work responsibilities?" Feel familiar? These are some of life's core concerns for each of us. A fear of failure is common. What is less common is the faith to endure life's trials and succeed.

### *"You're Fired!"*

For some, their greatest fear might be of never being able to have a family or losing a child. For others it may be never finding a soul mate or being a single parent, raising children alone. These are all profound fears, debilitating in their emotional effect on almost anyone.

I've mentioned this before, but in my case, my greatest fear after my divorce was not being able to provide for my family. Remembering the day I heard "you're fired" brings profound fear back to me again. Oh, they never say, "you're fired," but twice my computer wouldn't work.

Unjustified! You can say that too? Have you been separated or downsized after a takeover or a reorganization? Was your company sold? Consider a sales career. Salespeople are paid well. If you are responsible, consistent, work hard and like people, you will always have a job. For me, the fear of unemployment disappeared.

## *"Fortune 500 C-Suite Leader Available."*

If your career has advanced to where you want a C-level executive position, there is an interesting man on LinkedIn who has virtually taken the resumé frustration out of a job search. I would like to introduce you to Don Straits. In my search for LinkedIn executives to interview, his title and expertise made me curious. Then as we talked and he shared some people he was working with, my next trip was to his website to see what it was about. It was at the very least a creative approach, but what got my attention is that what his company put together would

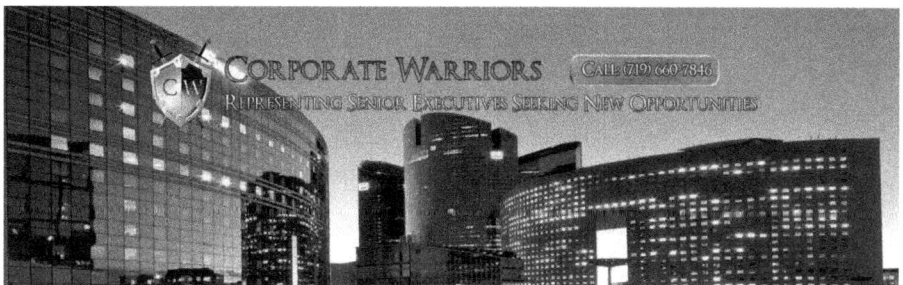

© Corporate Warriors. Used with permission.

allow an interested HR professional to get to know a person, their background, and their accomplishments before a face-to-face meeting.

With his visual *shout-out-kind-of-resumé approach,* Don helps current or former high profile executives position themselves to attract a C-level opportunity. Today's executive finds reemployment a frustrating process, a challenge. Don's seamless, fluid, creative presentations showcase your experience as you discover your amazing talents along with the viewer. Imagine if you created a blog but you're the interviewee "live," for everyone to see.

It was easy to distinguish Don from other Executive Headhunters in our interview. I wanted his opinions about his experiences like interviews I had with other "LinkedIn Influencers." As I began, he said,

"Instead of jumping right into the list of questions you sent, Bill, can I share my website with you first?" He took me there as he described his methods. I found that he was creating living *video resumés* for executives. As I sat there looking at the former CEO of Starbucks and the former CEO of the Four Seasons Hotel chain on the internet-based video blog-like format, in just a few minutes I felt like I'd met each of them. I could measure their characters as if I were looking for a new CEO for a major corporation. I soon learned how Don had also helped certain CEOs accept new opportunities they might not encounter otherwise.

Don had created a presentational approach I'd never seen before. I recommend you take a few moments to look at some of the amazing work Don has done for CEOs. As you do, imagine you have the privilege of working with Don Straits and he helps you land *The Big One* in some C-Level executive career position. Next, picture yourself not only as his client, but as someone your potential new boss can appreciate.

When you go to his website you'll see the casual nature of the commentary by accomplished executives. Perhaps you will see what I saw. Without answering my questions he answered the most important one in his video-format approach. What it said to me perhaps summarizes the advice each salesperson needs to accept:

### *"Be who you really are."*

Don Straits—"Fortune 500 C-Suite Leader Available."
   don@corporatewarriors.com
   https://www.linkedin.com/in/donstraits

# Top Sales Talent Must Take the Lead in Their Organizations and in Their Careers

Fixing what's broken about career searches requires a willingness to do things differently. Today's smart employers and candidates must use the internet as an integrated self-marketing platform to creatively tell their story and drive their search:

### Rethink the Resume
Don't just write a resume, build a digital portfolio. Candidates would do well to express their brand promise through a series of compelling stories, each one focused on one of their career-defining contributions and documented accomplishments.

### Let Your Personality Shine Through
When everybody appears interchangeable on paper, personality is a competitive advantage. Showcase your personality through videos, leadership insights, personal values and your contribution to the corporate culture.

### Take Advantage of Multimedia
Don't limit yourself to one medium. Your portfolio pieces can take as many forms as your imagination allows. Powerful visual aids can bring your track record of accomplishments to life in ways that words cannot, while recorded video introductions pull double-duty as a first-line candidate filter.

### High-tech & High Touch Approaches
Multiply your job search efforts considerably by combining your digital sphere of influence with the killer apps of the internet to zero in your desired roles, approach hiring managers at-scale and get your foot in the door with decision-makers in a meaningful way.

### Don't Schedule an Interview
Schedule business meetings instead. Approach decision makers, recruiters, VC's, PE's etc. with a value proposition on how you can impact the bottom line of the hiring organization

The structure of work itself is changing, and with it, so must the methods candidates use to secure their next career-defining role. Hopefully, these tips have opened your eyes to some of the methods that are working for the select few who dare to think differently.

## CORPORATE WARRIORS
### Are You Seeking New Leadership Challenges & Career Opportunities?

If you want to make a powerful impression on hiring organizations while differentiating yourself from the competition, the same strategies that have worked for our executive clients can work for you. Connect with us online to see what's possible and take your career search to the next level.

corporatewarriors.com/folios

**"The Best News for Sales Executives and Sales Managers!"**
**Wisdom from Dr. Marshall Goldsmith:**
**Managers Can Learn to Gain Interpersonal Skills!**

After a long conversation in which I learned about Dr. Marshall Goldsmith, about his passion to help others as well as the many business challenges he's faced and overcome, he simply said, "Here is the good news, we all can learn!"

This message could have come from a number of sources, but when I heard it from Dr. Marshall Goldsmith, a LinkedIn *Influencer* who has over 810,000 business followers, a man who's traveled to ninety-nine countries, consulting without pay *unless* the company he helped actually improved, I decided to share a profound true life story of one of his experiences that may encourage you, me and anyone venturing down a path to management.

## Hypothetical Scenario

If tomorrow you took over the position of an Army officer in an active theater of conflict, never having been in a live battle situation, what kind of a captain or general would you be? If you're now a sales manager, imagine that the VP of sales left the company and you got a phone call that they want you to accept that position. Never having had a national accountability before, what would be the first thing you would do? If you were hired as a CEO and you had to turn a floundering company around, or even if you stepped into a thriving one, are you prepared to make your first retail store visit? How will you be perceived? Will the word get around if it doesn't go well?

## "Real-life" Business Scenario

Imagine tomorrow is your first day. *Ride the Horses, Feed the Lions* challenges you to be authentic. Can you? This indeed happened to someone you've probably never heard of, Dr. Marshall Goldsmith. Dr. Goldsmith agreed to an interview for this book, taking time away from his grandchildren on a Sunday morning. It was the best time to reach him and I jumped at the chance. After telling me a bit about himself, answering questions and seeing the point of my interview, he shared a story about Hubert Joly, Best Buy's new CEO. Stay tuned for the whirlwind as we put ourselves in Joly's shoes. This is real life. It is *big time* media. Joly's troops are waiting to hear his words.

Goldsmith describes the field of battle:

"Let me share a perspective from an interview by CNBC's Courtney Reagan on September 17, 2017."

Speaking to CNBC, Joly outlined areas in the Best Buy Company in which he saw a potential for growth, such as *connected home markets* and *smartphones.*

"Our transformational strategy is mainly about fixing what was broken in Best Buy. The new strategy *pivots* and is focused on growth."

In that CNBC report, part of the headline read, "Wall Street isn't buying it."

I remembered Circuit City declaring bankruptcy in 2008 and shuttering all retail stores. I was managing Sears' San Francisco Home Improvements District at the time. Back in 1996 while I was in Sears' corporate offices, our Appliance Division had watched closely as Big Box stores grew market share, threatening Sears' position with consumers. Circuit City's demise caused rumors and realities to strike fear into Best Buy's stockholders. Marshall Goldsmith believed, at the time, that any new CEO faced an ongoing challenge, stating the obvious reality:

"Whatever is broken needs to be fixed."

Many new managers from the sales floor to a new chairman of the board faced the challenge of trying to emulate what they believed were qualities of this new CEO, Hubert Joly. In building a sales organization we often promote superstars in hopes their sales successes will translate into the new recruits and retain veterans who've carried our companies in the past. That doesn't always work. Some managers fear being perceived as a weak executive so they remain aloof. We might compare this to a U.S. Army general in an old World War II movie before a big battle:

"I can't get too close to my men. Some will die."

While that was a reality then, it doesn't work today. Aloof doesn't cut it on any level. Goldsmith continues:

"As Hubert Joly moved forward with his task of uniting the field sales force, as well as the management ranks, he began to get feedback about his management style, and it wasn't good. He was falling into the same intellectual trap as some other new sales managers and Army generals. He reflected poor interpersonal skills. His employees saw him as aloof."

### *Changes Hubert hoped to make in Best Buy's performance needed to start with him.*

As the infamous Paul Harvey of national radio fame would say.... "And now, for the rest of the story."

Hubert Joly took the employee feedback seriously. Was it possible for Hubert Joly to become an *authentic people-person?* Yes! He completely changed his management style, adopting new powerful interpersonal skills. Did employee perception of him change? Stay tuned for Goldsmith's answer:

"As reported from that store visit forward, employees excitedly anticipated visits of this new CEO."

Are the rest of us willing to be vulnerable enough to do the same, to change the way we manage and interact with those we seek to motivate?

The Peter Principle is a concept in management developed by Laurence J. Peter. The Peter Principle states, and I'm paraphrasing, that a person who is competent at their job will earn a promotion to a more senior position that requires different skills. If the promoted person lacks the skills required for their new role, then they will be incompetent at their new level and will not be promoted again. But if they are competent at their new role, then they will be promoted again, and they will continue to be promoted until they eventually reach a level at which they are incompetent. Why do I include this rather brash definition? It is, frankly, a reality check that attacks my *ego reality* and perhaps yours. As sales managers we typically came from the sales ranks. We were awesome, closing every sale...well, not every sale, but most. We may, after reading this book, look back and say... "Damn, I was a *lion* and didn't realize it. I'm way beyond even a *thoroughbred*."

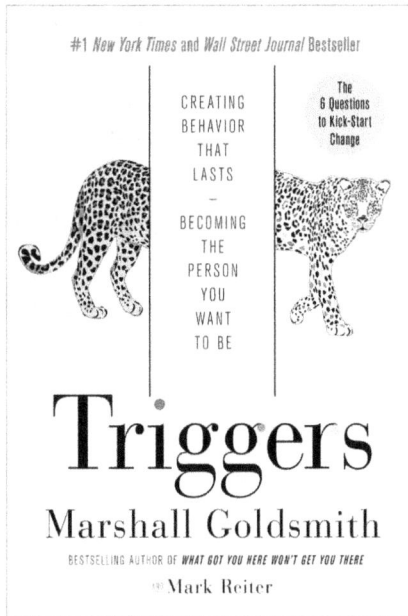

#1 *New York Times* and *Wall Street Journal* Bestseller

CREATING
BEHAVIOR
THAT
LASTS
—
BECOMING
THE
PERSON
YOU
WANT
TO BE

The
6 Questions
to Kick-Start
Change

# Triggers

## Marshall Goldsmith

BESTSELLING AUTHOR OF *WHAT GOT YOU HERE WON'T GET YOU THERE*

with Mark Reiter

© Dr. Marshall Goldsmith. Used with permission.

If it's true, we have a right to be proud, but in feeling overconfident perhaps we'll be reluctant to change and will lose the will to learn. Don't Forget Dr. Goldsmith's Good News:

### *"Managers can Learn and Gain new Interpersonal Skills!"*

If that wasn't surprising enough, as our conversation continued, he had one final statement to make:

### *"Managers can enjoy connecting with their people."*

In my interview with Dr. Marshall Goldsmith, I deviated from a planned list of ten questions such as:

"When you are sitting across the desk from a prospective new sales recruit, and after you look at their resumé, what is the final factor in hiring them?"

That was the key question for me, but instead I decided that I wanted to know one more about Dr. Goldsmith, so in a *pivot*, as Chad

Rawlins would say, or to change the subject, I asked him a much more personal question:

"Dr. Goldsmith, what drives you to do what you do?"

His response was simple and he didn't hesitate in giving me his answer. He shared:

"I want to help people improve. That's what drives me."

Dr. Marshall Goldsmith

https://www.linkedin.com/in/marshallgoldsmith

### *Brené Brown on Vulnerability as a Crucial Strength*

I encourage sales executives and sales managers to develop an entirely new environment by investing more time cultivating relationships that reflect authenticity, a rare commodity today. If you do this you will deserve, merit, and earn the trust of those who work *with you*. When you try to be more vulnerable, loyalty to you as an executive increases exponentially. That may be a theory in your mind, but it is a Brené Brown reality.

In June 2010, Brené Brown, a research professor at University of Houston's Graduate College of Social Work, gave a TEDx talk on "The Power of Vulnerability," condensing six years of research on shame resilience into 20 minutes. I will paraphrase what happened next:

Disarmingly hesitant at first, Brené Brown doesn't address the audience as much as she seems to confide in it, telling two interwoven stories. One is about her academic research into shame and vulnerability, the other about the spiritual and psychological crisis the work of writing the book precipitated in her, leading to a much deeper experience of authenticity and human connection. As she delivers her TEDx talk we get a little deeper.

"In this perfectionist culture, most of us believe we're 'not good enough...not thin enough, rich enough, beautiful enough, smart enough, promoted enough' to be worthy of love. So we can't afford to let our guard down, become *vulnerable*, because letting others see us as we really are would mean we'd be rejected out of hand. Better to avoid emotional risk and vulnerability, and numb ourselves to any pain we can't escape."

However, Brown's research had shown that some people have escaped that shame trap. But how? She takes the audience by their hearts and reveals the hard work ahead for all of us:

"They let themselves be vulnerable." Her TEDx indoctrination into our world of uncomfortable reality:

"Rather than always thinking *I'm not good enough*, they live in the belief that *I'm enough*. Grounded in this rock-bottom sense of their fundamental acceptability as human beings, for whom being good *enough* is plenty good, they can take hold of their courage and accept their vulnerability, live 'wholeheartedly' [a basic concept for Brown], loving without reservation or guarantees, living with the courage to be imperfect, unafraid to let others see their imperfections, opening themselves fully to whatever life brings, good or bad, pain or joy."

In short, Brown said,

"They were willing to let go of who they thought they should be in order to be who they were—which you have to absolutely do for connection."

*Escaping the Shame Trap* by Mary Sykes Wylie, September 19, 2016 excerpts from *Psychotherapy Networker*

## *Can you be vulnerable enough to... Ride the Horses and Feed the Lions?*

Will you recognize, recruit, relate-to, and retain thoroughbreds and those untamable lions you discover and hire onto your sales team? Across from the desk in an interview, will you ask yourself, "Do I like them?"

Remember Franklin-Covey's Shawn Moon and the *Barbeque Factor?* After measuring competencies and process discipline, he asked himself two questions,

"On Friday night after work, would I want to 'hang out' with them? Would I invite them over for a barbeque at our house?"

After reading *Ride the Horses, Feed the Lions*, will you say, "I'm already strong in interpersonal skills and attract loyalty. I reach out and connect with people. My unprompted, sincere feedback (we know each survey is coded so management knows who said what) on surveys is always positive. My rate of retention is above average".

Remember Shawn Moon's statistics of retention rates as VP Sales over Franklin-Covey's national sales team, 80% over three years? Shawn recently was hired as the new CEO at Zerorez. What do you think happens at Zerorez now? In sales organizations we NEVER see anything close to Shawn's retention levels under any leadership style. Is the difference people-skills? They work! Not just with salespeople; in the business and personal lives of managers too!

# ROGER K. ALLEN Ph.D.
*Live Joyfully. Love Fully.*

### A Benediction?
### "Making the World a More Benevolent Place"
### With permission, I share a post
### from Dr. Roger K. Allen, Ph.D.

"**Benevolence** is now my new word. [This] has been on my mind a lot in recent weeks and months, particularly given what we're going through as a nation and world. The simple definition of [benevolence] is:

"A desire to do *good to others*, to be charitable and to act kindly. I think of the word as expansive and encompassing. It is not like a watering hose we use to douse this or that plant but more like a 360-degree sprinkler head that shoots a spray indiscriminately outward. Benevolence casts a broad net of good will to all who come within its radius. As such it is an attitude, a *new paradigm*, a place to 'come from' that extends a deep sense of respect, warmth, generosity and concern

to others, as well as oneself. Most of us would agree that the world needs more benevolence."
  Roger K. Allen, Ph.D, *The Salesman's Choice*™
  https: //www.linkedin.com/in/drrogerallen
  roger@centerod.com

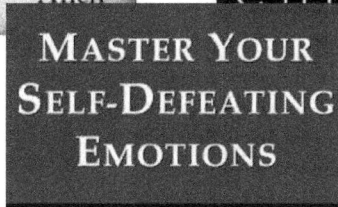

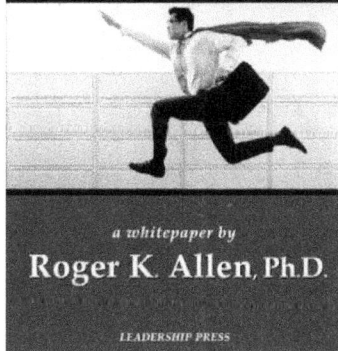

Covers © Roger K. Allen. Used with permission.

*"Your success depends on a support system,*
*wherever you call home.*
*Spend more time with those you love, who love you."*
**William D. Hatch**

Outstanding Managers, Million Dollar Sellers, and Stylistic Salespeople:
"Common Characteristics and Keys to Success"

Outstanding Managers

1. Listen Without Distractions.
2. Care by Believing in their People.
3. Make Time to Connect Personally.
4. Involve Others in Making Decisions.
5. Trust in their Decisions—Respect Them.
6. Show Appreciation: Validate Them.
7. Create Opportunities to Advance.
8. Have an "Open-Door Policy" for Feedback.
9. Replace Blame with Responsibility.
10. Empathize: Build Others' Self-esteem.
11. Understand that by Human Nature we Need Rewarding, Meaningful Work.
12. Set up Team Communication Time.
13. Are Emotionally Resilient and Handle High-Stakes Conversations Well.
14. Are Open-Minded. Not Quick to Judge. Understand by Asking Questions.
15. SHOW Genuine Concern for the Whole Person's Life Outside Work.
16. Are Authentic and Honest. If you can't share details, explain why.
17. Endorse Health-Wellness Programs.
18. Welcome New Ideas, Collaboration, and *Shake Things Up* Once in a While.

19. Are Not Afraid to Ask for Help and Perspectives from Others. Know their Impact. Admit their Mistakes. Are Vulnerable.
20. Strive to *See Things* from Employees' Perspectives. Know their Impact.
21. Detach from Negativity. Let go of Control when Necessary. Develop their "Softer Side" and Lead!

## Million *Dollar Sellers*

1.  Make Processes Simple for Clients.
2.  Commit!—the Michael Jordan Formula.
3.  Share Stories—the Best way to Communicate.
4.  Make Clients your Friends First!
5.  Treat Everyone "One Level Up!"
6.  Build a "Like" Platform. People do Business with People They Like!
7.  Don't just Explain—Show Them.
8.  LISTEN Carefully to Clients.
9.  Sell Smart: Have a Knowledge Library.
10. Learn More Outside of the Office.
11. Charm Gatekeepers—How Do You Treat Those Around Leaders at the Top?
12. Know the Whale is your Best Customer. Spend more time "Saving the Whales."
13. Not so Fast!—Super Salespeople interviewed almost universally SLOW down the sales process when they can.
14. Overcome No! Do it Differently.
15. Perseverance! Stick it Out. STAY.
16. Productivity—Master Your Day.
17. Use Personal Goal Setting Metrics.
18. Gold Mine—Golden Nuggets are what you learn from *lions*— Build on Successes.
19. Differentiate Themselves: Their Brand
20. Have Authenticity: You Can't Fake Real. The reality of million dollar salespeople comes as a result of careful preparation and hard work. Are the Real McCoy. In sales, *truth* is the foundation of authenticity. Authentic sales professionals are true to themselves."
21. Believe in Your Company, Yourself, and "Become your Product."

## *Characteristics of a Stylistic Salesperson*

1. They are **creative!** They only need your guidance on policy. They are problem solvers.
2. You can't **make** them; you **find** them. This is the best part of your journey. Training new people to become like robots is simply *not* fun, for you or them.
3. They are **people-people.** They are naturally sincere, authentic, warm and **charismatic.** For them, each appointment is like a first date.
4. They sell with **integrity** and honesty, are concerned about the customer's needs more than their own, and they feel they cannot be dishonest and succeed.
5. They need to be **motivated,** not managed. How would you manage Michael Jordan? Take an interest in them so they will "get you."
6. The need for **recognition** is different for each person. The challenge is how to reach them. In this sense each manager must be stylistic, too.
7. Want to **adopt them** or invite them for dinner? These are my tests. I hire on this basis when looking for a superstar.
8. You can't find these characteristics on their **resumé.** I admit that I never read resumés when hiring a salesperson. I look and listen for who they really are.
9. They're **happy** by nature. **50%** of how we handle rejection is how we are raised, **10%** of events are out of our control, but **40%** is our choice!
10. They want to **help** people. This is an intangible. Look for it. You don't have to push someone who **pulls others up.** They'll help you if you establish a relationship with them.

Get to know them personally. They're *thoroughbreds.* Don't rein them in right out of the gate. Let them set their own pace. Be on their team so they're on yours. Like most things, learning how to manage *Stylistic Salespeople* is on-the-job training. Each person is like a book with something unique on each page. Don't rush. Listen to stories they tell. Watch, learn, have fun!

### *Note to Sales Managers: They want you to get to know them!*

# HR Test Module—New Hire Candidates

New Hire candidates, please rate your
feelings 1-10 with 10 being the Strongest:

\_\_\_ I appreciate having other's ideas so I can add my approach or spin and innovation, making what I do or how I do things unique or different.

\_\_\_ I like to basically operate independently. Once I am trained I like to design my own approaches on how to connect with people and how I sell.

\_\_\_ I enjoy meeting and getting to know people I have never met. I can spend hours with a perfect stranger and connect with them personally.

\_\_\_ Friends say I'm naturally sincere, authentic, warm, and charismatic.

\_\_\_ I am seen as being comfortable in private and public social situations.

\_\_\_ Integrity and honesty are the foundation of who I am. It's what I've been taught and how I operate in my personal and business relationships.

\_\_\_ I am concerned about the customer's needs but not more than my own. I can succeed without really connecting.

\_\_\_ I respect managers. I don't need to be micromanaged, but I want to have a closer relationship with management than just as an employee.

\_\_\_ I enjoy being recognized but it's not the only reason I do what I do.

\_\_\_ After a two-hour appointment, customers often want me to stay for dinner, come back on Saturday for a barbecue, or meet family members.

\_\_\_ I listen basically to get the information I can use to "close the sale." I wait patiently until my customer is done talking so I can get right to it.

\_\_\_ I am naturally a happy person. It's how I was raised, but I choose it.

\_\_\_ I want to help people. I look for opportunities to solve problems. You don't have to push me to help pull others up.

Note to HR professionals: Take this test first yourself.

# Chapter Nineteen

## A Closing Statement

### *"A Revolutionary New Management Approach through Personal Goal Setting"*

This book is specifically for Sales Managers but applies to any level or type of manager who chooses to become connected with their associates. When facing the challenge of turning a company around or increasing revenues, the executive often resorts to cost-cutting measures. When I worked in Sears corporate headquarters, fears of some MBA students, graduating and facing the challenge of reducing costs in a sedentary employee base, generated this now hopefully worn-out doctrine from the 1990s:

"We have to do more with less."

There is a fixed cost for employees in any business. When revenues decrease, payroll seems to be the first place we look. Reducing staff or lowering commission rates results in lower morale. The outcome of this approach is always the "Talent Flight" or loss of your best employees, so performance is weaker, and the cycle continues as the CFO sends a team of MBAs out to find more areas to cut.

Another MBA doctrine from the 1990s was experienced at Sears. The new CEO wanted to infuse new retail management blood from outside the company into the Sears Tower organization, but how to do it? The doctrine goes as follows:

"If you can't achieve your stated goal, create a problem, the solution to which achieves your stated goal." What did they instruct Human Resources to do? "Add 1600 new hires from the best of the best in Retail."

HR accomplished that goal. Then CEO put out a Press Release stating Sears Headquarters was too heavy at the middle management level. HR instituted layoffs, buyouts and lateral promotions that moved veteran Sears management out or at least out of the way so that the new outside hires were given virtually all upward movement, or were placed in upper management positions over veteran middle management.

Turning around a company or a sales team's performance starts with you, the manager. The fastest way to increase revenues is by energizing your sales force. But how do we "teach them to fish" when it comes to goal setting? We know that if we're not in direct contact continually with our sales team they can become demoralized.

I personally discovered I actually needed to write down lofty personal goals. What I really needed, just like the Harvard MBA grads in the 1979 study, was to then have a way to be able to visualize my goals. In the upcoming book, *The 97 Club*, a plan imaginative enough to accomplish this is described, step by step, meeting by meeting, PowerPoint slide by slide so you can see its evolution from concept to reality. You can do this too.

https://www.linkedin.com/in/william-dilworth-hatch-45538637
WDHatch1.titanglobalgroup@gmail.com
www.WilliamDHatch.com

# About the Author

I hope you find me to be an ordinary person you can identify with. I now believe great people are average people with specific goals, have written them down, visualized them and addressed any unresolved personal issues that have held them back from embracing full confidence in themselves and their abilities. I believe if you write down personal goals it will impact your life. If you visualize them they will come to fruition.

One reason I'm sharing my career with you is that I believe "Middle Managers Carry the Water." You won't know me, even after you've read this book, but I know if anyone puts *people first*, before their own interests, they will succeed at work. If we invest in personal relationships, we will be remembered long after our final chapter is written. Family matters!

William Dilworth Hatch, VP, Titan Global Group LLC. is based in Denver. His musical theater roles in Illinois, Minnesota, Wisconsin, Colorado and New York have entertained thousands. He is a national sales trainer and marketing consultant, and an inspiring keynote speaker. Enjoy Bill's quick wit as he responds to attendee input. Bill brings to regional business seminars a background in Corporate Marketing, Brand Management, national Multicultural Advertising and Account

Management, Corporate Marketing Public Relations, National Sales promotional campaigns and distinguished successes managing three #1 Home Improvement Districts. He was founder, creative director and publisher of *Nuestra Gente,* the first ABC-audited, Spanish-language direct mail magazine in the United States with quarterly distribution nationally, 1993 to 2005, reaching ten percent of Hispanic/Latino households. He is a bilingual marketing presenter, fluent speaking and writing Spanish.

Having creative oversight of Spanish television, magazine, radio newspaper and direct marketing, Sears tapped Bill to create a national Sears general market campaign. Producer, writer and on-camera talent for 36 episodes of a 30-minute industrial video marketing series he wrote and collaborated with ad agencies such as Ogilvy & Mather, Young & Rubicam, Mendoza-Dillon y Asociados, Leo Burnett-Chicago, La Agencia de Orci, Burrell Communication Group, Bravo Group, Kang & Lee, and Focus Media.

Today he returns to pursue two passions. First, writing in order to consult and to motivate the sales industry, and the second becomes apparent when you look up his stage name, William Taylor Burton on IMDb, a site for budding AND veteran actors. Represented by four talent agencies nationwide, he's just started. His retail career:

1. Regional In-Store Trainer
2. Manager of Inventory Control
3. Menswear Regional Buyer–Automotive Buyer: Sears N.E. Zone
4. Softlines Store Manager–Nat'l Promotional Plan Mgr./Auto
5. National Sales Promotions Mgr. for 800 Stores. Graphics Budget: $14 mm
6. Corporate Retail Sales Promotions Manager
7. Special Assignment—"ET"
8. Asst. to VP. of Marketing Special Disney/Sears Project: Disney World MGM Studios Co-Venture
9. Nat'l Ad Launch: Sears, Your Money's Worth & A Whole Lot More
10. National Grand Re-opening
11. Nat'l In-Store Advertising Mgr.

12. Director Marketing PR: *Time Magazine* "Special Edition for Women"

13. Nascar/IROC/NHRA PR–DieHard/Craftsman Racing Plan

14. Director Ethnic Marketing, *L.A. Times* 1996 Sears #1 Ethnic Marketer

15. Publisher, *Nuestra Gente* ©*1993*, the first U.S. ABC-audited, Direct Mail Spanish language nationally distributed Magazine in history (1993–2005), first audited U.S. Spanish Sears TMC newspaper circulation in Hispanic Zip Codes in Los Angeles, CA; Chicago, IL; Miami, FL; Dallas, Houston and San Antonio, TX.

16. Acting Director Multicultural Mktg: Hispanic, Asian, Afro-American

17. Multicultural R.O.I. proposal grows ad budget from $27 to $70mm

18. Left Sears to start EMC2: Ethnic Marketing Consulting—4 accounts

19. Corporate Ethnic Equity Branding Manager—Kraft Foods, Illinois

20. Director Allstate Spanish Advertising: *La Agencia de Orci,* Los Angeles

21. Sears Commission Sales Rep: Ranked #12 of 1500 Reps—Denver

22. Sears Field Sales Manager

23. National Trainer Mid-South Region

24. District Sales Manager—San Francisco: Ranked #1 nationally in 2003

25. District Sales Manager—Washington DC: Ranked #1 Profit nationally in 2008

26. District Sales Manager—Denver, CO: Ranked #1 nationally in 2011

27. Recruited as Corporate National Trainer: Champion Windows in 2015

# Notables

*7 Habits of Highly Effective People,* first published in 1988 by Free Press, is a business and self-help book written by Stephen R. Covey. In it, Covey presents an approach to being effective in attaining goals by aligning oneself to what he calls "true north" principles of a character ethic that he presents as universal and timeless. Covey's best-known book has sold more than 25 million copies worldwide since its first publication in 1989. Stephen Richards Covey, a revered American educator, author, businessman, keynote speaker (October 24, 1932— July 16, 2012).

Allen, Roger K., Ph.D., author, consultant, coach and teacher, with thirty-five years professional experience, is the co-founder and President of the Human Development Institute (1980-1990). He provides counseling to a diverse client population. In public seminars on personal transformation and family relations, Roger is also co-founder and senior consultant with the Center for Organizational Design (1992-present).

He provides leadership and team development, strategic planning and organizational redesign to create cultures where each person is a contributing partner in their business. Roger has written numerous publications on topics of leadership, high performance teams, and organizational transformation. Roger, along with Preston Pond, has certified over eight hundred independent consultants worldwide authorized to use their consulting and development products, which have been delivered to hundreds of thousands of people.

Dr. Allen is the author of books addressing key interpersonal issues. Two are:

*The Hero's Choice, Mastering Your Self-Defeating Behaviors* and *Raising Responsible Emotionally Mature Children.* Roger is the facilitator of self-improvement courses and seminars. I've known Roger for almost twenty years. Because of his experience in human development, I went to a course of his called *Making Things Happen.* Attending just one of his seminars changed my life.

*Daring Greatly,* a New York Times Best Seller published in 2012 by Gotham Press in New York, was written by Brené Brown, a research professor at The University of Houston Graduate School of Social Work, an American scholar, author, and public speaker. In the introduction to her book Brown riffs on Theodore Roosevelt's words, which she says perfectly encapsulate her research into why we find being vulnerable such a hard thing to do. Casandra Brené Brown, born November 18, 1965.

*The Challenger Sale* is the first non-fiction book by Matthew Dixon, Brent Adamson, and their colleagues at CEB, Inc. Their book was published November 10, 2011 by Portfolio/Penguin. In the text, the book argues that relationship-building is no longer the best sales method. In selling complex, large-scale business-to-business solutions, customers are changing how they buy so salespeople must change how they sell. The authors' study found that sales reps fall into one of five profiles, and the Challenger Seller is the highest performer.

*Hartmann Personality Profiles,* The Color Code Personality Profile now also known as The Color Code or The People Code was created by Dr. Taylor Hartman. It divides personalities into four color groups: Red (motivated by power), Blue (motivated by intimacy), White (motivated by peace), and Yellow (motivated by fun). Although the different groups of people have different demographics, the general breakdown suggests that the Reds comprise 25% of the population, Blues 35%, Whites 20%, and Yellows 20% [Robert S. Hartmann Institute].

*Talent Unleashed,* a book co-authored by Shawn Moon, Exec. V.P., Strategic Markets at Franklin-Covey. "The 'talent conversations' in this book are highly practical tools for leaders who want to uncover untapped potential in their people—and develop it." Shawn is now the CEO of Zerorez, a dynamic, green, carpet cleaning system with headquarters in Salt Lake City, Utah. The process leaves no residue. The company is growing rapidly in the United States.

*LIFE Magazine, LIFE* was published weekly until 1972, as an intermittent "special" until 1978, and as a monthly from 1978 to 2000. When *LIFE* was founded in 1883, it was developed as similar to the British magazine, *Punch.* It was published for 53 years as a general-interest light entertainment magazine, heavy on illustrations, jokes and social commentary, and featured some of the greatest writers like Charles Dana Gibson, Norman Rockwell and Jacob Hartman Jr.

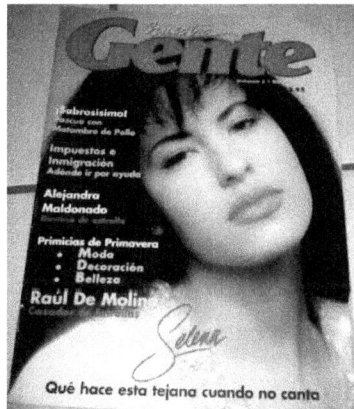

Qué hace esta tejana cuando no canta

*Nuestra Gente, magazine,* was a proprietary national U.S. Spanish language magazine published by Sears, Roebuck and Company's Multicultural Marketing Department. William Dilworth Hatch, the founder/publisher, created the publication, which was direct mailed to over 650,000 Spanish-dominant households, 4-6 times annually from 1993 to 2005 when it ceased due to the merger of K-Mart into Sears Holdings. It was the 1st ABC-audited national Spanish-language magazine in the United States.

A Los Angeles Times article, in a January 1996, Front-page Business Section declared Sears, Roebuck and Company "The Leader" in Ethnic Marketing to Hispanics and Asians.

*IPSO News: Independent Press Standards Organization,* an independent press standards organization based in England and Wales of the United Kingdom.

*Entrepreneur Magazine:* An American magazine and website that carries news stories about entrepreneurship, small business management, and business. The magazine, first published in 1977 by Entrepreneur Media Inc., is headquartered in Irvine, CA. The magazine's 12 annual issues are available by subscription and on newsstands. It is published under international licenses in South Africa, Mexico, Russia, India, Hungary, and the Philippines. Editor-in-chief is Jason Feifer. Its owner is Peter Shea.

# References

*Allure of the Seas,* Royal Caribbean Cruise Line launched in 2009; 1187 feet long with 18 decks. With sister ships *Oasis of the Seas* and *Harmony of the Seas*, they are the only three cruise ships with a "cut-out" profile of the aft portion, with staterooms being featured on the exterior and interior of these ships.

American Home Improvement Products, acquired by Sears early in 1999 having been a licensee with Sears since 1990. A.H.I.P. was based in Longwood, Florida.

Amre Inc. ended a 13-year relationship with Sears, Roebuck & Co. on Dec. 31, 1995 having been a licensee of Sears [Sears Home Improvements, Inc] since 1982.

The Baby-Boomer Woman and the Blog "She Economy."

Bannister, Sir Roger Gilbert (b. March 23, 1929), an English middle-distance athlete. He ran the mile in May 1954 at Iffley Road track in Oxford in 3 min 59.4 seconds.

Bellas, Michelle, MA. and Collard, Colin, MA., *Resolutions to Reality, The Most Comprehensive Guide to Achieving Your Goals,* 2011 Fireweed Group Inc.

Blanchard, Ken & Johnson, Spencer, *The One Minute Manager,* William Morrow & Co. 1982, USA. Its revolutionary paradigm shift encourages recognition of employees.

Brown, Mary and Orsborn, Carol., Ph.D., *Marketing to the Ultimate Power Consumer*

Collins, James C., *Good to Great,* William Collins & Sons Company, 2001, USA.

Costello, John, Sears Sr. Executive Vice President and General Mgr. of Marketing and former President of Nielsen Marketing Research USA, Northbrook, Illinois.

*Dave,* the movie, directed by Ivan Reitman, written by Gary Ross, stars Kevin Kline, Sigourney Weaver, and Frank Langella, distributed by Warner Brothers in 1993, produced by Northern Lights Entertainment and Lauren Shuler Donner Productions.

*Death of a Salesman*, a 1949 play written by Arthur Miller. It was the recipient of the 1949 Pulitzer Prize for Drama and Tony Award for Best Play. It premiered on Broadway in February 1949, ran 742 performances, and then returned to Broadway, winning 3 Tony Awards for Best Revival. Willy Loman was the main character.

*Glengarry Glen Ross*, a 1992 American feature film adapted by David Mamet from his 1984 Pulitzer Prize and Tony-winning play, directed by James Foley and produced by Jerry Tokofsky and Stanley R. Zupnik and the Zupnik Cinema Group. Al Pacino, Alec Baldwin and Jack Lemmon starred along with Ed Harris. The title is taken from real estate developers Glengarry Highlands and Glen Ross Farms.

Goldsmith, Dr. Marshall, Ph.D., New York Times Best-selling author.

Hawn, Goldie, actress and producer and Russell, Kurt, actor, writer and producer.

Hersey, Paul, *Situational Leadership.*

Hopkins, Tom, How to Master the Art of Selling, May 5, 2005, Warner Books, Published by Grand Central Publishing.

*La Agencia de Orci*, 11620 Wilshire Blvd. Ste. 600. West Los Angeles, CA, 90025 Purchase Demographics, MassMutual Financial Group–2007.

*Seabiscuit,* a 2003 American equestrian film directed by Gary Ross, based on the best-selling non-fiction book *Seabiscuit: An American Legend* by Laura Hillenbrand.

*"Sears, Your Money's Worth and a Whole Lot More,"* an advertising tagline in 1989 for Michael Bozic, Sears President, CEO by William Dilworth Hatch at Sears.

*The Secret,* written by Rhonda Byrne, published by Atria Books, November 2006.

Spray-tech Inc. Sears purchased it March 1998 after a relationship since 1982.

*Tin Men*, the movie, written and directed by Barry Levinson, produced by Mark Johnson by *Touchstone Picture, Silver Screen Partners III and Bandai Films*, starring Richard Dreyfuss and Danny DeVito.

*Tommy Boy,* the movie, directed by Peter Segal in 1995 with writers Bonnie and Terry Turner, starring Chris Farley as Tommy Boy.

Wallace, DeWitt and Bell, Lila, *Readers Digest*, founded 1922, Simon & Schuster.

Winfrey, Oprah and McGraw, Dr. Phillip; "Validate" from *The Oprah Winfrey Show.*

# LinkedIn Influencers

**Dr. Marshall Goldsmith,** NY Times Best Seller, Dartmouth Professor; *California*

**Peter Strohkorb**, Smarketing™ author *The OneTEAM Method®*; *Sydney, Australia*

**Shawn Moon**, Franklin-Covey Exec. VP, Sales, co-author *Talent Unleashed*

**Weldon Long**, NY Times Best Seller, author *The Power of Consistency*; *Colorado*

**Matthew Kelly**, VP Sales Fairway Architectural Railing Solutions; *Cincinnati*

**Mark Skovron**, Ph.D., CEO MaxGroup™ Business Solutions, author; *Phoenix*

**Michael S. Wooten**, CEO Landmark Results Group, entrepreneur; *Atlanta*

**Tim Wackel**, sales director, docent, keynote speaker, trainer, coach; *Dallas*

**Tony J. Hughes**, best selling author, keynote speaker; *NSW Australia*

**Jim Schleckser**, CEO, best selling author *Great CEO's are Lazy*; *the DC area*

**Chad B. Rawlings**, creator of Positive Mindsets for Success; *Salt Lake*

**Clint Geog**, Divisional VP., Terminix, Sears Home Services; *Raleigh, N.C.*

**Monica Pritchard**, VP Sales, Mktg., Prod. Development, Quality Edge; *Michigan*

**Olivier Riviére**, Grayling Marketing Director-Europe; *Paris*

**Don Straits,** CEO Corporate Warriors executive placement; *Denver*

**Steve Booz**, sales, marketing executive, Royal Bldg. Products; *Philadelphia*

# Index

www.ingramcontent.com/pod-product-compliance
Lightning Source LLC
Chambersburg PA
CBHW071337210326
41597CB00015B/1478